NATIVE FOODWAYS

SUNY series, Native Traces

Scott Richard Lyons, editor

NATIVE FOODWAYS

Indigenous North American Religious Traditions and Foods

Edited by
Michelene E. Pesantubbee
and
Michael J. Zogry

Published by State University of New York Press, Albany

Printed in the United States of America

For information, contact State University of New York Press, Albany, NY
www.sunypress.edu

Library of Congress Cataloging-in-Publication Data

Names: Pesantubbee, Michelene E., 1953– editor. | Zogry, Michael J., 1966– editor.
Title: Native foodways : indigenous North American religious traditions and foods / [edited by] Michelene E. Pesantubbee, Michael J. Zogry.
Other titles: Native traces.
Description: Albany : State University of New York, [2021] | Series: SUNY series, native traces | Includes bibliographical references and index.
Identifiers: LCCN 2020045651 (print) | LCCN 2020045652 (ebook) | ISBN 9781438482613 (hardcover : alk. paper) | ISBN 9781438482620 (pbk. : alk. paper) | ISBN 9781438482637 (ebook)
Subjects: LCSH: Indians of North America—Food. | Food—North America—Religious aspects.
Classification: LCC E98.F7 N378 2021 (print) | LCC E98.F7 (ebook) | DDC 970.004/97—dc23
LC record available at https://lccn.loc.gov/2020045651
LC ebook record available at https://lccn.loc.gov/2020045652

10 9 8 7 6 5 4 3 2 1

In Memory of Dr. Inés M. Talamantez

Contents

Acknowledgments

The editors would like to thank our colleague Jace Weaver and Amanda Lanne-Camilli, the acquisitions editor at SUNY Press, both of whom worked with us during the first several phases of the project. The editors also would like to thank James Peltz, associate director of the press, and Ryan Morris, senior production editor, who worked with us during the final stages of the project. Thanks as well to the chapter authors, and to all our colleagues in the Native Traditions of the Americas Unit of the American Academy of Religion. Michael J. Zogry would like to thank Renee Cyr, graduate research assistant, University of Kansas, for her assistance with one phase of the project.

Introduction

Michael J. Zogry

The essays in this volume discuss selected examples of significant confluences in Indigenous North American religious traditions and foodways. Methodologically diverse, this collection provides rich individual case studies informed by relevant historical, ethnographic, and comparative data. Many of the essays demonstrate how narrative and active elements of selected Native American religious traditions have provided templates for interactive relationships with particular animals and plants, rooted in detailed information about their local environments. In return, these animals and plants have provided them with sustenance. The remaining essays provide analysis of additional contemporary and historical Indigenous foodways, contributing to the ongoing scholarly discourse regarding issues of tradition and cultural change.[1]

Together, these essays make an important contribution to the expanding scholarly discourse on Indigenous, North American, global, and religious foodways. There are existing publications about Indigenous foodways, and about religious foodways. However, this is the first scholarly edited volume exclusively devoted to the interplay between Indigenous North American religious traditions and foodways.

There is no question that Indigenous foodways in North America have been impacted by colonial, in many cases European-derived, methods of developing and harvesting food resources. Though such efforts to force change began earlier, in the late eighteenth and early nineteenth centuries the widespread introduction of imported agricultural techniques, crops, and gender protocols disrupted Indigenous models of the same.[2] Federal policies and treaties aimed at "civilizing" Indigenous peoples strived to change nearly everything about them, including the food they ate and how they acquired it. For example, Article XIV of the 1791 Treaty of Holston between the United States and the Cherokee Nation stated:

> That the Cherokee nation may be led to a greater degree of civilization, and to become herdsmen and cultivators, instead of remaining in a state of hunters, the United States will from time to time furnish gratuitously the said nation with useful implements of husbandry.[3]

Simultaneously, a group of federal policies began a methodical, systemic attack on Indigenous land rights, families, education, and cultural systems in the United States. Regardless of the impetus for their institution, several of these policies bred predatory, corrupt treaty-making and lending practices, annuity models, and land allotment practices. Results included family units being torn apart, and entire nations being forcibly removed from traditional homelands.[4] As Neil Prendergast has summarized in *The Routledge History of American Foodways*, "even well after the nation's founding, the project of agriculture was also the project of empire."[5] Furthermore, this "barrage of federal policies aimed at dissolving American Indian culture, including foodways" has resulted in the majority of "twentieth-century civil rights efforts on the part of American Indians" being focused on "undoing this agriculturally inspired policy."[6]

Despite these challenges, at the time of this book's publication, cultural revitalization projects are underway in a number of contemporary North American Indigenous communities. Although such projects take many forms at present, those that focus on reviving or promoting community-wide engagement in foodways are the subject of the essays in this volume. Elizabeth Hoover and Devon A. Mihesuah explained the significance of this pairing as they defined the key subject of their coedited volume *Indigenous Food Sovereignty in the United States: Restoring Cultural Knowledge, Protecting Environments, and Regaining Health*. Due to the "focus on cultural relevancy and specific relationships to food systems, cultural restoration is imperative for Indigenous food sovereignty, 'generally more so than to non-indigenous food sovereignty.'"[7]

Furthermore, Indigenous food sovereignty,

> is not focused only on *rights to* land, food, and the ability to control a production system, but also *responsibilities to* and culturally, ecologically, and spiritually appropriate *relationships with* elements of those systems. This concept entails emphasizing reciprocal relationships with aspects of the landscape and the entities on it, "rather than asserting rights over particular resources as a means of controlling production and access."[8]

Hoover and Mihesuah cited the "four principles of Indigenous food sovereignty," formulated by scholar Dawn Morrison and the Working Group on Indigenous Food Sovereignty. The first principle is as follows: "the recognition that the right to food is *sacred*, and food sovereignty is achieved by upholding sacred responsibilities to nurture relationships with the land, plants and animals that provide food."[9]

Detailed explications of this statement occur in virtually every chapter of this present collection. Many Native American communities have traditions of living in symbiotic relationships with the plant and animal beings that surround them. The essays in this volume drive home the persistent reality, the manifest presence of animals and plants as meaningful partners in these cultural resource equations. Thus, the concept of humans interacting in person-to-person relationships with non–human living beings is important to consider carefully.

A useful conceptual term in this context is "other-than-human persons," coined by the anthropologist A. Irving Hallowell in his article "Ojibwa Ontology, Behavior, and World View," first published in 1960.[10] Michael McNally employs Hallowell's term in his essay for this collection, and several other authors also assert that in the cultures they discuss, animals and plants are understood to be other-than-human persons. In other words, people relate to these beings not as "its," but as "persons."

In fact, humans around the globe relate to non–human beings in the universe in myriad ways. Humans ask non–human beings for assistance, or to make specific events occur. Humans beg for forgiveness from, make promises to, and bargains with, forsake, reunite with, and doubt non–human beings. Some humans search for such beings throughout their lives, while others are born into traditions to which they belong for their entire lives. Some humans believe in a singular entity such as "God," while others believe in a multitude of gods and/or goddesses, or in the constant active presence of a spirit, entity, energy, or aspect of a universal element. In many cases, humans interact with these ancestors, animals and plants, celestial bodies, or one of various other manifestations as people—just not human people.

Among Native American nations, certain communities have been living in traditional homelands for centuries. In other cases these environmental relationships have developed after communities have settled in new territories, either by force or by choice. Often such relationships have been expressed in terms of kinship, and have encouraged attention to the health of plant and animal beings by means of daily practices as well as through performance of particular ritual actions. In reciprocal fashion those plant and animal beings have aided human health by providing food, medicine, and the raw materials for a variety of goods from which humans have constructed their built environments. Narrative traditions in such cultures often have detailed these relationships, featuring the animals and plants of particular landscapes as proactive characters.

People in many communities worldwide have long recognized the importance of ethically and morally sustainable practices with regard to animals and plants. Yet somewhere along the way there also have been disconnects; at times the message has gotten lost in translation between cultures. As a result, historically, Indigenous notions of relationships with other beings in the universe no doubt have contributed mightily to a generalized core motif in both classic popular and academic stereotypes, that of Indigenous peoples being "anti-scientific." This vague designation has provided a convenient counterpoint to postulated nonindigenous, "scientific," "educated," "rational" ideas and approaches in scholarship and other human endeavors. As a result, Indigenous explanatory frameworks often have been parsed variously as Disneyesque fantasy; the beliefs of the "savage," "heathen," or uneducated; or quaint, children's-book fare.

But of course the connections between Indigenous cultural narratives, ritual activities and particular food "persons" in these individual communities are *not* elements of a romanticized Disneyesque fantasy. They are in fact constituent parts of diverse cultural systems of relationships. They deserve to be taken seriously.

The essays in this volume emphasize how Indigenous community members assert authority in terms of interpreting their cultural practices and narratives, as well as their histories, and present circumstances. In this regard, the issue of "tradition" is complex. As they determine how best to chart a path forward into the future, often Indigenous communities are revitalizing associated beliefs, practices, and items, including foods, that are designated as being "traditional," "precontact," or "precolonial." It is certainly a valid question to consider the extent to which the cultural elements are in fact authentically any of these things, or if one can even know. And what does one make of cultural exchange? Does emphasis on such elements preclude recognition of the adoption or adaptation of elements from other cultures?

Archaeologists scour middens for bits of organic data, and check teeth in skeletal remains for evidence of what a particular community's ancestors ate. But can scholars, and for that matter members of the communities themselves, know for sure how their ancestors related to the sources of their foodstuffs, animal and vegetable? By the same token, assigning the designation "traditional" is a relative matter. One must consider what data is deemed appropriate to make such assertions, who is characterizing the information, and which a priori cultural assumptions are informing their views. Often what observers, visitors, and latecomers to a particular area documented when they arrived is designated a cultural fault line, an artificial Rubicon one must never cross in academic discourse. In the absence of physical or written historical evidence, are such data as oral history and cultural narratives of any utility at all?

Anyone with more than a passing interest in scholarship about Indigenous peoples knows that examples abound of discursive approaches in which authors either assail, pity, or champion Indigenous communities for refusing to adapt, while simultaneously bemoaning the loss of something authentic and pure due to what is characterized as an inevitable cultural slippage in the face of the steamroller of contact. All of these viewpoints assert authority over someone else's history.

James Clifford addressed these issues of history, evidence, and tradition in his book *Returns: Becoming Indigenous in the Twenty-First Century*. At the turn of the twenty-first century, many Indigenous communities have weathered the storm of very real challenges to their existence. They have defied the standard narrative of a "tragic" and "inevitable" fate, by,

> adapting and recombining the remnants of an interrupted way of life. They reach back selectively to deeply rooted, adaptive traditions: creating new pathways in a complex postmodernity. Cultural endurance is a process of becoming.[11]

This statement encapsulates the fundamental concept in Clifford's book, and is reflected in the book's title. Later in the book, to support this idea, Clifford invoked Stuart Hall's notion

> that a discursive linking of pasts and futures is integral to the positioning of collective subjects. Thus, to imagine a coherent future, people must selectively mobilize past resources—historical practices that take diverse forms and are expressed in unfamiliar idioms.[12]

Drawing from the work of Raymond Williams, Clifford argued that this multiplicity of cultural practices and expressions stops prevalent historical narratives in their tracks. For example, the long-standard narrative about the general "waning significance" of religion in society cannot account for the "many forms of religious practice today." Thus, "the global reach of Pentacostalism" simply does not compute. In the same way, when Indigenous communities look to their pasts to inform their futures, "[w]hen 'ancient' traditions are understood to be effectively 'modern,' the whole direction of Western historical development wavers."[13] In both cases, a standard narrative edifice is shaken, and begins to teeter under the weight of its own contradictions. Furthermore, when analysis shifts from Europe to

> the variegated and contradictory zones of colonial and postcolonial contact and struggle, Williams's sense of the "historical" is further complicated—thrown into dialogical relations of translation.[14]

At this point Clifford reminded readers of his own past assertion "that 'history' belongs, significantly, to others. Its discourses and temporal shapes are idiomatic and varied." He concluded, as follows:

> A concept of "historical practice" can help expand our range of attention, allowing us to take seriously the claims of oral transmission, genealogy, and ritual processes. These embodied, practical ways of representing the past have not been considered fully, realistically, historical by modern ideologies that privilege literacy and chronology. Historical practice can act as a translation tool for rethinking "tradition," a central process of indigenous survival and renewal.[15]

The chapters of this volume, as distinct as they are in terms of subject matter and method, share this commitment to treat as authentic the cultural products of Indigenous communities, and to accord them the same veracity as archaeological evidence and written evidence arranged in a linear chronology.

~

Conceptions of Indigenous peoples as being anti-scientific and anti-intellectual, resistant to change, and even childlike are rooted in centuries-old stereotypes. Scholarly, theological, and popular culture representations have contributed to the continued acceptance of characterizations with these underlying ideas buttressing them, while simultaneously romanticizing chosen characteristics as potent, symbolic elements of what it means to be "American."[16]

Corn also has morphed into a potent symbolic component of what it means to be "American." In a swift effort to illustrate the connection between tropes about Indigenous peoples and the symbol of corn, I now briefly survey early selected non-indigenous perspectives on corn and Indigenous botanical and cultivation knowledge. Along with scholarly critiques of them, I add review and critique of a 1953 magazine advertisement for corn and a 1959 account of animism written by Christian missionaries. I offer these observations to readers not to support a universal explanation, but simply as "food for thought."

Corn has held symbolic capital for many nonindigenous people in the United States throughout the nation's history. In this regard, historian Katherine Vester's finely detailed study of food and American identities, *A Taste of Power: Food and American Identities* offers an important summary. In a cogent discussion of the symbolism of corn in United States colonial history, Vester demonstrated how Indigenous foods, in particular corn, were depicted as powerful symbols for colonists as they strove to survive and then distinguish themselves from their European counterparts, in particular Britain. In the face of "widely circulating theories" that warned of regression "into a state of savagery . . . Anglo-Americans strived to demonstrate that they were not corrupted by living in an untamed landscape and in proximity to Indigenous peoples."[17] For such was the certain fate of "even the most civilized people . . . if exposed to insalubrious conditions of nature, climate, and food."[18]

Settlers of both Jamestown and Plymouth initially refused to eat corn. Fearing "for their humanity," those at "Jamestown would not eat corn even when faced with the prospect of starving." At Plymouth they "started cultivating corn only after all their European crops failed." Corn was cultivated and consumed in Europe at that time, but "mostly in rural areas and by the poor." Cornmeal was considered "too coarse for fine dining, and fit only for feeding animals."[19]

However, the tide turned for humble corn. In January 1766, Benjamin Franklin actually defended cornmeal in a letter sent to a London newspaper. Franklin, using "the pseudonym 'Homespun,'" verbally cloaked himself in corn husks when he responded to a published letter alleging that "Americans were dependent on English imports of tea, as their breakfast of cornmeal was indigestible without it." Sprinkling "the Native American names of Indian corn dishes," into his prose like seeds into the ground, Franklin wrote "'that Indian corn, take it for all in all, is one of the most agreeable and wholesome grains in the world.'"[20] In doing so, according to Vester,

> Franklin invokes the colonies' cultural difference from the mother country, perhaps menacingly, with the allusion to its "savage" heritage the way protesters would soon masquerade as Native Americans to dump English tea into the Boston harbor.[21]

It is possible that those protesters were masquerading as "Mohawks" in an effort to "honor" Indigenous people, similar to the claims of sports teams such as the Washington Football Team (which for too long was known as the "R-word"). However, it does seem more likely that they were doing so in order to avoid recognition and retribution, much like why Franklin was masquerading as "Homespun." Continuing its rehabilitation into a symbol of nascent national pride, corn made its way into "Yankee Doodle Dandy" renditions. It even was celebrated in Joel Barlow's 1793 post-Revolution "famous mock-epic 'The Hasty Pudding' . . . as a quintessential American food to describe the values the nation hoped to uphold."[22]

In terms of nonindigenous views of Indigenous botanical knowledge, the first account I offer is of the Jesuit Joseph-François Lafitau's 1716 "discovery" of ginseng. Christopher M. Parsons noted that, "in his *Mémoire*, Joseph-François Lafitau maintained the complex and ambivalent relationship with indigenous knowledge." He did so by "alternating between crediting himself with the intellectual heavy lifting and revealing his dependence on local networks of knowledgeable women."[23] According to Parsons, Lafitau

> suggested that the Haudenosaunee were largely unaware of the significance of their own botanical knowledge, and he denied that they were capable of joining a scientific discussion in their own right . . . Indigenous knowledge was incomplete and could only be understood through a comparative analysis that highlighted continuities and downplayed local particularities, yet it remained a valuable shadow of an original knowledge shared by all humanity.[24]

Two centuries later, the inferiority of Indigenous botanical knowledge in relation to "scientific" knowledge was a point of emphasis prevalent in boarding schools for Native American children. Jennifer Bess provided one example of this bias in an article about attitudes concerning corn cultivation at the Chilocco Indian Industrial School in Oklahoma in the early twentieth century. Bess cited a 1906 letter written by the superintendent of the school, Samuel M. McCowan, describing a World's Fair exhibit in which corn from students' home communities in New Mexico, Arizona, and elsewhere was displayed among other " 'native foods.' " As Bess characterized his commentary, "[i]n a statement typically dismissive of indigenous species and indigenous understanding of selective breeding, McCowan's verdict was that the corn 'was miserably poor.' " Of the exhibit he concluded, " '[t]he chief values seemed to be to illustrate the degenerate results of neglect and in-breeding.' " The Chilocco corn, on the other hand, was vastly superior. The School's "improvements and . . . engineering" had "produced kernels 'thick-skinned and filled to bursting with food elements.' "[25]

Bess argued that McCowan's

> ignorance of the maintenance of strains grown carefully by Hidatsa such as Buffalo Bird Woman (Wilson [1917] 1987), as well as Tewa, Pima, and Hopi farmers, for example, marginalizes not only a long history of empirically grown science, but spiritual and religious traditions connected to specific varieties.[26]

To further support the point, Bess quoted from a 1910 publication in which one of the boarding school teachers, J. W. Van Zant, spoke of an " 'age in which farming has become a science.' "[27] Finally, Bess pointed out that such disregard for Indigenous knowledge became part of the rhetoric of empire in the United States, even enshrined in reports to Congress:

> Even in the case of corn, ignorance, dissatisfaction, and marginalization of traditional environmental knowledge, including breeding practices, predate the foundation of the USDA and its quest for seeds as the Commissioner of Patents reported to Congress in 1838 that "there can be no doubt that the crop of Indian corn may be improved at least one-third, without any extra labor." (Conover 1924, 28).[28]

Though hardly comprehensive, these examples do demonstrate that there were negative evaluations of Indigenous botanical and cultivation knowledge which persisted from the early eighteenth century through the early twentieth. These accounts are consistent in the sense that all held steadfast to the dichotomy incontrovertibly subverting Indigenous knowledge to "science." This dichotomy is of course itself rooted in earlier images, in which Indigenous peoples themselves were portrayed as part of the landscape along with the flora and fauna.[29] The contrast, or dyad, became so ingrained in United States popular culture that through much of the twentieth century it featured prominently in food advertising campaigns.

There are many examples to choose from to illustrate the point, but in keeping with the theme of the symbolic significance of corn, here I offer for consideration a print advertisement for Green Giant brand "Niblets" corn that appeared on the back cover of the November 23, 1953 issue of *Life* magazine.[30] At the midpoint of the twentieth century *Life* magazine was a cultural juggernaut. It is difficult to characterize the scope of its significance as a media outlet. *Life* reported on cultural trends and set them as well. Photojournalistic essays combined succinct reporting, first with high-quality black-and-white, and then later, color photography. The format was wildly popular. For all of these reasons I think an advertisement for Green Giant brand "Niblets" corn on the back cover of the 1953 Thanksgiving issue of *Life* magazine provides an instructive popular cultural snapshot to illustrate my point.

This advertisement features a cartoonish drawing of a man with copper-colored skin, dressed in what appear to be buckskin clothes and moccasins, with a single giant feather attached to his headband. Crouched down on his haunches and hands, he stares with a stupefied grin on his face at a cornstalk inches from his prominent nose. To the right of the figure is a can filled with corn kernels, identified by a plain white label with the words "Niblets up to now" printed on it in plain black type. Underneath it in large print is the phrase "Indian discovered corn," followed by additional text in much smaller type.[31]

However, rather than read the fine print, the eye is drawn to a second can, seemingly suspended upside-down above the first, also filled with corn kernels. Writing is clearly visible on it, as well as an upside-down caption. This spurs the reader to turn the entire page upside down.

When one does so, suddenly the cartoon on the page reveals a second image conjoined upside-down with the first: the face of a man in glasses and a tie, staring down a can of corn and literally licking his lips in anticipation. Quick review: an image of a man in glasses and a tie staring longingly at a can of corn is combined with an image of a man in buckskin and feathers interacting moronically with a corn plant. This, in a nutshell, or a corn kernel, is the "anti-scientific"/"scientific" dichotomy.

This second can also has a white label, but this one, instead of having a label with plain black type, is colorfully illustrated with the eponymous Green Giant holding a large ripe ear of corn. Also colorfully imprinted on the label are the phrases, "Niblets brand / Fresh corn off the cob / NEW fresh-flavor process"; and the words "New Process Niblets" are printed next to the can. Finally, the caption underneath this second can reads "Science discovers New Niblets." Thus, the captions underneath both cans form a couplet: "Indian discovered corn" / "Science discovers New Niblets."[32]

To make sure the point of all of this was not lost on the readers, the fine print under both captions explains further. Under the first can the text reads,

> Indian discovered corn . . . but it remained for the Green Giant folks to make it a delicacy. They pioneered in seed breeding, flavor farming, and vacuum packaging to bring you corn-on-the-cob without the cob. Or, as it's better known, Niblets Brand whole kernel corn . . . finest corn up to now.[33]

And under the second can:

> Science discovers New Niblets . . . Now Green giant scientists have found a way to give America's most popular corn new natural color and flavor. They've developed a new "fresh-flavor" process that quick-cooks new Niblets in 7 minutes (instead of 35). See the difference . . . taste the difference at your dinner table tonight.[34]

A few observations: The singular term "Indian" seems to be a telling, though grammatically incorrect contrasting concept for "Science," rather than a typographical error or a crude attempt at stereotypical humor. In 1953, "seed breeding, flavor farming, and vacuum packaging," were wonderful new innovations, and the ability to bestow "new natural color and flavor" on the corn due to the " 'fresh-flavor' process" seemed almost magical. And what's more, it was faster to prepare! Almost too good to be true. But wait, the fact that it was touted as the "finest corn up to now" teased of further innovations just around the corner. Who knew corn could be so exciting?

The proposition that Indigenous people discovered corn, but it took the friendly folks down at Green Giant to turn it into a "delicacy," resolves the historical ambivalence about it discussed above. Corn had been modified successfully, just as many of the boarding school proponents had hoped to do with Native American children. By the 1950s corn certainly had come a long way, elevated from a food only fit for animals, to being worthy of Anglo consumption, to being considered American food.

The 1953 advertisement's basic message of "Indians *discovered* corn / Science made it better" continued to reflect the deeply engrained notion of the inferiority of Indigenous knowledge that had been codified centuries earlier. But it also gave it new life. Here in the advertisement for Green Giant brand "Niblets" corn, chosen for the back cover of the Thanksgiving holiday issue of the most popular magazine in the United States, the dichotomy is plainly and crudely rendered.[35]

Here too in the advertisement one can find an allusion to another critical element of the perceived anti-scientific Indigenous approach: the concept of other-than-human persons, discussed above. That man clad in buckskin might be interpreted as prostrating himself in front of the corn plant, that is, praying to it. Parsed as "animism," some theologians and scholars have deployed this concept to contrast Indigenous religions negatively with other religions, including Christianity.

My thoughts about this subject stem in part from reviewing a 1959 missionary publication titled *Introducing Animism*. The authors of the text were Rev. Eugene A. Nida and William A. Smalley; at the time they were the secretary and an associate secretary for translations of the American Bible Society. Text on the front and back inside covers announced that the book would provide a global survey of the phenomenon:

> The word "animism" is not easily defined. The authors . . . explain that it has two separate and valid meanings. One is the definition of anthropologists, who designate it as the belief in spirits.

> More popularly, the word has a broader meaning as the name for all kinds of primitive religions.[36]

In a section titled, "Weaknesses in Animistic Beliefs," the missionary authors provided a list of reasons for the "inherent weakness in the primitive religions."[37] This statement is worth quoting at some length:

> In the first place, there is no fundamental moral basis in animism . . . a religious belief that is scientifically preposterous may still enjoy a long and comfortable life, for worshipers seem quite capable of suspending the scientific part of their minds while worshiping. However, they cannot suspend judgment on what is morally contemptible while at the same time being challenged by a deep religious sentiment that is basically good and just. As in the case of the religions of ancient Greece and Rome, the vulnerable point was the traditional mythology, filled with the absurd moral antics of the gods. By the process of allegorizing, an attempt was made to adjust such myths to the science of the day, but they could not be refurbished to meet the moral challenge posed by the Christians.[38]

This remarkably forthright passage encapsulates a theological argument against animism. According to the authors, animistic beliefs, like "the religions of ancient Greece and Rome," lack a "fundamental moral basis," due to their "traditional mythology." Akin to "the absurd moral antics of the gods," these beliefs could not "meet the moral challenge posed by the Christians." This was beyond not aligning with the prevailing "science of the day."

The authors concluded that for converts, "becoming a Christian has meant a step from basic mistrust of an irresponsible spirit world to growing confidence in an eternal God."[39] So in this case the contrast is belief in "an eternal God" versus belief in spirits. These statements reflect negative interpretations of both "other-than-human persons" and Indigenous knowledge versus "the science of the day." One might modify the "Niblets" dyad accordingly: "Indians discovered Animism / Christianity discovers Morality."

Over the sixty or so years since the 1953 magazine advertisement and the 1959 missionary handbook, such ideas and attitudes about Indigenous knowledge and "scientific credibility" still have found traction in scholarship. Vestiges of this "anti-scientific" assessment have continued to surface in the scholarly discourse regarding Indigenous foodways. As Suzanne Crawford O'Brien and Kimberly Wogahn assert in their essay for this collection: "anthropological scholarship has largely misrepresented Native land management practices, first denying their existence, and where admitting they exist, placing these cultivation practices on the 'backward, less-developed side of the imaginary evolutionary scale.'"[40]

However, a shift is occurring. In his article about Lafitau, Parsons identified a group of contemporary scholars whose

> work has reconceptualized the nature of scientific activity in a multicultural, epistemologically diverse Atlantic world, answering the call to use "recent methodologies in history, anthropology, and archaeology" to adequately capture traces of the knowledge of indigenous actors who remain underrepresented in histories of the rise of Western science.[41]

Certainly many of the essays in this collection are illustrations of such approaches in Native American communities. Parsons concluded with a statement that I think encapsulates important features of the current state of the discourse:

> Environmental and Native American histories can demonstrate the local ramifications of the creation of global science in early America and the Atlantic world. These are particularly important lessons to bear in mind in an era when ecologists and Native Americans are again being asked to collaborate in a bid to better know and protect American environments.[42]

In an article on contemporary tribal watershed management, Amanda Cronin and David M. Ostergan discussed the important point of the gradual acceptance of Traditional Ecological Knowledge, or "TEK":

> TEK is slowly gaining Western recognition as a valid and integral component of ecosystem management. Even as some writers caution against direct applicability of management based on TEK, Dennis Martinez of the National Park Service views integration of TEK as vital to a global reconciliation with Indigenous peoples.[43]

The authors then quoted Martinez: " 'Native cultures, although badly fragmented by the impacts of industrial societies, still hold onto significant ecological wisdom based on long ecological experience in particular places. To ignore that millennia-long local experience and knowledge is to risk doing poor science.' "[44]

James R. Veveto and Kevin Welch presented one good contemporary illustration of this point in a book chapter detailing revitalization efforts underway among members of the Eastern Band of Cherokee Indians in western North Carolina. The authors described the contemporary strategy of what they referred to as the " 'memory banking' of farmers' cultural and agroecological knowledge about traditional cultivars to complement the more traditional scientific *ex situ* conservation strategy of collecting and storing folk crop varieties in seed bank facilities."[45] Likewise, several of the essays in this volume illustrate how this notion of "memory banking" traditional knowledge and employing it in conjunction with "traditional scientific" knowledge is being put into practice in many Indigenous North American communities.

~

In a chapter of *The Routledge History of American Foodways*, Angela Jill Cooley asserted that "food historians need to take up the challenge to write more region-based histories of food—starting with the American Indian story."[46] She cited Rayna Green's chapter in *The Larder: Food Studies Methods from the American South*: "Green laments the lack of research on native food practices in the south." Cooley cited Green's discussion of how "the 1960s emphasis toward giving proper recognition to the cultural endeavors of historically marginalized populations . . . virtually ignored indigenous communities." Cooley concluded, "future scholarly attention to American Indian foodways will broaden our understanding of regionalism" in terms of food studies.[47] Such attention also will contribute to the growing body of scholarship on religion and food.[48]

In many cases the experiences of Native Americans reflect those of people worldwide in that they raise concerns about international issues that impact everyone on the planet. Issues such as access to affordable, healthy food and clean water are global concerns. More attention to the study of religions and food will add valuable additional specific perspectives and data to the discourse. This collection was conceived as part of that effort.

it illustrates that not all foodways that once were significant have been revived by Indigenous nations.

Yaupon is currently experiencing a popular culture regional resurgence in certain areas of the country as an enjoyable, restorative beverage. As Vick explains, historically, it was said to lack any medicinal properties other than as a diuretic. This past assessment also speaks to the heart of the "anti-scientific" stereotype I sketched out above. However, as Vick notes, "contemporary research . . . has shown that yaupon holly foliage possesses a high antioxidant capacity," as well as "anti-inflammatory properties shown to have potential to inhibit colorectal cancer and inflammatory bowel disease (IBD)."[62]

As this book was going to press, purely by coincidence I discovered an example of yaupon's current popular culture appeal, and the use of old stereotypes to market it. In the aisles of a chain store that features food, drink, and household items from around the globe, I found it staring at me at eye level on a shelf: Yaupon Brothers' American Tea Company Fire Roasted Warrior's Yaupon Tea. The label was a parchment-like color and was decorated with some generic geometric design images (that someone thought looked "Indigenous") and the accompanying drawing like the label text was monochromatic, in black ink. Depicted were two individuals with what looked to be hides covering their waists down to their knees. They were crouched over a kettle perched on an open fire, mixing and stirring something into the kettle. On the back a portion of the text read,

> Florida's native Timucua people roasted Yaupon leaves over an open fire before going into battle . . . In tribute to the ancestral tribes of Florida, we've brought this powerful blend to you. Sweet and smoky with an intensity that will awaken your inner warrior. Make it part of your daily ritual.

Around the bottom of the round container it read: "Naturally Caffeinated-Wild & Organic-Grown in Florida-Antioxidant Super-Food."[63]

Once more I want to return to the image of the Green Giant Niblet advertisement in *Life* magazine discussed above. It's been nearly seventy years since that ad appeared, but the Yaupon Brothers' Warrior's Yaupon Tea, with its stereotypical views of Indigenous religions as well as Indigenous foodways, would fit right alongside it. While much has changed since the 1950s, the example of yaupon proves that old stereotypes, both written and illustrated, remain difficult to exorcise from cultural usage.

Dennis Kelley's chapter 8, "The Semiotics of Resistance: On the Power of Frybread" discusses what is likely one of the most controversial Indigenous North American foods: frybread. Kelley incorporates both historical data and contemporary cultural debate to produce a well-balanced assessment of the debate surrounding frybread. In a section of his essay titled "Frybread as Sign," Kelley zeroes in on "the central puzzle in the frybread tale":

> how it fits into the current discourse on food sovereignty, health and wellness programs in Indian Country, and concerted efforts to regain traditional food gathering and preparation techniques as acts of cultural revitalization.[64]

Kelley argues in his chapter's introductory section that the

> chapter will turn on that seeming contradiction: a traditional Native food that was imposed on Native people within the last 150 or so years. But therein lies the bigger issue that goes to the theme of this book. Frybread has become one of the symbolic touchstones that connects American Indian communities to both their discrete ethnic identities and traditions, and to the reality of their colonized status. And it is this aspect, I will argue, that gives frybread its power and significance.[65]

Kelley's contribution acts as an effective complement to the rest of this volume, providing an important critical perspective as it addresses issues of contemporary identity signification and urbanization in the context of the foodways revitalization discussion. As mentioned above, the topic elicits strong opinions from scholars and the general public alike. Interested readers are encouraged to consult the work of Devon A. Mihesuah for an important, and very different, perspective in the discourse about frybread, including discussion of the "fry bread myth."[66]

Michelene E. Pesantubbee's Epilogue provides the perfect coda to this collection. In addition to amplifying key points the authors discussed in the preceding chapters, Pesantubbee incorporates points of information about foodways from eight additional Indigenous nations. Interested readers can note these references and use them as invitations to learn more about these cultures. Taken together, Pesantubbee's references illustrate another important point: There is no monolithic, singular "Indigenous

North American" or "Native American" foodway. Likewise, there is no monolithic, singular "Indigenous North American" or "Native American" religion. There are a multitude of Indigenous nations in North America. Like nations large or small elsewhere in the world, while certain elements of their cultures are similar, other elements are as different and distinct as those of any other two nations.

Finally, Pesantubbee also incorporates a key reference to the methodological influence of Dr. Inés Talamantez, when she notes of the authors in this volume,

> They all have been trained, as Inés Talamantez taught, to direct their research toward the needs of the communities they study as those communities identify them.[67]

A few words about the book project and the individual to whose memory it is dedicated are in order. This volume is the result of two consecutive years of paper sessions presented by the Native Traditions in the Americas Unit at the American Academy of Religion Annual Meeting. My coeditor Michelene Pesantubbee and I served together as national cochairs of the Native Traditions unit during this time, and I would like to thank for her work on this project, as well as her collegiality.

As this book was going to press, Dr. Inés M. Talamantez unexpectedly passed. Dr. Talamantez was a longtime professor in the Department of Religious Studies at the University of California, Santa Barbara (UCSB), where she helmed the PhD track specializing in Native American religious traditions. The UCSB program is unique in that it is the only institution in the United States that offers such a subject emphasis.

Dr. Talamantez was a founding member of, and an inspirational and tireless advocate for both the Native Traditions in the Americas and the Indigenous Religions units of the American Academy of Religion. Dr. Talamantez had a lifelong passion for and dedication to the subject matter. She was an insistent advocate for the academic study of Indigenous peoples' cultural, religious, and intellectual traditions. She demanded that they be taken seriously and be incorporated into broader conversations in the academic study of religions.

In addition to being a colleague of all the contributors to this volume, Dr. Talamantez served as a mentor and teacher to many. She was the dissertation advisor for several contributors, including me. In the epilogue to this volume, as noted above, Michelene Pesantubbee spoke to the methodological influence of Dr. Talamantez on her students. To reiterate, Dr. Talamantez insisted that her students "direct their research towards the needs of the communities they study as those communities identify them."

This approach required that her students venture out of their comfort zones, beyond libraries and archives, and into the communities they studied. It dovetailed with another of her methodological principles: the necessity of incorporating fieldwork, or cultural consultation, into one's research program. Her profile statement on the UCSB website sums up her approach to her work: "my emphasis on teaching and mentoring is critical to my work, as is field research."[68]

I would like to share a brief personal story that helps to illustrate Dr. Talamantez's significance to her colleagues and her generosity of spirit. It was the last time I saw her, at the AAR Annual Meeting in November 2018. The custom for many years has been that at least once during the conference, a large group of colleagues associated with the Native Traditions unit, both professors and students, all go out to dinner after the final sessions of the day ended. This occasion was a great evening, one in which Dr. Talamantez, as usual, was surrounded both by many people she had known for a long time as well as by some new faces. Several tables had been pushed together to accommodate the group, and during the meal, all around what was now one large table, everyone was part of a conversation, catching up with colleagues and making new acquaintances.

At the center of it all sat Inés, the focal point and magnet of this social energy. People vied for her attention, and she took time to speak with everyone. Wherever she went, whomever she met, Inés always left a lasting impression. She was just that kind of person.

When the meal ended and people were saying their goodbyes and heading out into the night, Inés and I took a few minutes to catch up a bit. I had not yet had a chance to speak with her, so we sat off to the side and talked. She asked about my family, as she always did. On this night at the AAR, as our conversation drew to a close, I told her about the plan to dedicate this volume to her. Her face lit up and she beamed.

The contributors to this volume thank and strive to honor Dr. Inés Talamantez with this collection. Dr. Talamantez was instrumental in shaping

45. James R. Veveto and Kevin Welch, "Food from the Ancestors: Documentation, Conservation, and Revival of Eastern Cherokee Heirloom Plants," in *Seeds of Resistance, Seeds of Hope: Place and Agency in the Conservation of Biodiversity*, eds. Virginia D. Nazarea, Robert E. Rhoades, and Jenna E. Andrews-Swann (Tucson: University of Arizona Press, 2013), 67.

46. Angela Jill Cooley, "Food and Regionalism," in *The Routledge History of American Foodways*, eds. Michael D. Wise and Jennifer Jensen Wallach (New York: Routledge, 2016), 322.

47. All, Cooley, "Food and Regionalism," 322.

48. See, for example, Benjamin Zeller, Marie Dallam, Reid Neilson, Nora L Rubel, and Martha Finch, eds., *Religion, Food, and Eating in North America*, Arts and Traditions of the Table: Perspectives on Culinary History (New York: Columbia University Press, 2014); Todd LeVasseur, Pramod Parajuli, and Norman Wirzba, eds., *Religion and Sustainable Agriculture: World Spiritual Traditions and Food Ethics* (Lexington: University Press of Kentucky, 2016).

49. Andrea McComb Sanchez, "Balance and a Bean: Restoring *Himdag* through Traditional Farming and Sacred Knowledge," 33, 34.

50. McComb Sanchez, "Balance and a Bean," 41.

51. McComb Sanchez, "Balance and a Bean," 43.

52. Crawford O'Brien, "Of Coyotes and Culverts," 61.

53. Crawford O'Brien, "Of Coyotes and Culverts," 64.

54. Both, Michael McNally, "Where Food Grows on the Water: *Manoomin/* Wild Rice and Anishinaabe Peoplehood," 75.

55. White Earth Land Recovery Project Native Harvest Website, quoted in McNally, "Where Food Grows on the Water," 95, note 40.

56. McNally, "Where Food Grows on the Water," 75.

57. Both, Lawrence W. Gross, "Harvesting Wild Rice," 99.

58. All, Gross, "Harvesting Wild Rice," 104, 100, 104.

59. David S. Walsh, "They Call Us 'Caribou Eaters': Negotiating Tłı̨chǫ Dene Relationships with Caribou," 124.

60. Walsh, "They Call Us 'Caribou Eaters,'" 123.

61. Suzanne Crawford O'Brien and Kimberly Wogahn, "Bringing a Berry Back from the Land of the Dead," 142.

62. R. Alfred Vick, "Yaupon," 170.

63. Yaupon Brothers' American Tea Company Fire Roasted Warrior's Yaupon Tea, Yaupon Brothers LLC, www.YauponBrothers.com.

64. Dennis Kelley, "The Semiotics of Resistance: On the Power of Frybread," 198, 198–199.

65. Dennis Kelley, "The Semiotics of Resistance," 196.

66. Devon A. Mihesuah, "Comanche Traditional Foodways and the Decline of Health," in *Indigenous Food Sovereignty in the United States*, eds. Elizabeth Hoover and Devon A. Mihesuah, 239. See for example, Devon Mihesuah, "Indigenous

Health Initiatives, Frybread, and the Marketing of Non-Traditional "Traditional" American Indian Foods," *Native American and Indigenous Studies* 3, no. 2 (Fall 2016): 45–69. Also see Mihesuah's comments about fry bread in "Searching for *Haknip Achukma* (Good Health): Challenges to Food Sovereignty Initiatives in Oklahoma," in *Indigenous Food Sovereignty in the United States*, eds. Elizabeth Hoover and Devon A. Mihesuah, Hoover and Mihesuah, eds., 98, 99.

67. Michelene E. Pesantubbee, "Epilogue," 212.

68. Inés Talamantez Faculty Profile, https://www.religion.ucsb.edu/people/faculty/ines-talamantez/. Also see this UCSB Facebook post for reflections on her life: https://www.facebook.com/ucsbreligion/posts/10156942340097880?__xts__[0]=68.ARBuH5DSb7qI-T5oGk_SKDLoUY5LP6t_K4GlWDsKrk07HeyYZwcTsK-RH61ySMbpLcWO5iDZBx35E0Tkdbi6yzCsytylvTN2IJ52_NkeUVb40Slq4N0mb-Nn6Uo9SdfNYCJbbE66_HD6VAYfehP9d_XNPOogA4E8PrS01Jw6kV5Db_UI3H-h0x5b48szdWnxLZRi5y4qICC_jaimygdNVFLd6bu376f57aqNXJgfmVOc-bHRDTW4efz26174d1TXQLnKG9qDx0TnlMEUc7xU-6vCB6GKJMkHXZLnM2t-06NAsMWA1aTHoPtJNbEj9pTlfl8QH342kXh0tLyRvYQ&__tn__=-R.

Bibliography

Basso, Keith. *Wisdom Sits in Places: Landscape and Language among the Western Apache.* Albuquerque: University of New Mexico Press, 1996.

Berkhofer, Robert. *The White Man's Indian: Images of the American Indian from Columbus to the Present.* New York: Vintage Books, 1978.

Bess, Jennifer. "Indigenizing the Safety Zone: Contesting Ideologies in Foodways at the Chilocco Indian Industrial School, 1902–1918." *Journal of the Southwest* 55, no. 2 (Summer 2013): 193–244.

Clifford, James. *Returns: Becoming Indigenous in the Twenty-First Century.* Cambridge, MA: Harvard University Press, 2013.

Cooley, Angela Jill. "Food and Regionalism." In *The Routledge History of American Foodways*, edited by Michael D. Wise and Jennifer Jensen Wallach, 311–25. New York: Routledge, 2016.

Cronin, Amanda, and David M. Ostergren, "Tribal Watershed Management: Culture, Science, Capacity, and Collaboration," *American Indian Quarterly* 31, no. 1 (Winter, 2007): 87–109.

Deur, Douglas, and Nancy Turner, *Keeping It Living: Traditions of Plant Use and Cultivation on the Northwest Coast of North America.* Seattle: University of Washington Press, 2005.

Franklin, Benjamin. *The Writings of Benjamin Franklin*, vol. 4. New York: Macmillan, 1906.

Hallowell, A. Irving. "Ojibwa Ontology, Behavior, and World View." In *Teachings from the American Earth: Indian Religion and Philosophy*, edited by Dennis

Tedlock and Barbara Tedlock. New York: Liveright, 1975, 141–78. Originally published in Stanley Diamond, ed., *Culture in History: Essays in Honor of Paul Radin*. New York: Columbia University Press, 1960.

Hill, Christina Gish. "Precolonial Foodways." In *The Routledge History of American Foodways*, edited by Michael D. Wise and Jennifer Jensen Wallach, 9–22. New York: Routledge, 2016.

Hoover, Elizabeth, and Devon A. Mihesuah, "Introduction." In *Indigenous Food Sovereignty in the United States: Restoring Cultural Knowledge, Protecting Environments, and Regaining Health*, edited by Elizabeth Hoover and Devon A. Mihesuah, 3–25. Norman: University of Oklahoma Press, 2019.

Kamal, Asfia Gulrukh, Rene Linklater, Shirley Thompson, Joseph Dipple, and Ithinto Mechisowin Committee. "A Recipe for Change: Reclamation of Indigenous Food Sovereignty in O-Pipon-Na-Piwin Cree Nation for Decolonization, Resource Sharing, and Cultural Restoration." *Globalizations* 12, no. 4 (June 2015): 559–75.

LeVasseur, Todd, Pramod Parajuli, and Norman Wirzba, eds., *Religion and Sustainable Agriculture: World Spiritual Traditions and Food Ethics*. Lexington: University Press of Kentucky, 2016.

Martinez, Dennis. "Protected Areas, Indigenous Peoples, and the Western Idea of Nature." *Ecological Restoration* 21, no. 4 (December 2003): 247–50.

Mihesuah, Devon A. "Indigenous Health Initiatives, Frybread, and the Marketing of Nontraditional 'Traditional' American Indian Foods." *Native American and Indigenous Studies* 3, no. 2 (2016): 45–69.

———. "Searching for *Haknip Achukma* (Good Health): Challenges to Food Sovereignty Initiatives in Oklahoma." In *Indigenous Food Sovereignty in the United States: Restoring Cultural Knowledge, Protecting Environments, and Regaining Health*, edited by Elizabeth Hoover and Devon A. Mihesuah, 94–121. New Directions in Native American Studies. Norman: University of Oklahoma Press, 2019.

———. "Comanche Traditional Foodways and the Decline of Health." In *Indigenous Food Sovereignty in the United States: Restoring Cultural Knowledge, Protecting Environments, and Regaining Health*, edited by Elizabeth Hoover and Devon A. Mihesuah, 223–52. New Directions in Native American Studies. Norman: University of Oklahoma Press, 2019.

Morrison, Dawn. "Indigenous Food Sovereignty: A Model for Social Learning." In *Food Sovereignty in Canada: Creating Just and Sustainable Food Systems*, edited by Hannah Wittman, Annette Aurélie Desmarias, and Nettie Wiebe, 97–113. Halifax, NS: Fernwood, 2011.

Nida, Eugene A., and William A. Smalley, *Introducing Animism*. New York: Friendship Press, 1959.

Parsons, Christopher M. "The Natural History of Colonial Science: Joseph-François Lafitau's Discovery of Ginseng and Its Afterlives." *William and Mary Quarterly* 73, no. 1 (January 2016): 37–72.

Perdue, Theda. *Cherokee Women: Gender and Culture Change, 1700–1835*. Lincoln: University of Nebraska Press, 1998.

Prendergast, Neil. "Food and the Environment." In *The Routledge History of American Foodways*, edited by Michael D. Wise and Jennifer Jensen Wallach, 261–75. New York: Routledge, 2016.

"Proclamation on the Treaty of Holston, 11 November 1791." *Founders Online*, National Archives. Accessed September 29, 2019. https://founders.archives.gov/documents/Washington/05-09-02-0100.

Prucha, Francis Paul. *The Great Father: The United States Government and the American Indians*, abridged ed. Lincoln: University of Nebraska Press, 2014.

Raster, Amanda, and Christina Gish Hill. "The Dispute Over Wild Rice: An Investigation of Treaty Agreements and Ojibwe Food Sovereignty." *Agriculture and Human Values* 34, no. 2 (June 1, 2017): 267–81. https://doi.org/10.1007/s10460-016-9703-6.

"Treaty with the Cherokee: 1791" [Treaty of Holston]. The Avalon Project: Documents in Law, History, and Diplomacy. Lillian Goldman Law Library, Yale Law School. Accessed November 8, 2019. https://avalon.law.yale.edu/18th_century/chr1791.asp. Source: *Indian Affairs: Laws and Treaties*, vol. II. (Treaties), compiled and edited by Charles J. Kappler, LL M, Clerk to the Senate Committee on Indian Affairs (Washington, DC: Government Printing Office, 1904).

Van Zandt, J. W. "Farm Department." *Indian School Journal* 10 (June 1910).

Vester, Katherine. *A Taste of Power: Food and American Identities*, California Studies in Food and Culture. Oakland: University of California Press, 2015.

Veveto, James R., and Kevin Welch. "Food from the Ancestors: Documentation, Conservation, and Revival of Eastern Cherokee Heirloom Plants." In *Seeds of Resistance, Seeds of Hope: Place and Agency in the Conservation of Biodiversity*, edited by Virginia D. Nazarea, Robert E. Rhoades, and Jenna E. Andrews-Swann, 65–84. Tucson: University of Arizona Press, 2013.

Yellow Bird, Michael. "'What We Want to Be Called': Indigenous Peoples' Perspectives on Racial and Ethnic Identity Labels." *American Indian Quarterly* 23, no. 2 (Spring 1999): 1–22.

Zeller, Benjamin, Marie Dallam, Reid Neilson, Nora L. Rubel, and Martha Finch, eds. *Religion, Food, and Eating in North America*. Arts and Traditions of the Table: Perspectives on Culinary History. New York: Columbia University Press, 2014.

Zogry, Michael "Lost in Conflation: Visual Culture and Constructions of the Category of Religion," *American Indian Quarterly* 35, no. 1 (Winter 2011): 1–55.

1

Balance and a Bean

Revitalizing *Himdag* through Traditional Farming and Sacred Knowledge

Andrea McComb Sanchez

In the summer of 2013, Tohono O'odham Community Action (TOCA) released the inaugural issue of its magazine, *Native Foodways*. TOCA was formed in 1996 as an independent grassroots organization, "dedicated to creating a healthy, culturally vital and sustainable community on the Tohono O'odham Nation."[1] This magazine, one of the many projects TOCA was involved in, was about creating "a tool for sharing between and among all people committed to the revitalization of Native food, culture, and community."[2] Among those who contributed to this groundbreaking issue were author, activist, and environmentalist, Winona LaDuke; chef and founder of the Native American Culinary Association (NACA), Nephi Craig; and chef, author, and Native foods historian, Lois Ellen Frank. It contains articles on Hopi and Coast Salish food traditions, food sovereignty, prickly pear harvesting, and basketry. This magazine, writes Terrol Dew Johnson, a member of the Tohono O'odham Nation and the magazine's publisher and editor-at-large, "is about more than what we eat."[3] That is because food itself is about more than just eating. Food is connected to and in many cases central to songs, dances, ceremonies, and sacred narratives. It is about personal and communal wellness, family, strength, economics, and Native sovereignty and is inextricably linked to traditional culture, worldviews, and religious beliefs and practices. Food is sacred. The term *foodways* is used to incorporate these interconnected elements that are involved in the production and consumption of food.

The Tohono O'odham, the People of the Desert (Tohono is "Desert" and O'odham is "People"), call their traditional life ways the *O'odham Himdag*, loosely translated as "The People's Way," and elements of *himdag* such as ceremonies, sacred narratives, stories, songs, and the language itself "are directly rooted in the systems of food production."[4] The knowledge needed for food production is part of environmental knowledge more broadly and the Tohono O'odham's collective knowledge of their environment makes up what can be labeled Traditional Ecological Knowledge, Indigenous Knowledge, or Native Science (hereafter referred to as TEK), which is an important part of the *O'odham Himdag*.[5] This chapter will discuss Tohono O'odham foodways with particular attention paid to the tepary bean. It will also briefly address some of the ways these food systems were and continue to be threatened by colonialism and environmental change and some revitalization efforts within the Tohono O'odham Nation.

TEK refers to the knowledge, beliefs, and practices of communities that developed from direct experience and long-term observation of the local environment. According to Fikret Berkes, TEK is "a cumulative body of knowledge, practice, and belief, evolving by adaptive processes and handed down through generations by cultural transmission, about the relationship of living beings (including humans) with one another and with their environment."[6] This local, relational, and situational knowledge is a process rather than a collected body of content.[7] Further, it is part of a way of life that has developed and is tied to a particular place, and where human beings are acknowledged as just one part of the greater whole; thus human beings need to be cognizant of the responsibilities that come with being human and work toward maintaining proper relationships not only within their own smaller human communities but with other-than-human animals, ancestors, spiritual beings, plant beings, water, and the land itself. Among indigenous people this has been passed on through songs, sacred narratives (also called myths), oral histories and stories, ceremonies, community laws, the structure of language, as well as through hunting, gathering, and agricultural practices. This demonstrates the interconnection of community identity, worldviews, religious beliefs and practices, and ecological values.

The Tohono *O'odham Himdag*, or Desert People's Way, "consists of the culture, way of life, and values that are uniquely held and displayed by the Tohono O'odham people."[8] *Himdag* incorporates everything that makes the Tohono O'odham who they are as a distinct people; it refers to their individual and collective life's journey and emphasizes living in balance and interacting correctly with the world. The people credit I'itoi with teaching them *himdag*; he is called Elder Brother and people look to him in times of need. According to one version of a sacred narrative I'itoi was one of the first three beings to be created along with Buzzard and Coyote, and in ancient times he called the Tohono O'odham from the underworld into the Sonoran desert.[9] The stories of his life and exploits make up an important part of O'odham sacred narratives, as do the teachings found within. The *O'odham Himdag*, as taught by I'itoi, includes knowledge about the land and how to have correct relationships with the land, knowledge about medicinal plants, the seasons, basketry, correct community relations, games, language, the past and the future, songs, stories, healing, ceremonies, and foodways. All of these and more are integrated and interconnected and tied to the Sonoran desert, the Tohono O'odham traditional homeland.[10] As Ruth Underhill wrote in her famous book *Papago Woman*, "it is the land that possesses the people. Its influence, in time, shapes their bodies, their language, even, a little, their religion."[11]

The Tohono O'odham have lived in the Sonoran desert for countless generations, or as many would say since time immemorial, in a region that averages five to ten inches of rainfall per year. Throughout this time knowledge, practices, and belief systems emerged out of their experiences and relationships with this land, with water, with all the different beings that share the desert, and with each other. One example of this, and an example of TEK, is the traditional calendar that is based around descriptions of temperature, rainfall, and the activities of plants and animals. This calendar is not fixed and the Tohono O'odham New Year begins roughly in late June or July with the ripening and harvest of *bahidaj*, red saguaro fruit located at the top of the tall cactus, and the arrival of the monsoon rains. The end of the previous year is marked by the ripening of the *bahidaj* and is called *Ha:ṣañ Ba:k Maṣad*, Saguaro Fruit Ripening Moon. Once the *bahidaj* is harvested, the new year begins with the coming of the monsoon rains, which start the next phase called Jukiabig *Maṣad* or Big Rains Moon. *Jukiabig Maṣad* is followed by *Sopol' Eṣabig Maṣad* (Short

Planting Moon), *Wasai Gakidag Maṣad* (Dry Grass Moon), *I'al Ju:pig Maṣad* (Small Rains Moon), *S-ke:g S-he:pijig Maṣad* (Pleasant Cold Moon), *Ge'e S-he:pijig Maṣad* (Big Cold Moon), *Gakimdag Maṣad* (Animals Loose Their Fat Moon), *U:walig Maṣad* (Deer Mating Moon), *Ce:dagi Maṣad* (Green Moon), *Uam Maṣad* (Yellow Moon), *U'us Wihogdag Maṣad* (Mesquite Bean Harvest Moon), and finally back to *Ha:ṣañ Ba:k Maṣad* (Saguaro Fruit Ripening Moon).[12] As will be discussed later, the ceremonial activities of the people during Saguaro Fruit Ripening Moon and into Big Rains Moon are thought to be responsible for bringing the rains; and rain is essential for agriculture within the Tohono O'odham homelands.

Like many indigenous people of the southwest the Tohono O'odham traditionally relied on a combination of harvesting wild foods, hunting, and farming. The Tohono O'odham are typically distinguished historically from their O'odham neighbors, the Akimel O'odham and the Hia C-ed O'odham, by their two-village system with winter villages located near mountains and springs where people relied on hunting and gathering, and their summer villages located near the flood plains for planting.[13] And like many other Native American groups the most important of their crops were the three sisters: maize, beans, and squash. While corn or maize was one of their most important crops, it was rivaled by a bean commonly called the tepary bean. This name refers to *Phaseolus acutifolius*, little brown, white, red, yellow, and black colored beans grown throughout the southwestern United States and northern Mexico since pre-Columbian times. The tepary bean is especially important to the Tohono O'odham because of its unique tolerance to drought.[14] In fact, the tepary bean is one of the most heat- and drought-tolerant crops in the world, along with having the highest protein content of any bean. The name "tepary" is thought by some to come from the Opata word *tepar*.[15] Other scholars argue that the word "tepary" comes from the Tohono O'odham phrase *t'bawĭ* (or *t'pawi*) "it's a bean."[16] The tepary bean, originally a wild plant, is particularly suited to the Sonoran Desert not only because of its tolerance to drought, in fact too much water will actually inhibit the production of the beans, but because of its ability to produce both pods and pollen in heat that consistently averages above 105 degrees during the growing season.[17] Whether the word *tepary* derives from the Opata or the Tohono O'odham language, since before Spanish colonial times the bean itself has been most closely linked to the Tohono O'odham, who call the bean *bawĭ* (also spelled *pawi*). The two main varieties cultivated by the Tohono O'odham were and continue to be the brown *wepegi bawĭ*, and the white *tota bawĭ*.

Further connecting the tepary bean to the Tohono O'odham is its link to the name given them by the Spanish, "Papago." The designation Papago is thought to be derived from the Pima language, and could be the Spanish transliteration of the phrase *papawi o'otam*, "tepary bean people," or from a condensation of *papavi kuadam*, "tepary bean eaters," or from the phrase *papawi'koa*, which means "eating tepary beans."[18] Whatever the origination of the name "Papago," which was officially rejected and replaced by their name for themselves in 1986, the association between the Tohono O'odham and the tepary bean is insinuated within this moniker.

Because of the aridity of the region tepary beans were historically planted only during monsoon season, which is approximately late June through September. For the remainder of the year the people gathered cholla buds and prickly pear fruit, mesquite bean pods and acorns, and hunted animals such as rabbits, deer, and javelina.[19] The time before monsoon season, May and into June, as well as being called *U'us Wihogdag Maṣad* (Mesquite Bean Harvest Moon) is also known as *Ko'ohk Maṣad* "the Painful Moon" because of the difficulty of finding food. During this extremely hot and dry time mesquite trees, whose pods and the seeds inside were ground into meal, provided the majority of the people's sustenance.[20]

Since the Tohono O'odham predominantly did not live along permanent streams or rivers, they relied instead on dry farming and *Ak Chin* farming, or floodwater farming. During monsoon season in the Sonoran Desert, rain pummels the earth and water is carried through channels and then released at the mouth of these washes. It was here, after the first rains, the Tohono O'odham planted their fields, creating an irrigation system on land that averages five to ten inches of rain a year.[21] These fields could be utilized year after year because soil is renewed through the mud and sand brought by the floodwaters. *Bawĭ*, the tepary bean, is particularly suited to this type of agriculture and to the unpredictability of water, because while water is needed for germination, which happens during the initial flood, the plant will actually produce more beans if deprived of water. It required extensive knowledge of storms and the different types of runoff they produced to know where and when and what to plant in different places within the flood plains. *Bawĭ* had to be planted immediately after water flooded the plain and planted in a location where subsequent flooding was less likely to carry the beans away. This required knowledge about cloud types and the nature and amount of rain that would come from different cloud types. It involved monitoring the clouds over the mountains to know when the floodwaters were coming so people could quickly prepare the fields by digging channels to catch

from the ribs of dead saguaros, filling their baskets with the pulp and leaving the skins with the red side pointing toward the sky to further help draw the rain.[28] The pulp is cooked that same day, reduced to jam, seeds, and syrup. The boiled syrup is poured in jars and set aside until the appropriate time to pull down the clouds. When the proper time is determined by the knowledge keepers the syrup is brought to the ceremonial house where it is mixed with water and set to ferment. This is accompanied by prayers, songs, and other ritual activities performed by ceremonial specialists and *mamakai* (medicine men) that are necessary to bring the wine into being and then pull down the clouds. To aid in the transformation people outside the ceremonial house dance and sing for four nights, after which the sacred wine needs to be completely consumed by the entire community, minus the children.[29]

It is the ceremonial consumption and expulsion of the wine that calls the clouds; the saturation of the body with the wine is thought to produce the saturation of the earth with the monsoon rains. As Maria Chona said, "Much, much liquor we made, and we drank it to pull down the clouds . . . people must make themselves drunk like plants in the rain, and they must sing for happiness."[30] Once the ceremony brings the clouds, the people can plant their crops.

This entire process involves religious elements. Before picking the fruit the saguaro is asked to bless the harvest, and only fruit at the correct stage of ripeness is ever taken, leaving the rest for the animals and birds. Every part of it from picking, to fermenting, to drinking, is accompanied by songs, by dancing, and by the recitation of sacred narratives that tell of rain, of growth, and of I'itoi, the one who in distant times taught them *himdag*.[31] According to Maria Chona it was I'itoi who taught the people about the saguaro and taught them the ceremony, telling them that all the wine must be drunk during this ceremony and none made again until the following year.[32] This and more is evoked through songs and recitations. Christine Johnson, an elder of No:lig village recalls a particular song that is sung to the saguaro with the words "They are ripening red / standing so visible in the distance / cloud rises over me / and moistens the earth."[33] She says,

> [t]his is a song to encourage the saguaro to be strong and to bear fruit and to thank the saguaro for its harvest, and for helping to bring the rain; which will help the seeds grow; which will help us grow our crops and help grow the materials

> to make our baskets which we use to carry the ripe saguaro fruit. In our family we sing this song before any saguaro fruit is harvested, as we pick the ripe fruit, and as we dance the dance to encourage the saguaro to grow.[34]

Songs, as the strongest form of vocalization during ceremonies, are aimed at the beings who are the subjects of the sacred narrative, such as I'itoi and *ha:ṣañ* (saguaro). The ritual recitations of sacred narratives during ceremonies are aimed at both these beings and humans; they are meant to reach the ears of the spiritual beings as well as teach the people who are listening.[35] Christine Johnson tells us this song is sung for *ha:ṣañ*, it is sung before the fruit is harvested, while picking the fruit, and as the people dance; because without the saguaro and the rain it brings there would be nothing, no crops, no baskets, and therefore no people.

But not all songs are sung in a strict ceremonial context. As Christine Johnson again relates, "Song is an everyday thing. We use it to wake up, to go to sleep. There are songs about planting, harvest, rain, rainbows, clouds. In my age group, it was an everyday thing. You sing to get up, sing to go walking, sing to cook."[36] And like all beings in the traditional Tohono O'odham universe, the tepary bean, *bawĭ*, who could not exist without the rain brought forth by the saguaro wine ceremony, has its own songs and its own stories. Some of these songs ask I'itoi for a good harvest and for the earth to be blessed; others describe the planting and harvesting process. People sing these songs as the ground is being prepared for the beans and as the beans are placed within the holes. People sing as they tend and weed the fields, when they pull the dried and brown bean plants from the earth and when they are placed on a flat hard surface and pounded with sticks or stomped on to release the beans from their pods. People sing when the beans are placed in baskets and tossed in the air to remove the debris. There are even songs for cooking beans. The songs in part describe the desired event and are thought to help bring about that desired event. Through these songs every aspect of the agricultural process is attended to, is paid attention to.[37]

The proper ways to plant and harvest *bawĭ* are found within traditional narratives. Long ago there was a grandfather who treated his grandchild terribly. The child left and went to live up above but when he saw that his grandfather was searching for him he returned to give him a gift. "Take care of it," he told his grandfather, "and when it multiplies, eat it and be filled and think of me." He gave his grandfather some seeds and told him to plant them by his head when he slept, and to watch so nothing will remove then. He told him that after a short while the plant will grow and blossom and bear beans, it will then dry and its seeds will scatter. The grandfather should gather the seeds and wait one year "until the rain moistens the earth," then bury four of them together, watching so animals do not eat or trample them, or grass and weeds choke them. The boy then teaches his grandfather the proper way to harvest them. "When they ripen, pull up and pile them where you've cleared a place. Then get a stick to beat them with. The seed will be removed. When the wind blows, you will take them in your hands and throw them up, and it will blow away the stalks and leave the seed." He then instructs him to take the beans, store them away, and do the same thing next year. When he has repeated this four times there will be enough and he can finally eat the beans.[38]

Within this narrative we can see many important lessons such as proper and improper kinship behavior and agricultural instructions. These instructions include the correct way to plant beans, to harvest them, along with guidelines regarding how many can be eaten while keeping enough to plant the following year. Through this narrative we are given more than basic agricultural knowledge and we are shown how foundational *bawĭ* is to Tohono O'odham lifeways, to the *O'odham Himdag*. After imparting this knowledge to his grandfather he tells him, "Then you will eat it, and be full from me. You will be alive and happy from me, your grandchild, who is the white bean. That gray streak stretched across the sky is my home." The narrative continues,

> [s]o that is why the white bean is the child of the Desert People [Tohono O'odham]. It is born here and grows here and endures dryness. When it doesn't rain enough, the white bean still comes up. The Desert People will always eat it and live here. The Milky Way is said to be the white bean. He lives clear across the sky. Beans grow in abundance and we see them scattered across the sky.[39]

Bawĭ, is a relative of the Tohono O'odham and, like the people, is connected to and is an integral part of the Sonoran Desert. Both the bean and the people belong here. All things in the desert endure dryness and *bawĭ* endures it better than most, giving itself to the people, providing for the people even in years of very little rain.

Bawĭ is not just a food, it is an integral part of the ecosystem, of the people, and is an essential component to the *O'odham Himdag*. The Tohono O'odham community includes more than just human kinship groups, and the conception of *bawĭ* as a distant child, as found in the sacred narratives, includes it within the extended community that is rooted in the Tohono O'odham homeland where songs and ceremonies along with other forms of Traditional Ecological Knowledge work to establish conditions necessary for the people and the land to not only survive but thrive. As stated in the TOCA and TOCC report, "Virtually all elements of traditional culture—ceremonies, stories, songs, language—are directly rooted in the system of food production. O'odham culture is truly an *agri/* culture."[40] These relationships are thought to be thousands of years old, and are part of a cultural continuity that has always been both added to and changed. The most drastic of these additions and changes in recent memory came with the arrival of Europeans and Euro-Americans.

When Father Eusebio Francisco Kino arrived in the late seventeenth century he brought with him not only a new religion, Catholicism, but he and his contemporaries also introduced cattle, sheep, and European agricultural methods and crops.[41] Wheat added another form of food that was harvested at a different time, extending the growing season significantly, and cattle and sheep provided food and materials for clothing. While only a minority of the Tohono O'odham population during this time owned grazing animals, those who did, in addition to settler colonists, utilized and related to the landscape in different ways, and where animals grazed the ecosystem changed. In earth that is undisturbed by cattle or sheep, plants, particularly grasses, are an obstacle to the flood waters, forcing them to disperse across the earth. When these obstacles are not there, the water tends to concentrate more significantly into channels that run into the arroyos (washes) and the rivers. As more and more water is concentrated into these channels they become deeper and faster, more water gets channeled into them, which causes more erosion, and the cycle continues. This means that the overall surface area of the land gets less saturated with water, since it is whisked away more quickly. In addition, the mouths of the arroyos become narrower and more defined eliminating the floodplains that are conducive to agriculture.[42]

During the Spanish and Mexican periods (1687–1821 and 1821–1848, respectively), the impact of grazing was minimal because there were too few herds to significantly alter the larger ecosystem; many Tohono O'odham successfully continued and expanded on their agricultural practices and cattle herds and cowboy culture grew. After the United States' conquest of the region however, which was finalized in the Treaty of Guadalupe Hidalgo in 1848 and the Gadsden Purchase of 1854 where the traditional lands of the Tohono O'odham were cut in half by the new border with Mexico, environmental impacts increased significantly with the cattle boom of 1873–1891 and the arrival of the railroads in 1880. Rivers were damned and diverted and wells were dug to water the cattle, depleting the availability of ground water. This began to dramatically alter the ecosystem, particularly the riparian habitats. Devastating floods became more common because of erosion, while other areas ceased to see water at all. Farming methods were altered to divert this water to bean, squash, and cornfields for trench irrigation and more wells were dug to water the fields and for ranching. Within a brief period of time most of the water was diverted off the newly formed reservation, where wells ran dry and *Ak Chin* farming became more difficult.[43]

Water loss was only one factor that affected people's ability to farm. Many Tohono O'odham were recruited into federal work programs such as the migrant farmworker program, taking them away from their fields. The boarding schools separated children from their families, language, and traditions, and while at these schools students were prohibited from speaking their language or engaging in any aspect of their culture. The children not only did not learn their agricultural techniques and the cultural and religious practices associated with this way of life, but they were taught that these were inferior, primitive, and had no value; many were taught these traditional ways were evil.[44] World War II also took many people away from their land and their crops, and thus from their songs, ceremonies, and sacred narratives.

In 1930, O'odham farmers were growing around 1.4 million tons of tepary beans on 20,000 acres; in 1949 there were only 2,500 acres of tepary beans; and in 2001 there were less than 100 acres producing only around 110 pounds of beans.[45] The introduction of commodity foods (white flour, lard, American cheese, white sugar) further separated people from the land and undermined agriculture. In the 1960s diabetes was virtually unknown, but today the Tohono O'odham community has the highest rate of adult-onset diabetes in the world, with more than half of the population affected.[46] The loss of food sovereignty, the right and ability of people to have sustained access to healthy and culturally appropriate food as defined and controlled by the community, occurred relatively quickly.

Lois Ellen Frank, a Native American foods historian and chef, divides Native American foodways into four periods of history. The first is precontact or ancestral foodways; the second is first-contact foodways, where Native people incorporated much of what was introduced by colonists into their traditional diets; the third and most destructive is the Commodity food period, the era of reservations, starvation, and creatively using what few resources were available to survive, which led to the advent of frybread. The current moment is the fourth period, which she calls New Native American cuisine. Today people are rediscovering and reinventing indigenous food and emphasizing the connections between cultural health and physical health. This is not just about revitalizing food but revitalizing everything associated with that food.[47]

For many Tohono O'odham embracing the interconnectivity found within the *O'odham Himdag* encourages the revitalization of agriculture and foodways, more broadly, that are in harmony with the environment and with community wellness. The saguaro harvest and wine ceremony, which brings the New Year and makes agriculture possible in the Sonoran Desert are currently only being celebrated by a small portion of the population. The reason fewer people participate in this ceremony is that so few people currently grow their own food: "People did not stop planting the fields because the ceremony was dying out; the ceremony began to die out when people stopped planting their fields."[48] Everything is interconnected, the land, ceremonies, sacred narratives, songs, basketry, and community wellness and all "are directly rooted in the systems of food production."[49] Part of food sovereignty is the ability of communities to fulfill their responsibility to maintain healthy and proper relationships with the land, plant-beings, and animal-beings through correct and balanced living and actions, much of which has sacred origins and elements.

Formed in 1996, Tohono O'odham Community Action is working toward revitalization. One of their many initiatives is the New Generation of O'odham Farmers Program, established in 2009 its stated purpose is restoring *himdag*—because learning about farming is learning about *himdag*.[50] The two different tracks in this program, the "Intensive Farming Apprenticeships" and the "Farming and Gardening Internships," teach people farming techniques along with the cultural knowledge necessary to understand and practice these methods correctly. Many people involved in this program also teach workshops and hold storytelling sessions both in the local classrooms as well as in the fields themselves.[51] TOCA introduced farming and cooking at the tribal alternative school, teaching about food in connection with the O'odham language, the land, traditional songs, stories, and basketry.[52] They also continue to work with the Tohono O'odham Nation and the school food service provider Sodexo to serve locally grown traditional foods at least once a week in public schools across the reservation. And according to the TOCA website certain traditional foods, like the brown tepary bean quesadilla made with a whole wheat tortilla, became so popular that Sodexo added it to their regular menu rotation.[53] Serving and eating traditional foods provides opportunities to teach not just about the health benefits of those foods, but about ceremonial songs and sacred narratives connected to those foods. Terrol Johnson, TOCA CEO recalls, "We told the children among other things, that the stars are tepary beans Coyote tossed into the sky. We made sure they were familiar with the tepary bean at all levels."[54]

Traditional Tohono O'odham farming practices are not just about creating a healthy food source and practicing environmentally friendly farming techniques. They are about renewing the people's relationship with the land, language, songs, ceremonies, and sacred narratives and through this revitalizing *himdag*. Perhaps a better word for food here is *sustenance*. For the Tohono O'odham traditional foodways sustain people's bodies and their physical health, but they also sustain their stories, land, ceremonies, and communities. Foodways sustain the *O'odham Himdag*.

Notes

1. "Tohono O'odham Community Action—GuideStar Profile," accessed January 21, 2016, http://www.nativefoodways.org.

2. Terrol Dew Johnson, "Welcome to Our Magazine," *Native Foodways: Celebrating Food, Culture & Community*, Premier Issue, Summer 2013, 5. The magazine's publication run was three issues: Summer 2013, Winter 2013/2014, and Spring 2015.

3. Johnson, "Welcome," *Native Foodways*, 5.

4. Tohono O'odham Community Action and Tohono O'odham Community College (TOCA and TOCC), "Community Attitudes toward Traditional Tohono O'odham Foods," (Sells, AZ: Tohono O'odham Community Action and Tohono O'odham Community College, 2002), 11.

5. The use of TEK here is not meant to reference the category as it is currently being used within governmental organizations, particularly in Canada, to acknowledge the existence of indigenous knowledge about the natural world without understanding how it is interconnected with other aspects of indigenous lifeways and notions of sovereignty. Instead it is meant to emphasize the presence of this knowledge and its interconnection.

6. Fikret Berkes, *Sacred Ecology*, 3rd ed. (New York: Routledge, 2012), 7.

7. Berkes, *Sacred Ecology*, 7.

8. Tohono O'odham Community College, "Himdag Policy," December 20, 2015. http://www.tocc.edu/himdag_policy.html.

9. See James Griffith, *Belief and Holy Places: A Spiritual Geography of the Pimeria Alta* (Tucson: University of Arizona Press, 1992), 14–22.

10. Tohono O'odham Community College, "Himdag Policy," December 20, 2015. http://www.tocc.edu/himdag_policy.html.

11. Ruth Underhill, *Papago Woman*, Case Studies in Cultural Anthropology (New York: Holt, Rinehart and Winston, 1979), 3.

12. TOCAonline "Tohono O'odham Traditional Calendar: A Reflection of Food and Culture," December 20, 2015, http://www.tocaonline.org/traditional-calendar.html.

13. The Akimel O'odham (River People) were known as a one-village people because they had permanent villages located along the Gila, Salt, and Santa Cruz Rivers. The Hia C-ed O'odham (Sand Dune People) lived in the desert east of the Lower Colorado River, where there are no rivers and rainfall averaged zero to five inches per year. They were known as a no-village people because they were constantly on the move. See Trudy Griffin-Pierce, *Native Peoples of the Southwest*, 1st ed. (Albuquerque: University of New Mexico Press, 2000), 166–68.

14. Edward Franklin Castetter and Willis Harvey Bell, *Pima and Papago Indian Agriculture* (Albuquerque: The University of New Mexico Press, 1942), 57, 73.

15. Gary Paul Nabhan, *Gathering the Desert* (Tucson: University of Arizona Press, 1985), 112–13.

16. Castetter and Bell, *Pima and Papago Indian Agriculture*, 91; Nabhan, *Gathering the Desert*, 113.

17. Nabhan, *Gathering the Desert*, 112–13.

18. Castetter and Bell, *Pima and Papago Indian Agriculture*, 91; Nabhan, *Gathering the Desert*, 113.

19. Tohono O'odham Community Action and Tohono O'odham Community College (TOCA and TOCC), "Community Attitudes toward Traditional Tohono O'odham Foods," 8; Castetter and Bell, *Pima and Papago Indian Agriculture*, 57.

20. Castetter and Bell, *Pima and Papago Indian Agriculture*, 44–45.

21. Castetter and Bell, *Pima and Papago Indian Agriculture*, 44–45; David Rich Lewis, *Niether Wolf nor Dog: American Indians, Environment, and Agrarian Change* (New York: Oxford University Press, 1994), 123–28.

22. Ruth Underhill, *Papago Indian Religion*, Columbia University Contributions to Anthropology (New York: Columbia University Press, 1946), 41.

23. Camillus Lopez, "Tohono O'odham Culture: Embracing Traditional Wisdom," in *Thinking Like a Watershed: Voices from the West*, eds. Jack Loeffler and Celestia Loeffler (Albuquerque: University of New Mexico Press, 2012), 148.

24. Toka is a traditional O'odham sport played by women. Each player uses an *usaga* (stick) to hit the *ola* (puck) through a goal; both are handmade

from mesquite wood. This is an ancient sport that is regaining popularity among the women of the Tohono O'odham Nation and its sister tribes. It most closely resembles field hockey.

25. This narrative is taken from several sources and reworded by the author. Lopez, "Tohono O'odham Culture," 145–47; Dean Saxton and Lucille Saxton, *Legends and Lore of the Papago and Pima Indians* (Tucson: University of Arizona Press, 1973), 211–15; Tohono O'odham Community Action, Mary Paganelli Votto, and Frances Sallie Manuel, *From I'itoi's Garden: Tohono O'odham Food Traditions* (Sells, AZ: Tohono O'odham Community Action (TOCA)/Blurb, 2010).

26. This version is taken from Lopez, "Tohono O'odham Culture," 147–48. Another similar version can be found in Saxton and Saxton, *Legends and Lore*, 79–84 and 215–19.

27. Lopez, "Tohono O'odham Culture," 148.

28. Underhill, *Papago Woman*, 40; Underhill, *Papago Indian Religion*, 41.

29. Underhill, *Papago Woman*, 41–51; Underhill, *Papago Indian Religion*, 41–67.

30. Underhill, *Papago Woman*, 40.

31. Underhill, *Papago Indian Religion*, 41.

32. Underhill, *Papago Woman*, 26.

33. TOCA, Votto, and Manuel *From I'itoi's Garden*, 117.

34. TOCA, Votto, and Manuel *From I'itoi's Garden*, 117.

35. Donald M. Bahr, *Pima and Papago Ritual Oratory: A Study of Three Texts = Ó 'odham ha-ñiokculida: mámce ab wáikk há'icu Ámjeḍ* (San Francisco: Indian Historian Press, 1975), 5–6.

36. TOCA Votto, and Mauel, *From I'itoi's Garden*, 117.

37. For more information on specific songs see Ruth Underhill, *Singing for Power; the Song Magic of the Papago Indians of Southern Arizona* (Berkeley: University of California Press, 1938).

38. Saxton and Saxton, *Legends and Lore*, 21–23.

39. Saxton and Saxton, *Legends and Lore*, 23.

40. Tohono O'odham Community Action and Tohono O'odham Community College (TOCA and TOCC), "Community Attitudes toward Traditional Tohono O'odham Foods," 11.

41. For more on Father Kino see Herbert Eugene Bolton, *The Padre on Horseback*. 1932 (Chicago: Loyola University Press, 1963).

42. Winston P. Erickson and Tohono O'odham Nation of Arizona Education Department, *Sharing the Desert: The Tohono O'odham in History* (Tucson: University of Arizona Press, 1994), 3.

43. See Erickson, *Sharing the Desert*; Bernard Fontana, "History of the Papago," in *Handbook of North American Indians*, vol. 10, ed. Alfonso Ortiz (Washington, DC: Smithsonian Institution, 1983), 137–48; Lewis, *Neither Wolf nor Dog*, 133–67.

44. For more on the boarding schools see David Wallace Adams, *Education for Extinction: American Indians and the Boarding School Experience 1875–1928* (Lawrence: University Press of Kansas, 1995).

45. Tohono O'odham Community Action and Tohono O'odham Community College (TOCA and TOCC), "Community Attitudes toward Traditional Tohono O'odham Foods," 9.

46. David Fazzino, "Continuity and Change in Tohono O'odham Food Systems: Implications for Dietary Interventions," *Culture & Agriculture* 30, no. 1–2 (2008): 38–46.

47. Lois Ellen Frank, "The Discourse and Practice of Native American Cuisine: Native American Chefs and Native American Cooks in Contemporary Southwest Kitchens" (PhD diss., University of New Mexico, 2011), 5–11.

48. TOCA, Votto, and Manuel, *From I'itoi's Garden*, 11.

49. Tohono O'odham Community Action and Tohono O'odham Community College (TOCA and TOCC), "Community Attitudes toward Traditional Tohono O'odham Foods," (Sells, AZ: Tohono O'odham Community Action and Tohono O'odham Community College, 2002), 11.

50. Stephanie Woodard, "Traditional Foods Go to School," *Native Foodways: Celebrating Food, Culture, & Community* (Winter 2013/14): 24.

51. TOCAonline, "New Generation of O'odham Farmers: Food System Leadership in Action," July 13, 2016, http://www.tocaonline.org/new-generation-of-o-odham-farmers.html.

52. Stephanie Woodard, "Traditional Foods Go to School," 24.

53. TOCAonline, "Traditional School Meals," July 13, 2016, http://www.tocaonline.org/traditional-school-meals.html.

54. Stephanie Woodard, "Traditional Foods Go to School," 24.

Bibliography

Adams, David Wallace. *Education for Extinction: American Indians and the Boarding School Experience 1875–1928*. Lawrence: University Press of Kansas, 1995.

Bahr, Donald M. *Pima and Papago Ritual Oratory: A Study of Three Texts = Ó 'odham ha-ñiokculida: mámce ab wáikk há'icu Ámjeḍ*. San Francisco: Indian Historian Press, 1975.

Berkes, Fikret. *Sacred Ecology*. 3rd ed. New York: Routledge, 2012.

Bolton, Herbert Eugene. *The Padre on Horseback*. 1932. Chicago: Loyola University Press, 1963.

Castetter, Edward Franklin, and Willis Harvey Bell. *Pima and Papago Indian Agriculture*. Albuquerque: University of New Mexico Press, 1942.

Di Cintio, Marcello. "Farming the Monsoon: A Return to Traditional Tohono O'odham Foods." *Gastronomica* 12, no. 2 (Summer 2012): 14–17.

Erickson, Winston P, and Tohono O'odham Nation of Arizona Education Department. *Sharing the Desert: The Tohono O'odham in History*. Tucson: University of Arizona Press, 1994.

Fazzino, David. "Continuity and Change in Tohono O'odham Food Systems: Implications for Dietary Interventions." *Culture & Agriculture* 30, no. 1–2 (2008): 38–46.

Fontana, Bernard L. "History of the Papago." In *Handbook of North American Indians*, edited by Alfonso Ortiz, vol. 10, 137–48. Washington, DC: Smithsonian Institution, 1983.

Frank, Lois Ellen. "The Discourse and Practice of Native American Cuisine: Native American Chefs and Native American Cooks in Contemporary Southwest Kitchens." PhD diss., University of New Mexico, 2011.

Griffin-Pierce, Trudy. *Native Peoples of the Southwest*. 1st ed. Albuquerque: University of New Mexico Press, 2000.

Griffith, James S. *Belief and Holy Places: A Spiritual Geography of the Pimeria Alta*. Tucson: University of Arizona Press, 1992.

Johnson, Terrol Dew. "Welcome to Our Magazine." *Native Foodways: Celebrating Food, Culture & Community*. Premier Issue, Summer 2013.

Lewis, David Rich. *Neither Wolf nor Dog: American Indians, Environment, and Agrarian Change*. Oxford, UK: Oxford University Press, 1994.

Loeffler, Jack, and Celestia Loeffler. *Thinking Like a Watershed: Voices from the West*. Albuquerque: University of New Mexico Press, 2012.

Lopez, Camillus. "Tohono O'odham Culture: Embracing Traditional Wisdom." In *Thinking Like a Watershed: Voices from the West*, edited by Jack and Celestia Loeffler, 134–50. Albuquerque: University of New Mexico Press, 2012.

Nabhan, Gary Paul. *Gathering the Desert*. Tucson: University of Arizona Press, 1985.

Saxton, Dean, and Lucille Saxton. *Legends and Lore of the Papago and Pima Indians*. Tucson: University of Arizona Press, 1973.

Tohono O'odham Community Action, and Tohono O'odham Community College (TOCA and TOCC). "Community Attitudes toward Traditional Tohono O'odham Foods." Sells: Tohono O'odham Community Action and Tohono O'odham Community College, 2002.

Tohono O'odham Community Action, Mary Paganelli Votto, and Frances Sallie Manuel. *From I'itoi's Garden: Tohono O'odham Food Traditions*. Sells, AZ: Tohono O'odham Community Action (TOCA)/Blurb, 2010.

Underhill, Ruth. *Papago Indian Religion*. New York: Columbia University Press, 1946.

———. *Papago Woman*. Case Studies in Cultural Anthropology. New York: Holt, Rinehart and Winston, 1979.

———. *Singing for Power; the Song Magic of the Papago Indians of Southern Arizona*. Berkeley: University of California Press, 1938.

Woodard, Stephanie. "Traditional Foods Go to School." *Native Foodways: Celebrating Food, Culture, & Community* (Winter 2013/14).

2

Of Coyotes and Culverts

Salmon and the People of the Mid-Columbia River

SUZANNE CRAWFORD O'BRIEN

> Some elders predict a day when Coyote will come back and smash all the dams built along the Columbia, washing away environmental pollution and once again bringing the Salmon upriver.
>
> —Mourning Dove, *Coyote Stories*

Act One: Coyote and Creation

In a commonly told creation story maintained by the Native people of the middle Columbia River, when Creator decided to make human beings, Creator sent Coyote down from a mountain to ask all the plants and animals for gifts that they would be willing to bestow on this newest creation. These little human things were small and weak, and they were going to need help. In one version of the story, Coyote descends from the mountain, speaking first with Eagle (who offers the gift of sight), then with Elk (who offers his hide), Owl (who gives hearing), Beaver (who offers his teeth), and finally reaches Salmon in the Columbia River. When asked, Salmon replies: "Of course I will. I want to provide two gifts. The first is my body, so the humans will have food that will make them

Act Two: Coyote Learns the Rules

Showing that respect, however, is not always easy. The realities of life, of the desire to get ahead, and the sometimes-capricious nature of human technology and innovation can complicate matters. Salmon are resilient creatures. But they are also part of a complex and interdependent ecosystem: if one strand of the web is broken, the entire system can unravel. This may sound like a twenty-first-century problem, and in many ways it is, but the ancestors of the people of the mid–Columbia River knew this to be true as well. Stories abound on the Columbia River in which Coyote, acting out of greed and impatience, breaks the rules of respect that maintain the web of relationships on which everyone depends. Very often, the cost is his supper. In 1894 Franz Boas recorded lower Chinookan Coyote tales in which our hungry canine violates proper protocol. After catching a silver-side salmon he takes it home and cuts it crosswise, and steams it. When he returns to the river the next day, the salmon are gone. His feces (which are usually his best counselors) tell him that he has violated a ritual restriction. Silver-side salmon are to be cut lengthwise and roasted, and can only be steamed once enough have gone upriver. On the second day, he again cooks the fish inappropriately, and they again disappear from the stream. His feces once more give him a proper cooking lesson, and he learns the right way to prepare the fish. It takes Coyote several tries before he gets it right. Such stories serve as lessons of the proper way to treat the fish, so as to show them proper respect.[20]

On the Columbia River today, these traditional restrictions on when to fish and how to process the fish that are caught are integrated both into fisheries management techniques and into the religious calendar of the Columbia River people. Ceremonial restrictions and first-salmon ceremonies ensure both a continued healthy salmon run and a good spiritual relationship with the fish. In 1808, Lewis and Clark observed a first salmon ceremony at Wishram Village, just above the Dalles. As they noted, "There was great joy with the natives last night in consequence of the arrival of the Salmon; one of those fish was caught; this was a harbinger of good news to them. They informed us that these fish would arrive in great quantities in the course of about 5 days. This fish was dressed and being divided into small pieces was given to each child in the village. This custom was founded in superstitious opinion that it will hasten the arrival of the salmon."[21] In 1843 Henry Perkins learned of a similar practice at Celilo Falls. "Before any of the common people are permitted to boil, or even to cut the flesh of the salmon transversely for any purpose the tu-a-ti (*twati*) medicine man of the village, assembles the people and after invoking the Tah (*taax*) or the particular spirit which presides over the salmon, and who they suppose can make it a prosperous year or otherwise, takes a fish just caught and wrings off its head."[22] At Wishram, villagers celebrated the arrival of the salmon run by ritually filleting and cutting the fish into small bites, distributing them to all the children. The first salmon was afforded special honor, because "those fish had been endowed by the Great Spirit with powers that made them bolder and better able to swim to the spawning grounds, from which their fingerlings would return to the sea . . . The Chinooks believed that they should place a berry in the mouth of the first salmon caught to nourish it on what they believed to be its foodless journey to the spawning grounds."[23] James Selam recalled that a particularly strong swimmer would then be given the task of swimming above Celilo Falls with the remains of the first fish. He would dive deep, and deposit the remains midriver, demonstrating the respectful care the people took, and signaling that other salmon should come up river as well.[24] The first salmon feast is still honored throughout the Plateau, including an annual ceremony at Celilo Village, celebrating the first salmon of the spring.[25]

The harvesting of first foods was considered *Áut-ni kutkút*, "sacred work," done by carefully selected individuals. Such ceremonial leaders were chosen for the depth of their knowledge surrounding particular resources, as well as their spiritual relationship with them.[26] Before these *Áut-ni kutkútłama* ("sacred workers") could harvest first fish, roots, berries, or elk, they had to undergo rites of purification. "The sanctioned or authenticated workers were required to go to the sweathouse for five consecutive days. If the cleansing ceremony was not adhered to, then it was believed that bad luck and bad feelings would come to others . . . approaching the Life Giver with a dirty spiritual life was an abomination."

Coyote stories likewise teach about the importance of relating to salmon with a proper spirit. After observing a people's hunger, Coyote created Willamette Falls, establishing a valuable fishing site. He also created a magical trap, capable of catching an enormous haul of salmon without any effort. He grew impatient, however, for the trap worked too well, catching fish faster than he could start a fire to cook them. Having grown irate, he cursed the trap. Offended, it stopped working. From then on, Coyote and the humans that followed had to brave the rapids to catch their fish.[27] Attitude matters.

Virginia Beavert-Martin affirmed this tradition when she related the teachings of her mother Ellen Saluskin. According to Beavert-Martin, it was vital that food gatherers "purify their mind and body," because such foods worked as "a healing medicine to the spirit and body" for those who were suffering physically, mentally, or spiritually.[28] The *Áut-ni kutkútłama* offered songs of thanksgiving to the Creator, expressing thanks for the provision of the holy food. It was only when the songs had been sung that "the untrained, unsanctioned or lay members were then permitted to harvest."[29] At important fishing sites like Kettle Falls and Celilo Falls a salmon chief held this important task, governing both ritual activities and fishing itself. The salmon chief opened and closed fishing on a daily and an annual basis, and limited fishing during the night, after a death, or on Sundays.[30] Such controls on fishing were belittled by Euro-Americans of the nineteenth and early twentieth centuries, but contemporary fishery biologists and ecologists recognize the importance of such practices, which provided the opportunity for sufficient numbers of salmon to proceed to spawning grounds upriver.[31]

While fishing itself is often the purview of men on the Plateau, processing and preserving salmon is the domain of women. And when working with salmon, it is also vital that the individual maintain a good spirit and positive thoughts. As Yakama elder Romana Kiona has emphasized,

> It's a culture thing. You cannot use harsh words over a food product in our culture. 'Cause whoever is going to eat that is probably going to get those vibes or they may get ill or something. If you look at our culture, if you're in one of our churches, and in the kitchen, if someone gets angry or sad, they need to leave the kitchen. Cooking and working with our foods is an important attitude thing. And if we feel sad or mean or mad, we might as well just leave the kitchen because you are going to hurt somebody . . . if anybody is mean in the kitchen or sad, they're going to give those vibes [to other people] when they eat that food. And that's what our elders taught us.[33]

Maintaining relationships with the salmon people thus does not end with fishing, but carries on into the processing and preparation of those fish. As Michelle Jacob explains, inherent within this teaching "is also the message that food preparers must have a positive and gentle spirit while working with foods (who have sacrificed themselves for their people), as well as the people who consume the food after it has been prepared."[32]

Act Three: Coyote Steals the Salmon

But despite the people's willingness to show respect and observe proper protocol, salmon runs are unpredictable and vulnerable to human actions that interfere with their ability to spawn upstream. This vulnerability is demonstrated in other Coyote stories of the mid-Columbia River. In these stories, Coyote is not the Creator's emissary, but rather a figure driven by greed and avarice. Here, his actions account for the absence of salmon, and the destruction of valuable runs. Coyote is often blamed for the absence of salmon within certain tributaries. In many such stories, Coyote sees an attractive woman. And, typical of Coyote, he attempts to seduce her or claim her for a wife. When she refuses, Coyote retaliates by banning salmon from the waterway on which the people live.[33] In "Coyote Becomes Chief of the Salmon," for instance, we are told that he creates falls along the Okanogan, Kettle, and Columbia Rivers, "because in all these places maidens refused him."[34]

Here, Coyote's actions are a direct contrast with those in the creation account, where Salmon, Elk, Owl, and Eagle act out of compassion, generosity, and self-sacrifice. Looking at these stories, a pattern soon emerges: whenever Coyote is motivated by greed, impatience, or arrogance, the result is a diminishing of resources for everyone—including himself.[35] Mid-Columbia Indian culture is guided by core values of kinship, interdependence, and equity. When Coyote violates these ethics, it leads to scarcity. As Rodney Frey has argued, "When Coyote's intentions are to assist others, to 'prepare for the coming of people,' he generally succeeds; when his intentions are for himself alone, he is likely to fail. But even in his failure, Coyote offers important lessons to those listening to his story. He sets forth what one should or should not do in certain situations."[36] Thus, Coyote is both revered and reviled. Louis Simpson was Edward Sapir's primary consultant when he gathered stories on the Columbia River around 1905. Simpson expressed both respect for Coyote and "a degree of scorn," particularly when relating stories of Coyote's folly. When Coyote acts inappropriately, Simpson noted, he suffers social and moral isolation, and is excluded from the relations of reciprocity that defined this region's cultural ethos.[37]

In the Columbia River region, such stories serve as metaphors for considering the impact thoughtless actions can have on salmon runs. The fourteen dams on the Columbia River and sixteen dams on the Snake River were a death knell for many fish, preventing their passage upstream. It is estimated that, prior to colonization, between 15 and 30 million salmon returned annually to the Columbia and Snake Rivers. By the 1970s, that number was reduced to three million, literally decimated, because of overfishing and dams that obstructed fish passage. Today, 2 and a half million anadromous fish find their way up the Columbia, but 80 percent of these are hatchery fish. Wild salmon remain endangered.[38]

The historic fall of salmon populations on the Columbia River parallels the history of tribal fishing rights. The threat to tribal fishing rights began in 1855 with the signing of treaties, as villages along the River granted rights to the newly arrival settlers. Settlers would be permitted to fish in the river, to build homes, and settle in the territories. Thirty years later in the 1880s, Euro-American policy makers further sought to disrupt Native ways of living on the land, using the General Allotment Act and other suppressive policies to undermine their subsistence rights. In 1886 Commissioner of Indian Affairs John Atkins argued in support of the Allotment Act, saying that "The Indian must be imbued with the exalting egoism of American civilization so that he will say 'I' instead of 'We' and 'This is mine' instead of 'This is ours.' "[39] The Allotment act was intended to break up any sense of collective ownership and responsibility toward the land, with the goal of ensuring an individual would "abandon his tribal relations."[40] This loss of collective land ownership often meant a loss of access to traditional resource gathering and fishing locations, despite the fact that these had been guaranteed in their treaties. The tribes had reserved the right to fish, hunt, and gather in usual and accustomed places, but their ability to fish would be challenged again and again, as settlers blocked Native access to the river, built hugely extractive fish wheels, and dammed the rivers. By 1900 dozens of fish wheels and five canneries would line the Columbia, overtaking many ancient fishing sites.[41]

When The Dalles Dam was completed in 1957, it flooded one of the oldest continuously occupied communities in the world, with archaeological evidence dating back more than 10,000 years.[42] The dam destroyed the ancient fishing sites at Celilo Falls and Five Mile Rapids, inundating countless unexcavated archaeological sites.[43] Warm Springs tribal members were awarded damages to compensate for the loss of Celilo Falls: after legal fees and related costs, each tribal member received a mere $145.50.[44] As Warm Springs tribal member George Aguilar writes, "A ghastly silence has reigned at this place for nearly half a century, as the dam's backwaters snuffed out landmarks that told of many Coyote stories . . . If our Chinookan ancestors saw the current condition of the Columbia River, they probably would sing and perform the Chinook funeral and death song."[45]

Act Four: Coyote Frees the Salmon

We can't stop there. After all, the most well-known mid-Columbia Coyote stories are about *liberating* salmon. In those tales we see a role reversal, where Coyote uses his ingenuity and creativity to free salmon runs that had been locked away by the greedy and self-interested. In one of the most common stories, variations of which are told from southern Oregon to northeastern Washington, Coyote encounters three gluttonous sisters who have dammed up the salmon, preferring to keep them for themselves. Coyote disguises himself as a baby, manages to gain entrance to their home, and day-by-day surreptitiously chips away at the dam. Finally, the dam is breached and the salmon are freed. "It is not right for you to have all this salmon penned up in one place!" he scolds the women. "Things are going to change."[46]

I'd like to suggest we consider these salmon liberation stories as another lens through which to think about Native people's relationship with salmon, for just as Coyote uses his ingenuity to rescue the salmon, so Columbia River tribes are using their creativity and intellectual acumen to solve contemporary salmon problems.

An example of this is the way in which Native people have had to get their Coyote on in the courtroom. The legal fight to protect both salmon and 1855 treaty rights to salmon fishing has a long and complicated history in the Pacific Northwest that goes back as far as the 1887 case *United States v. Taylor*. In this case a white homesteader had erected barbed-wire fencing across his property, preventing Yakama tribal members from accessing the river. The Supreme Court of Washington found for the Yakama, stating treaty rights to fish guaranteed access, even across private lands.[47] The 1905 case *United States v. Winans* was meant to appeal this decision, and was the first of nine tribal fishing rights cases that would make it to the U.S. Supreme Court. Three key principles were decided in the Winans case. "The first stated that treaties must be construed as the Indians understood them at the time and 'as justice and reason demanded,' since the United States exerted superior power over the 'unlettered' tribal representatives. The second, known as the reserved rights doctrine, held that treaties were 'not a grant of rights to the Indians, but a grant of rights from them—a reservation of those not granted." Finally, the court also ruled that Yakama "retained their existing rights to cross the land, to fish at usual and accustomed places, and to erect temporary houses for curing their catch."[48]

Contemporary legal victories affirming treaty rights to salmon fishing in Washington State were made possible because of the famous fish-in movements of the Pacific Northwest, which pushed the case into the public eye. On the Columbia River and throughout Puget Sound and the Salish Sea tribal peoples fished, in defiance of state laws that restricted their ability to do so. Tribal leaders like Billy Frank Jr., Janet McCloud (Yet-Si-Blue), and David Sohappy had to employ the best of Coyote's stubbornness, creativity, and attitude to carry on the fight. Decades of struggle, arrests, and harassment from state authorities came to a head in two vital court cases.

The first of these, *Sohappy v. Smith* (later *United States v. Oregon*) was decided in 1969, determining that treaty-tribes along the Columbia River had the right to a "fair share" of fish, and with minimal regulation. The ruling also made clear that tribes must be allowed the opportunity to be comanagers of salmon resources, and participants in their regulation.[49] Sohappy was a grandnephew of the Wáashat prophet Smohalla, and adhered to the seasonal round and spiritual teachings of his ancestors. He was raised to be a firm believer in the Wáashat tradition, and participated in the first food ceremonies. For Sohappy, the legal battle was not merely about subsistence, but was about culture, tradition, and faith. As he said in 1976, "No man should be required to obtain a permit from any other man to practice his religion. . . . I know of no other church or religion for which to exercise it the permit of any governmental body or person or tribe is required, and I don't think it just that one be required to apply for and obtain a permit before exercising one's ceremonial fishing rites and rights."[50]

The Sohappy ruling did not make clear what exactly a "fair share" of the fish entailed. This matter was settled in the Boldt Decision of 1974 (*U.S. v. State of Washington*). The Boldt Decision affirmed the rights of treaty-tribes in Washington State to "fifty percent of the annual harvest," that the state could regulate tribal fishing "only if all other means of conservation had been exhausted," and affirmed the right of tribes to self-regulate fishing practices.[51] These legal findings led to the formation of two important intertribal governing bodies that continue to bring treaty-tribes together to protect salmon and restore salmon habitat: the Columbia River Intertribal Fish Commission (CRIFC) and the Northwest Indian Fisheries Commission (NWIFC).[52] Tribal rights were further clarified in a 1982 case *U.S. v. Anderson*, which affirmed that treaty rights to salmon also meant that the state and federal government had an obligation to protect salmon habitat, in effect stating that tribes had a treaty right to healthy rivers that could sustain life. In this case, it meant that temperatures must be regulated by the release of water from dams to ensure the safety of fish.

In his essay on treaty fishing rights, Yale Lewis argues that the 1855 treaties guaranteed tribes three rights: the right to access fish, the right to have the fish harvest equitably apportioned, and the right to healthy habitat. Lewis contends: "If the tribes had a habitat right, they could use it to make the fishing right meaningful, demanding that the state take simple, cost-effective steps to protect fish habitat, such as fixing culverts."[53] The first of these rights was assured in *United States v. Winans*. The second in the Sohappy and Boldt decisions. The third was affirmed in *United States v. Anderson*, and reaffirmed in *Northwest Indian Fisheries Commission v. State of Washington*.

In 2001, the NWIFC brought a lawsuit against the state of Washington, demanding that the state repair or replace culverts that were blocking fish passage. The case addressed barrier culverts running under state roads that ran through treaty tribes "usual and accustomed" fishing places. The state acknowledged the need to repair or replace the culverts, but said it would take an estimated one hundred years to do so. For twelve years, the case worked its way through the courts. Finally, in March of 2013, federal judge Ricardo Martinez issued a permanent injunction, ordering the state to repair nearly 1,000 state-owned fish-blocking culverts within the next seventeen years, an action that would provide salmon access to thousands of miles of salmon habitat. Tribal people, environmentalists, and salmon advocates hailed the decision as a major victory. But within two months the state of Washington appealed the ruling, citing its high cost and current budget restrictions. In 2016, the Ninth Circuit Court of Appeals again found for the tribes, supporting the claim that the state must replace culverts that impede salmon passage.[54]

The ingenuity of Coyote is not limited to the courtroom, but is also illustrated by initiatives put forth by the Columbia River Intertribal Fish Commission. *Wy-Kan-Ush-Mi Wa-Kish-Wit* (Spirit of the Salmon Plan), is an initiative that prioritizes tribal culture, values, and sovereignty, and draws on traditional knowledge to restore salmon populations.[55] The CRIFC defines "traditional ecological knowledge" (or TEK) as that which is "rooted in a familial relationship with the plants, animals, and the environment. Traditional ecological knowledge is passed down the generations through oral traditions such as storytelling, songs and ceremonies." It includes cultural values, worldviews, and practical knowledge that provide stewardship principles for hunting, fishing, gathering, and cultivating. The authors of this program point out that it has a great deal in common with Western science in that it relies on questioning, non-static view of facts, interpretation of evidence, and quantitative thinking. What Traditional Ecological Knowledge has that science lacks, however, is its explicit moral and ethical worldview, wherein "social, spiritual, cultural, and natural systems are intertwined and inseparable."[56]

When treaty-tribes of the middle Columbia River frame their sustainability efforts around Traditional Ecological Knowledge it means in part that they are integrating traditional knowledge of the seasons and how they are tied to cultural practices into their sustainability efforts. For instance, consulting the oral testimony of elders is helping tribal scientists assess the impacts of climate change, as plants and animals shift in altitude or appear at different times of year than in previous generations. A Traditional Ecological Knowledge perspective also demands that fisheries managers take a whole ecosystem perspective, rather than singling out a single species. It demands a whole watershed perspective that considers biological diversity, the complex way species connect across habitats and throughout a riverine network, and the nature of health within an interconnected ecological community.

Integrating a Traditional Ecological Knowledge value of adaptive management has also led to the creation of tribal fish hatcheries that are more ecologically integrated, recognizing the distinct needs of a particular place. For instance, rather than the factory-production model that dominates at most hatcheries, tribal programs recognize the sacred irreplaceable nature of local places and populations. CRITFC members use only wild, local-origin brood stock, for example, and include the ritual and ceremonial aspects of Indigenous religious life within this very modern approach to fisheries management.

The interplay of sacred traditions and ecological knowledge is perhaps most powerfully illustrated by the use of Wáashat first foods ceremonies as a model for fish and wildlife management. The Wáashat religious movement was revitalized and given a formalized structure by Smohalla in the nineteenth century, though it draws on centuries- if not millennia-old practices of engagement with the natural landscape. The high holy days of the Wáashat ceremonial calendar are the first foods ceremonies, held to honor the sacred foods on which the peoples depend. During a First Foods ceremony, songs are sung in sets of seven, and oratory is given regarding each food and its importance for the people. James Selam emphasized that all holy foods were of equal importance, and refused to rank one above any other. "All the foods are most important," he argued. They are, however, served in a particular order: "čuuš (water), núsux (salmon), pyakí (bitterroot), lukš or xawš (the lomatium roots), xamsí (bare-stemmed lomatium), and wíwnu (huckleberries)."[57]

As Eric Quaempts, director of Natural Resources for the Confederated Tribes of the Umatilla explains, the order in which the food is brought to the table re-creates the ecosystem as a whole, providing both a philosophical and practical way of thinking about the interconnection of the bioregion. The distribution of foods, one dish at a time, in careful order, both recalls the sacred stories of creation and provides a picture of the ecosystem in miniature, moving from the lowest elevation (water at the river bottom) to the tributaries where salmon are caught, to the foothills where game are hunted, the high prairies where roots are gathered, and the mountainous terrain where berries can be found. The Umatilla, guided by this religious practice, reorganized their natural resources program so that it emphasized each of these key foods. They went even further, merging various tribal programs and departments to create a more integrated system. By employing TEK and drawing on the spiritual knowledge within traditional ceremonies, tribal fisheries and wildlife managers are bringing the ethical and spiritual principles of their ancestors into conversation with contemporary sciences.[58]

Another example of Coyote-like ingenuity can be found within tribal grassroots activist organizations working to revitalize traditional knowledge and ceremonies and to restore salmon habitat. In her book *Yakama Rising*, Michelle Jacob reflects on efforts within her own tribal community to do just that.[59] *X̱wayamamí ishích* is a nonprofit activist organization that works to heal community and ecosystem "by offering seasonal workshops that bring elders and youth together to teach community members about traditional food gathering and preservation." Jacob contends that *X̱wayamamí ishích* resists the devastation wrought by colonialism, working to restore kinship relations, Indigenous languages, and traditional food practices.[60] Settler colonialism has undermined Yakama culture in many ways, restricting access to traditional foods, imposing destructive gender norms that undermined traditional Plateau egalitarianism, and providing a food-system comprised of omnipresent junk food, all of which continue the "erosion of traditional Yakama social and economic systems."[61] Because of this, activists such as those at *X̱wayamamí ishích* "view their work in spiritual terms."[62] The program restores traditional food knowledge, reinforces traditional teachings about the importance and value of women's roles in Indigenous society, and affirms the value of every individual. They are guided by five key principles: humility, faith, grassroots empowerment, place-based teachings, and intergenerational teaching and learning. A primary lesson the program hopes to convey is the notion that "spirits of people and our foods are interconnected. Ill feelings will be spread to others, so it is important to bring positive, kind feelings to share with others. By teaching the youth these important cultural lessons, the youth learn to respect the foods as sacred gifts, they respect each other, and, perhaps most importantly, they respect themselves as they realize their spirits matter and are interconnected with others."[63]

Contemporary social and ecological challenges can be overwhelming. But tribal leaders and advocates such as these insist that the solution is to be found in strengthening ceremonies, going back to traditional foods, and becoming reacquainted with Mother Earth. As Elsie David, member of the Rock Creek longhouse said a recent interview: "I don't think I would know a great deal of my culture if I just lived on cow and nontraditional food. My grandma used to say, 'You're not going to know anything about our people if you don't eat our food.' If you're going to eat cows, you're going to be dumb like a cow."[64] Such an approach rejects the extractive and hierarchical worldview of settler colonialism, and demonstrates the recognition that restoring balance and reviving Indigenous foodways will, as Jacob tells us, "connect [the people] respectfully with the land—with Mother Earth—and will help lead the people to a better place."[65]

Notes

1. Charles Sams, "Wakanish NaknooweeThluma: 'Keepers of the Salmon,'" *Oregon Historical Quarterly* 108, no. 4 (Winter 2007): 645; 644–48. See also, http://www.critfc.org/salmon-culture/we-are-all-salmon-people/.

2. http://www.critfc.org/for-kids-home/for-kids/why-salmon-are-important-to-the-tribes/#sthash.6aGEeSBn.dpuf.

3. See Andrew Fisher, *Shadow Tribe: The Making of Columbia River Indian Identity* (Seattle: University of Washington Press, 2013) for an excellent discussion of the complex, interwoven history of the people of this region.

4. Fisher, *Shadow Tribe*, 15.

5. Fisher, *Shadow Tribe*, 16.

6. Fisher, *Shadow Tribe*, 25.

7. Fisher, *Shadow Tribe*, 19.

8. Fisher, *Shadow Tribe*, 20.

9. George W. Aguilar Sr., *When the River Ran Wild! Indian Traditions on the Mid-Columbia and the Warm Springs Reservation* (Seattle: University of Washington Press, 2005), 90.

10. Edward Sapir, *Wishram Texts, and Wasco Tales and Legends*, Publications of the American Ethnological Society (1909): xi. See also Aguilar *When the River Ran Wild*, 226.

11. Aguilar, *When the River Ran Wild*, 229, quoting Edward Sapir, *Wishram Texts*, 2: 242–24.

12. Aguilar, *When the River Ran Wild*, 104.

13. Aguilar, *When the River Ran Wild*, 108–9.

14. Aguilar, *When the River Ran Wild*, 111.

15. Eugene Hunn, *N'chiWana: The Big River, Mid-Columbia Indians and Their Land* (Seattle: University of Washington Press, 1990), 154–55.

16. Virginia Beavert Martin, "Native Songs Taught by Ellen Saluskin," in *Spirit of the First People: Native American Music Traditions of Washington State*, eds. Willie Smyth and Esme Ryan (Seattle: University of Washington Press, 1999), 69.

17. Brycene Neaman, "Song Traditions of the Yakama," in *Spirit of the First People: Native American Music Traditions of Washington State*, eds. Willie Smyth and Esme Ryan (Seattle: University of Washington Press, 1999), 79.

18. Fisher, *Shadow Indians*, 84.

19. Melville Jacobs, "A Few Observations on the World View of the Clackamas Chinook Indians," *Journal of American Folklore* 68, no. 269 (1955): 288.

20. Franz Boas, *Chinook Texts*, Smithsonian Institution (1894): 105. See also Susan Staiger Gooding, "Interior Salishan Creation Stories: Historical Ethics in the Making," *Journal of Religious Ethics* 20, no. 2 (Fall 1992): 358 for a summary of Sahaptin coyote stories.

21. Reuben Gold Thwaits, ed., *Original Journals of the Lewis and Clark Expedition* 1804–1806, vol. 4 (New York: Antiquarian Press [1904] 1959), 300. See also Hunn, *N'chiWana*, 153.

22. Henry K. Perkins, "Diary and Letters: 1838–1843," edited by Robert T. Boyd. Manuscript, Pacific Lutheran University, Tacoma, Washington. Book 1: 7. Quoted in Hunn, *N'chiWana*, 153.

23. Aguilar, *When the River Ran Wild*, 114.

24. Hunn, *N'chiWana*, 154.

25. Aguilar, *When the River Ran Wild*, 122. See Suzanne Crawford-O'Brien, "Salmon as Sacrament: First Salmon Ceremonies in the Pacific Northwest," in *Religion, Food and Eating in North America*, eds. Benjamin Zeller, Marie Dallam, Reid Neilson, Nora L Rubel, and Martha Finch (New York: Columbia University Press, 2014). See also Hiens, 125.

26. Fisher, *Shadow Tribe*, 20.

27. Clark, *Indian Legends*, 99.

Salmon Economies *American Indian Law Review* 24, no. 2 (1999/2000): 357–419.

55. http://plan.critfc.org/2013/spirit-of-the-salmon-plan/about-spirit-of-the-salmon/traditional-ecological-knowledge-and-science/.

56. http://plan.critfc.org/2013/spirit-of-the-salmon-plan/about-spirit-of-the-salmon/traditional-ecological-knowledge-and-science/.

57. Hunn, *N'chi Wana*, 209. See also Aguilar, *When the River Ran Wild*, 152. Water is powerfully symbolic because of its ability to give life. Seven is a ritual pattern number for the Wáashat, signaling completion and wholeness. "Seven appointed men hunt for deer and fish for salmon for the first salmon feast; seven chosen women dig for roots or gather berries for the first root and first berry feasts." The earthen floor of the longhouse is also important representing the presence of Mother Earth. Aguilar, *When the River Ran Wild*, 147.

58. Eric Quaempts, Tulalip Nature Resources Director, presentation at second annual *The Living Breath of Wəłəbʔaltxʷ Indigenous Ways of Knowing Cultural Food Practices and Ecological Knowledge Symposium*, University of Washington, September 26–27, 2014. See also Eric Quaempts, Krista Jones, Scott O'Daniel, Timothy Beechie and Geoffrey Poole, "Aligning Environmental Management with Ecosystem Resilience a First Foods Example from the Confederated Tribes of the Umatilla Indian Reservation, Oregon, USA," *Ecology and Society* 23, no. 2 (June 2018): 29–48.

59. Michelle Jacob, *Yakama Rising* (Tucson: University of Arizona Press, 2013).

60. Jacob, *Yakama Rising*, 83, 87.

61. Jacob, *Yakama Rising*, 95.

62. Jacob, *Yakama Rising*, 102.

63. Jacob, *Yakama Rising*, 97.

64. Fisher, *Shadow Tribe*, 151.

65. Jacob, *Yakama Rising*, 90.

Bibliography

Aguilar, George W., Sr. *When the River Ran Wild! Indian Traditions on the Mid-Columbia and the Warm Springs Reservation*. Seattle: University of Washington Press, 2005.

Barber, Katrine, and Andrew Fisher. "From Coyote to the Corps of Engineers." *Oregon Historical Quarterly* 108, no. 4 (2007): 522.

Beavert-Martin, Virginia. "Native Songs Taught by Ellen Saluskin." In *Spirit of the First People: Native American Music Traditions of Washington State*, edited by Willie Smyth and Esme Ryan, 62–71. Seattle: University of Washington Press, 1999.

Boas, Franz. *Chinook Texts*. Washington D.C.: Smithsonian Institution, 1894.

Clackamas Chinook (no individual name). "Coyote Builds Willamette Falls and the Magic Fish Trap." In *Indian Literature of the Oregon Country*, compiled and edited by Jarold Ramsey, 93. Seattle: University of Washington Press, 1977.

Clark, Ella E. *Indian Legends of the Pacific Northwest*. Berkeley: University of California Press, 1953.

Columbia River Intertribal Fish Commission. http://www.critfc.org/salmon-culture/we-are-all-salmon-people/. Accessed June 1, 2015.

———. http://www.critfc.org/for-kids-home/for-kids/why-salmon-are-important-to-the-tribes/#sthash.6aGEeSBn.dpuf. Accessed June 1, 2015.

———. http://plan.critfc.org/2013/spirit-of-the-salmon-plan/about-spirit-of-the-salmon/traditional-ecological-knowledge-and-science/. Accessed June 1, 2015.

Connelly, Thomas, and Mark Tveskov. "Mapping the Mosier Mounds: The Significance of Rock Feature Complexes on the Southern Columbia Plateau." *Journal of Archaeological Science* (1997): 289–300.

Crawford-O'Brien, Suzanne. "Salmon as Sacrament: First Salmon Ceremonies in the Pacific Northwest." In *Religion, Food and Eating in North America*, edited by Benjamin Zeller, Marie Dallam, Reid Neilson, Nora L. Rubel, and Martha Finch, 114–33. New York: Columbia University Press, 2014.

Ferguson, Jennifer K. *Book of Legends*. Colville Confederated Tribes, 2007. Accessed May 30, 2015. http://www.colvilletribes.com/book_of_legends.php.

Fisher, Andrew. *Shadow Tribe: The Making of Columbia River Indian Identity*. Seattle: University of Washington Press, 2013.

Fisher, Andrew. "'This I Know from the Old People': Yakama Indian Treaty Rights as Oral Tradition," *Montana Magazine of Western History* 49, no. 1 (Spring 1999): 2–17.

Frey, Rodney. *Stories that Make the World: Oral Literature of the Indian Peoples of the Inland Northwest*. Norman: University of Oklahoma Press, 1995.

Gooding, Susan Staiger. "Interior Salishan Creation Stories: Historical Ethics in the Making," *Journal of Religious Ethics* 20, no. 2 (Fall 1992): 253–387.

Gould, Marian K., and Franz Boas. *Folk Tales of the Salishan and Sahaptin Tribes, Okanogan, and Sanpoil Tales*. Washington, DC: Smithsonian Institution, 1917.

Hines, Donald. *Ghost Voices: Yakima Indian Myths, Legends, Humor and Hunting Stories*. Issaquah, WA: Great Eagle Publishing, 1992.

Hunn, Eugene. *N'chiWana: The Big River, Mid-Columbia Indians and Their* Land. Seattle: University of Washington Press, 1990.

Jacob, Michelle. *Yakama Rising: Indigenous Cultural Revitalization, Activism and Healing*. Tucson: University of Arizona Press, 2013.

Jacobs, Melville. "A Few Observations on the World View of the Clackamas Chinook Indians." *Journal of American Folklore* 68, no. 269 (1955): 283–89.

Lewis, Yale O., III. "Treaty Fishing Rights: A Habitat Right as Part of the Trinity of Rights Implied by the Fishing Clause of the Stevens Treaties," *American Indian Law Review* 27, no. 1 (2002/2003): 281–311.

Meyer, Tony. "Federal Court Upholds Tribal Treaty Rights in Culvert Case," Northwest Indian Fisheries Commission (April 2, 2013). http://nwifc.org/2013/04/federal-court-upholds-tribal-treaty-rights-in-culvert-case/. Accessed May 30, 2015.

Mourning Dove. *Coyote Stories*, edited by Jay Miller. Seattle: University of Washington Press, 1990.

Myers, W. E. "Coyote Frees the Salmon." *Oregon Historical Quarterly* 108, no. 4 (Winter 2007): 543–45.

Neaman, Brycene. "Song Traditions of the Yakama." In *Spirit of the First People: Native American Music Traditions of Washington State*, edited by Willie Smyth and Esme Ryan, 72–80. Seattle: University of Washington Press, 1999.

Perkins, Henry K. "Diary and Letters: 1838–1843." Edited by Robert T. Boyd. Manuscript, Pacific Lutheran University, Tacoma, Washington.

Quaempts, Eric, Krista Jones, Scott O'Daniel, Timothy Beechie, and Geoffrey Poole, "Aligning Environmental Management with Ecosystem Resilience, A First Foods Example from the Confederated Tribes of the Umatilla Indian Reservation, Oregon, USA," *Ecology and Society* 23, no. 2 (June 2018): 29–48.

Sams, Charles. "Wakanish NaknooweeThluma: 'Keepers of the Salmon.'" *Oregon Historical Quarterly* 108, no. 4 (Winter 2007): 644–48.

Sapir, Edward. *Wishram Texts, and Wasco Tales and Legends*. New York: Publications of the American Ethnological Society, 1909.

Simpson, Louis and Dell Hymes. "Bungling Host, Benevolent Host: Louis Simpson's Deer and Coyote." *American Indian Quarterly* 8, no. 3 (1984): 171–98.

Thwaits, Reuben Gold, ed. *Original Journals of the Lewis and Clark Expedition 1804–1806*, vols. 3–4. New York: Antiquarian Press, (1904) 1959.

Trafzer, Cliff. *Grandmother, Grandfather, Old Wolf: Tamanwit Ku Sukat and Traditional Native American Narratives from the Columbia Plateau*. East Lansing: Michigan State University Press, 1988.

Wilkinson, Charles. *Messages From Frank's Landing: A Story of Salmon, Treaties and the Indian Way*. Seattle: University of Washington Press, 2006.

Wilkinson, Charles. *Blood Struggle: The Rise of Modern Indian Nations*. New York: W. W. Norton, 2006.

Wilson, Rollie. "Removing Dam Development to Recover Columbia Basin Treaty Protected Salmon Economies." *American Indian Law Review* 24, no. 2 (1999/2000): 357–419.

3

Where Food Grows on the Water

Manoomin/Wild Rice and Anishinaabe Peoplehood

Michael D. McNally

> Food for us comes from our relatives whether they have wings or fins or roots. That is how we consider food. Food has a culture. It has a history. It has a story. It has relationships.
>
> —Winona LaDuke

Introduction

These words of Anishinaabe writer and activist Winona LaDuke serve as an excellent epigraph for a chapter in this volume, because *manoomin*, wild rice, is not only the traditional staple food of Minnesota's Anishinaabe, or Ojibwe, community (variously Ojibwa, Ojibway, Chippewa; plural Anishinaabeg); it is a *sacred* food.[1] But even as I utter "sacred food," I risk the hackneyed image that so often comes with the term sacred. *Manoomin* is not only a sacred food in the sense of a soul food or a healing food or a ceremonial food—although it is all these things. It is, at the end of the day, more than a food source. It has culture; it has history; it has story; and LaDuke can speak in these terms because as we'll soon see, the wild rice plant is no "it" at all, but a subject, a moral person.

Many Anishinaabe speakers gloss the term *manoomin* as "good berry," and this grain is distinct indeed from what most of us know from boxes of Uncle Ben's, a monoculture crop based on a hybrid strain bred in labs at the University of Minnesota in the 1950s. That crop is now grown largely in paddies in California's Central Valley in some cases flooded with waters diverted from salmon stocks in the North. *Manoomin*, by contrast, grows in the shallows at the edges of many of Minnesota's more than ten thousand lakes and slow rivers. *Zizania aquatica* is not only a bellwether species for the health of those waters; *manoomin* captures their distinctive flavors—a trained palate can literally taste the place of particular lakes or rivers. The grain that ripens each late August/early September occasions traditional harvests and ricing camps at traditional gathering grounds both on the state's seven Ojibwe reservations and in ceded territories where usufruct rights were wisely reserved by Anishinaabe treaty signatories in the nineteenth century. *Manoomin* is regarded as a medicine, a ceremonial food, and a soul food for the feasts following the ceremonies. In the Anishinaabe migration story, the spiritual calling to move west until the old people found "food growing on the water" weaves the *manoomin* plant, the landscape, and Anishinaabe peoplehood into a tight braid. The harvest of *manoomin* remains one of the most important traditional practices, both for a sense of Anishinaabe peoplehood and subsistence on their traditional lands, and more recently for sustainable tribal economic development. But again, what is often understood as a resource to be managed for human flourishing is no mere resource.

And here is the larger way that a religious studies approach to food can perhaps help us better understand and appreciate indigenous valuations of foods and the plants and animals that comprise those foods. Foods, especially so-called sacred foods, can be seen to bridge the conceptual categorizations that both structure and constrain our thinking: material and spiritual, natural and supernatural, economic and religious. Attending to this specificity, as we shall see, will require a more nuanced approach to such inherited oppositions as material/spiritual, sacred/profane, nature/culture, and economy/religion. As important as undoing the surety of such oppositions, and as important has been the consideration of foodways to such important work, I want to suggest as well that the language of law, environmental science, and politics, where the issues are played out, and in particular the language of *resource* function as discourses that obscure the urgency and reach—call it *religious*, or call it *"fire in the belly"*—of Anishinaabe commitments to *manoomin*.

For Anishinaabe people, *manoomin*, like other plants and animals, is an other-than-human person, and as a person holds a place in the moral circle of concern.[2] Ecological and genomic research challenges to the *manoomin* plant have generated important spirited activism within Minnesota's Ojibwe community. Drawing on the place of *manoomin* in Anishinaabe myth and ritual, on the one hand, and the contested history of wild rice "resource development," on the other, this chapter will explore that spirited activism in an effort to come to terms with the limits and possibilities of natural and cultural resource discourses.

In this chapter, I want to draw on a range of Anishinaabe voices to identify the very different starting points for activism on a number of contemporary issues where the health, integrity, and peoplehood of *manoomin*, and thus the health, integrity, and peoplehood of Anishinaabe people, are in serious question. The first issue concerns the most recent agricultural science work, genetic modification of the plant; the second involves the potential expansion of copper and nickel open-pit mining in Northern Minnesota, with toxic discharges posing serious threats to *manoomin* on reservation lands, but also on ceded lands downstream from the proposed mining sites in the Superior National Forest, where Ojibwe tribes retain court-recognized treaty rights, including rights to resource comanagement. Along with these more acute issues, *manoomin* activism has much to do with broader health and healing of Anishinaabe people and with the sustainable economic development of tribal operations.

I will leave it to others to relate the ecological, legal, and political nuances of these issues. My more specific purpose here is to use religious studies categories of analysis—myth, ritual, ethical practice, and notions of sacred community—to frame more effectively the sophistication and indeed the *specificity* of Anishinaabe relationships with and commitments to this food and this plant. For as society weighs the goods of genetic engineering or of extractive industries with the threats they present to wild rice, it is crucial to see how *manoomin* is more than a factor in risk assessment or in managing resources of instrumental value. Fittingly, then, we begin not with the issues but with two sacred stories that "center" Anishinaabe approaches to those issues.[3]

Narrative

Long ago, when we lived on the shores of the Great Salt Water (the Atlantic coastline), the Seven Fires Prophecy was given to

> us. The First Fire reads: "You will know the chosen ground has been reached when you come to a land where food grows on water." We then set forth on our Great Migration that began over 500 years ago. We traveled down the St. Lawrence River, into the Great Lakes region, and thence came to Anishinaabe Aki where we found the food that grows on water.[4]
>
> Nenabozho, our Great Uncle, was the first to find manoomin. Hungry, Nenabozho visited his friend Zhiishiib (Duck) for food. Zhiishiib served Nenabozho with manoomin naboob. It was the most delicious naboob Nenabozho had ever eaten. Later, Nenabozho set out to find the food that Zhiishiib had served him. After several days, Nenabozho, hungry, followed a flock of ducks to a lake. He found tall, slender plants growing from the water. "Eat us, Nenabozho," the plants said. "We're good to eat." Eating some, he realized it was the food Zhiishiib had given him. "What do you call yourselves," Nenabozho asked the beautiful plants. "We are called manoomin, Nenabozho," the manoomin aadizookaanag answered.[5]

There are three facets to these stories I want to focus on. First, as stories about the Trickster, they conform to what we might identify as an indigenous category of story congruent to that of the theoretical category of "myth."[6] Ojibwe tradition differentiates *aadizookanag*, sometimes called Winter Stories, from *dibaadjimowin*, other stories that can matter and blend family memory, history, and traditional practices, but without the strictures on when and how they are taught. *Aadizookanag*, a category gendered animate, refers both to the story and to the spiritual beings referenced in the story: where animals aren't just animals and plants aren't just plants but are capitalized spiritual beings: Duck, not ducks, *Manoomin*, not wild rice. Such stories happen in the "long ago" (*mewinzha*), a myth time in this case where the Trickster, son of a human mother and a spirit father, could speak fluently with plants and animals prior to the communicative divide that only certain spiritually gifted people can traverse.

Second, the first story, part of the sacred migration story that places Anishinaabe people in their current territory "where food grows on the water," connects Anishinaabe people and this plant, this food, in a most specific way. Anishinaabe Akiing, the Land of the Anishinaabe, is in this story neither a utopian no-place like a Garden of Eden, nor the terrain of historical contingency. Although Ojibwe teachings do not dispute ethnohistorians' tracking of their migration to the region in the sixteenth and seventeenth centuries, this story suggests that Anishinaabe people are "called" to living on this land; a vocation, if you will, not a happenstance of history. As the late White Earth tribal historian Andy Favorite aptly put it, "Wild rice is part of our prophecy, our process of being human, our process of being Anishinaabe . . . we are here because of the wild rice. We are living a prophecy fulfilled."[7] Indeed, grammatically Anishinaabe Akiing, the place where food grows on the water, can be translated as "the land of the people," or "the people of the land," where the belonging goes both ways. Reciprocity with the land.

Third, it is crucial in these stories that the plants and animals of Anishinaabe Akiing precede human beings; indeed the Trickster models for Anishinaabe people how to regard plants and animals as "people," and indeed people who are prior to the human people. Plants and animals are, in this story, the Trickster's teacher. It is Zhishiib, Duck, who instructs the Trickster that one can eat *Manoomin*, and it is the *Manoomin*-people themselves who invite the Trickster to feed on them. Note that the Trickster does not "name" "it," but he asks "them" their name, and it is they who teach him how to live well on Anishinaabe Akiing. The Trickster, and the Anishinaabe people for whom he is sacred hero, fits into a world of plants and animals that precedes him. They are, it happens, Trickster's elders, and this establishes a key Anishinaabe teaching: to learn to live well, humans should take plants and animals as their teachers.[8] A climate change report by one Anishinaabe organization put it thus: "We consider beings in the natural environment to be elders and teachers who can teach us valuable lessons . . . We have always been the younger siblings and students."[9]

Indigenous Ways of Knowing and Valuing

The personhood of plants may be hard to get Modern Western heads around, but it is crucial to do so in order to better understand the urgency of issues affecting *manoomin* and the limits of the discourse of resource. In the Ojibwe language, gender involves a distinction not between masculine and feminine (in fact Ojibwe makes no such grammatical distinction), but between animate and inanimate. Words classed as animate take he/she and him/her as pronouns and engage different verbs to describe transitive actions. My late Ojibwe teacher Larry Cloud Morgan often said that thinking of the world in the Ojibwe language constrained him to think

> harvest begins. The manoomin is taken from the lakes, threshed, and stored along with the corn, squash, pumpkin, and beans. Throughout the summer the meat is dried and stored and the herbs and medicine secured. The fish is dried and the acorns hung. The kin-nik-a-nik is scraped and prepared for daily use.[15]

This presentation of culture in terms of nature and its seasons is encoded in this indigenous knowledge category, and it bears a few words of clarification here before we return to the subject of *manoomin.*

Bimaadiziwin is an everyday word that can be translated rather flatly as *life* or *nature—bimaadizi*—he/she is alive. As Ojibwe nouns are fashioned from the verbs that drive the language, *bimaadiziwin* implies a kind of motion that passes by, and thus has been conceptualized and translated as "the circle of life." Crucially, this circle of life closely associated with seasonal cycles is also closely associated with Anishinaabe cultural practices of the seasonal round that follow those seasons. The nineteenth-century missionary, Frederic Baraga, who compiled the first Ojibwe dictionary, rendered Anishinaabe Bimaadiziwin as "the Savage Life," of course wrongly identifying such a way of life with savagery but correctly noting the important ways that Anishinaabe culture follows nature. For me it is the way that culture participates in nature that makes this term so instructive; for the life on the land, the seasonal round, is no mere economic resource strategy, though it is that, too. Neither is it merely an elegant cultural ecology, where human ways are modeled and regulated to be in a symbiotic balance with the environment, though it is that, as well. Ignatia Broker, whose description of the cycle of natural seasons above enjoins the cycle of cultural practices that follow those seasons, thickens the meaning of the practices. Culture, following nature, is not arbitrary but a matter of vocation: "We believe in the circle of life. We believe that all returns to its source; that both good and bad return to the place where they began. We believe that if we start a deed, after the fullness of time it will return to us, the source of the journey. If care is not used when the circle is begun, then the hurts along the way will be received in the end. Such is the belief of the true Ojibway."[16] Indeed, as Lawrence Gross's fine chapter in this volume shows, the economic sustenance and ecological balance indicated by the ricing season is also a morally compelling and aesthetically beautiful matter.

Hallowell glossed *bimaadiziwin* as "the Good life." Ojibwe literary critic Scott Lyons suggests how the imaginative and productive dimensions of culture are not so much "tied to" but rather participating in and through nature.

> Perhaps it would not be going too far to suggest that Ojibwe speakers do not have a culture at all. Rather it may be more accurate to say that they spend their time "culturing . . . producing more life, living in a sustainable manner as part of the flow of nature—and never separate from it."[17]

In the Ojibwe case, what a modern Western analysis might distinguish as the economic and religious dimensions of this category are similarly inextricable. As Hallowell put it,

> The central goal of life for the Ojibwa is expressed by the term *bimaadiziwin*, life in the fullest sense, life in the sense of longevity, health and freedom from misfortune. This goal cannot be achieved without the effective help and cooperation of both human and other-than-human persons, as well as by one's own personal efforts.[18]

If *manoomin*, and the other plants and animals of Anishinaabe Akiing, are construed as nonhuman persons in an Ojibwe-language moral, spiritual, and physical universe, it makes sense to think of Anishinaabe Akiing not so much in terms of such abstractions as "nature" or "the land" as it does to think of Anishinaabe Akiing as a community of persons. Or, as Hallowell put it, "another society" in which the Ojibwe live. I have explored the extension of human relations to the sociality of the other-than-human persons elsewhere, but suffice it to say that the same gestures and principles of respect, which involve both ethical restraint and ceremonious decorum, extend to the nonhuman world.[19] As with the ceremonialized ethics of the Confucian and neo-Confucian traditions, the Ojibwe tradition makes demands both ethical and ritual in terms of *manoomin*. I turn now to the ritual dimension.

Ritual

Manoomin as Ritual Food

If as a staple *manoomin* is an ordinary, everyday food, it is also an extraordinary food: a special gift of the Creator that ties Anishinaabe people to their lands through nourishment, taste, and life. And the extraordinariness of *manoomin* extends well beyond being merely a "comfort food" or even a "soul food." According to LaDuke, *manoomin* is ideally the "first food for a child when they can eat solid; last food eaten before you pass into the spirit world."[20] *Manoomin* is regarded as a medicine, *mashkiki*, a term that can enjoin both material and spiritual properties and powers to heal and to do things in the world. White Earth elder and activist Joe Lagarde, points out that *manoomin* and *nibi*, water, are the only two things required at every ceremony. According to Erma Vizenor, one-time tribal chair of the White Earth Nation, "manoomin accompanies our celebrations, our mourning, and our initiations, our feasts, as a food and as a spiritual presence."[21]

Autumnal ceremonies of the *Midéwiwin* society, the key traditional Anishinaabe ceremonial complex, are timed in thanksgiving for the *manoomin* harvest. *Manoomin* specifically is called for in ritual offerings to drums at their feasts, at naming ceremonies, funerals, and other occasions where spirits are fed with spirit plates. *Manoomin* grains have been used in the ritualized practices of medicine bundles, for its talismanic and centering properties in the Civil War, both World Wars, and the Korean and Vietnam Wars. But its medicine power is no merely supernatural affair. Thomas Vennum reports that *manoomin*, both the grain as well as other parts of the plant, has held a place in the *materia medica* of Anishinaabe healers: for babies having difficulty nursing, for poultices, and so on.[22] And just as the significance of the *manoomin* harvest has become accentuated in the current historical moment, so too has *manoomin*'s medicinal associations become even more marked in light of diabetes, heart disease, depression, and other health effects of historical trauma. As a food of the land, of Anishinaabe Akiing, *manoomin* has come to hold particular healing at this particular historical moment.[23] I turn now not so much to the "ritual" of harvesting *manoomin* as to its ritualization, following Catherine Bell's nuanced attention to how people don't so much practice ritual as ritualize practices.[24]

Ritualized Harvest

Manoominikewin, "making wild rice" or simply "ricing," is more than an elegant ecology or economic activity whereby Ojibwe people have eked out a living. Scholars have pointed out how the rice harvest has included principles of Anishinaabe law regarding property and rights;[25] of political organization and women's leadership;[26] and of traditions of natural resource management.[27] Family stories elaborate on what managers refer to as cultural resources as well: the way that *manoominikewin* includes special traditional places, rice camps associated with traditional dwellings (wigwams) and extended families, specialized practices such as "jigging" or "dancing" parched rice to separate the hulls from grain in special moccasins, and storytelling.

To be sure the harvest has been an important economic practice, but *how* it has been economically important has changed in time. In the early subsistence times, a cache of *manoomin* could get people through the harsh season of late winter, when game was scarce or hard to access due to thick melting and refreezing snow, uncertain lake ice, and when other food stocks had run dry. Beginning with the fur trade but extending down to today, *manoominikewin* produced a surplus trade good that underwrote survival in new ways. Indeed, in the twentieth century and today, the making of wild rice has been remembered for being a time of plenty, when cash from rice sales could fund school supplies, and where the want of the rest of the year was wanting. One woman remembered:

> The people are generally in good spirits. There is less of a financial strain and stress because of the rice that is sold. Many people are able to supplement their children's clothes, pay bills and maybe even buy a car to be able make it to school, job, next seasonal work, hospital and grocery store. For one time of the White Man's billing year—it's not so hard making ends meet.[28]

But as indicated by the cultural resources, places, and practices involved with the harvest, it would be missing much of the point to reduce its significance to this economic purpose. *Manoominikewin* has a special place in what could justly be called an Anishinaabe liturgical calendar and not simply a resource-maximization strategy. The moon that time of year is called *manoominike giizis*. As one Anishinaabe woman put it, "The work is hard but to have some free food, and to engage in the traditions of our ancestors and to really be connected to this good earth. . . . well it makes up for all that sweat and strain, surely. This is the time of year when families get together, stories and jokes are told, the memory is flexed and (sometimes stretched)."[29] A number of powwow celebrations, at the Leech Lake reservation community of Ball Club, at Nett Lake and at Red Lake, are called "Migwetch Mahnomen" (thank you, *manoomin*) days.

Manoominikewin was characterized by specific ritual practices that were season specific. Paul Peter Buffalo told Tim Roufs, "we used a certain method when we go out into the field to look for medicines, wild rice, and other crops of the season which will be turned over to the Indian when they are mature. When we look at a crop we are always ready to say '*migwitch*.'"[30] Maude Kegg of the Mille Lacs Band insisted that rice camps were governed by ritualized gestures of respect and prayer for *manoomin*, including a first fruits offering of sorts.

> When [the old lady who did the parching] finished the rice, no one was supposed to eat any, so I was forbidden to eat any. First she gave a feast in which she offered tobacco and talked about the manitous and thunderbirds, and the sun, and all such things, and put tobacco out. When she finished speaking, we ate the rice.[31]

Earl Nyholm told Anthony Paredes about the Bad River ricing camps of his youth: "It seemed that the old people really enjoyed that time of the year. . . . They would really go about the whole process like it was sacred; they really put themselves into it."[32]

Behind Nyholm's observation is a nod to timeless Anishinaabe traditions, but behind it, too, is an observation that for those elders, *manoominikewin*, and by extension the taste and meaning of the food it produces, had other things at stake than may have been the case in 1710, 1810, or even 1910. Sacralization is surely in this case a function of desecration, and I turn now to *manoomin*'s history, which is one of profound political, cultural, religious, and environmental interruptions. As LaDuke put it, *manoomin* has a history, this history is crucial both for the continuous affirmation of the relationship between Anishinaabeg and *manoomin* and the new legal, political, and environmental registers in which that timeless relationship was newly affirmed.

History

Interruptions and Reaffirmations of Relationship

Throughout early fur trade encounters with French, English, and later Americans, *manoomin* became not merely a matter of subsistence but an important trade item to victual the posts, but importantly the indigenous relationship with *manoomin* continued to be subject to the ecological, moral, and spiritual regulation of Anishinaabe tradition. Even with the encroachments of timber interests and settlers, Anishinaabe leaders affirmed their relationship with *manoomin* in treaties, providing for continued access to it in the ceded lands of the nineteenth-century treaties. The 1837 Treaty, for example, provided, "The privilege of hunting, fishing, and gathering the wild rice, upon the lands, the rivers and the lakes included in the territory ceded, is guaranteed to the Indians, during the pleasure of the President of the United States."[33]

There is a much longer story than can be told here of indigenous struggles to assert rights they reserved, either explicitly or implicitly, in treaties to continue hunting, fishing, and gathering in ceded territories. In Minnesota, the full force of this provision of the 1837 Treaty was affirmed in 1999 by the US Supreme Court over the protestations of the State of Minnesota.[34]

While the ink on the treaties was still drying, the U.S. Army Corps of Engineers in the 1880s begin building a series of dams on the lakes of the upper Mississippi watershed, especially those that dammed up Lake Winnibigoshish and Leech Lake, and sent the region's Anishinaabeg into a tailspin. The dams were built to secure reliable flows over St. Anthony Falls to power Minneapolis's grain mills and to render the Mississippi navigable by barge to St. Paul at all times of year. Raising Leech Lake four feet and Lake Winnibigoshish fourteen feet, the two dams alone flooded 200,000 acres of the choice reservation lands, and especially wild rice fields at the edge of those lakes. A series of paltry federal offers to compensate the Anishinaabe for the losses to their livelihoods and reservation lands were experienced by Anishinaabe leaders as insulting. But they were part of a larger federal strategy, broadly supported by the region's missionaries, to dissuade Anishinaabe people from continuing the practices of the seasonal round deemed inimical to civilization and instead to take up allotments at the White Earth Reservation, where they were to become farmers.

Winnibigoshish and Pillager band Anishinaabe, who in any case chose to remain on their flooded lands, found ever more rigorously enforced rules against off-reservation travel, even to customary ricing camps on ceded lands where hunting and gathering rights were expressly protected in treaty language, especially as state game laws sought to regulate "natural resources" for the benefit of sport hunting and fishing. Bruce White has referred to this maneuver as the "criminalization of the seasonal round."[35]

The dams, the handling of the damages from the dams, and the subsequent criminalization of the seasonal round—all were part of a concerted effort to remove Anishinaabe people from the traditional practices of *mino-bimaadiziwin*. As Albert Jenks put it, "wild rice, which had led to [the Ojibwe people's] advance thus far, held them back from further progress."[36] And all this happened even as state officials promoted access by non-Indians to a food that came to have increased association with the state's culture and economic development, and of recreational duck hunting. In an effort to address Anishinaabe poverty during the Great Depression, the federal government reversed its previous policies discouraging *manoominikewin* and other practices of the seasonal round and actively promoted an "improved" and "modernized" form of wild rice production, including the creation of wild rice cooperatives to step up processing and incorporate broad distribution networks for Indian produced rice. "Seemingly overnight," writes historian Brenda Child, "government officials and the State Forest service in Minnesota yielded to an Ojibwe economy it had worked for the previous half-century to destroy."[37] In and through these apparent reversals of policy, however, Child shows how the gendered basic aims of assimilation policy, organizing labor to promote women's domesticity and men's agricultural production, remained intact. Anishinaabe women continued to assert themselves in the cooperatives, but the authority they had long exercised over the harvest had been "modernized" under male control.[38]

By the 1970s, after official federal policies of relocation toward the fuller economic assimilation of Native people into the labor force, fully half of the American Indian population was living in urban areas like Chicago and Minneapolis. But even this demographic sea change did not wrest relocated Anishinaabe people from their connection to ricing. Indeed the distance from traditional ricing grounds accentuated its cultural importance, and as Thomas Vennum Jr. observed, the late August/early September rice harvest time became an even more marked time for return to reservation communities, a time to take off from work, and in some cases even to face losing their job or early weeks of school out of fidelity to the tradition of *manoominikewin*.[39]

The broader cultural identification of non-Native Minnesotans with wild rice had been building all the while, but it became associated with the state's economic development in the late 1960s and 1970s, with the selective cross-breeding at the University of Minnesota to produce hybrid strains that could permit controlled cultivation in paddies and that were of uniform size and shape and of stronger hulls to sustain mechanized harvesting.[40] The state legislature declared "wild rice" to be the State Grain in 1977.

Given the efficiencies of mechanized cultivation of paddy rice, the bottom fell off the market for Indian-harvested *manoomin* from natural stands. According to the White Earth Land Recovery Project, the wholesale price "dropped from $4.44 per pound in 1967 to $2.68 a pound in 1976, destabilizing the wild rice economy of the Ojibwe." Ojibwe activists won a statutory labeling requirement to distinguish cultivated "paddy rice" from natural stand *manoomin* that could be labeled "wild rice" for sale in Minnesota.[41]

Continued Threats to Wild Rice

The diversity of strains of *zizania aquatica* in any given locale makes it a hardy survivor of "natural" environmental fluctuations, but the plant is unusually sensitive to environmental changes resulting from a variety of human actions. When non-Indians, whose harvest was not regulated by indigenous women elders or ricing chiefs, took to the rice stands to get their crop, they often devastated those stands through use of wide and motorized fishing boats, and later mechanized harvesters, indiscriminately knocking rice regardless of ripeness and doing permanent damage to affected plants. This led Minnesota's Anishinaabeg to press for state regulations that require hand harvesting. The state legislature passed a statute in 1939 to protect the plant in public waters from destruction by indiscriminate harvests, but also made the state Department of Conservation, rather than local leadership with local knowledge, the regulatory authority to set the season and issue permits, much to the dismay of the Anishinaabe leaders.[42]

Manoomin is particularly susceptible to changes in water quality; a Minnesota Department of Natural Resources study identifies the downstream implications of sulfide mining pollutants exceeding ten parts per million, which is currently Minnesota's water-quality standard for rice, as particularly hazardous, as would be the fluctuations in groundwater level and fluctuations in water level. Climate change has impacted the Minnesota region most noticeable in terms of an increased geographic concentrations of rainfall events, with increased droughts in other locations, all presenting challenges to *manoomin* stands. Other human impacts that present challenges are increases in recreational boating, fishing, and lakefront development, where wild rice stands can be regarded as an obstacle.

In addition to these threats, however, a number of activists consider research into and development of genetically modified organisms that capitalize on *manoomin*'s genome, which was mapped in 2000 at the University of Minnesota, a principal threat operating in the multiple registers this chapter has identified: environmental, spiritual, and ethical.[43]

The concern, rooted in indigenous experiences with rice and corn strains in Southeast Asia and Mesoamerica, is that genetically modified supercrops will overtake genetically diverse strains of *manoomin* in natural stands. The contamination could be through blow over by wind, or by migratory waterfowl, which do not discern differences between natural stands and other sources. Advocates of genetic modification point out that nutritional and health benefits associated with particular units of information in the *manoomin* genome can be put together with other beneficial characteristics found in other genomes to produce better and better foods, potentially equipping humankind to better address global nutritional and health concerns. With so much at stake, one shouldn't take such claims lightly, and to be sure Anishinaabe *manoomin* activists have not. But for these activists, *manoomin* is not merely a resource for the human project. As Joe Lagarde puts it,

> today the traditional teachings of Anishinaabe communities and Western science and genetic research are at an impasse. A tribal nation seeks to preserve and protect a sacred gift from becoming the next genetically modified agricultural crop redesigned for those who see wild rice only as another cash crop in need of modification so as to improve yield, pest resistance, uniform maturation, resilience and creating seed that assures these "improvements." To Western science, the mere thought that something spiritual might impede scientific research is absurd, unnecessary, and only would serve as an unnecessary obstacle to inevitable progress. To Anishinaabe people, the sacred relationship with the manoomin is central and cannot be ignored in any discussion on the natural gift as it has been given.[44]

Genetic engineering would not only threaten contamination through cross pollination with natural stands of *manoomin*, it also represents an ownership trend where the original caretakers of *manoomin* are dispossessed in favor of patented ownership of genetically engineered strains by the corporations sponsoring the research. As Winona LaDuke put it, "the Ojibwe now find themselves at the center of an international battle over who owns lifeforms, foods, and medicines that have throughout history been the collective property of indigenous peoples."[45] Hewing to their understanding of *manoomin* as a being and thus not a resource to be owned, activists and the White Earth tribe have disclaimed at this time pursuing the protection of *manoomin* through specific property law claims of either intellectual or cultural property law. Instead their efforts have been broadly dialogical with scientists at the University of Minnesota, appealing to principles of research ethics and stakeholder interests in a public research institution, as well as to international law bodies. The activism of Lagarde and others, especially at White Earth, bore fruit in a 2007 Minnesota state law that anticipates threats to natural stands still regarded as potential. The law requires that an Environmental Impact Statement be completed prior to any state-permitted release of genetically engineered wild rice, along with a state Department of Natural Resources study to the potential threats to natural stand wild rice.

In addition to genetic modification, another looming threat to the well-being of *manoomin* is the proposal to license a number of copper- and nickel-mining operations in Northeastern Minnesota, in the ceded territories of the 1854 Treaty. The treaty specifies that Lake Superior Ojibwe "shall have the right to hunt and fish therein, until otherwise ordered by the President."[46] The Bois Forte, Grand Portage, and the Fond du Lac bands, and the 1854 Treaty Authority (comprised of Grand Portage and Bois Forte) have joined forces with environmental groups like Friends of the Boundary Waters to challenge licensure of the mining operations in the Superior National Forest, citing concerns about groundwater and watershed contamination. For proponents, jobs in Minnesota's economically depressed Iron Range and a renewed sense of mining purpose for the region are summoned to speak in mining's favor.

For environmentalist opponents, the major concern is damage to the one of the nation's more precious wilderness areas, the Boundary Waters Canoe Area Wilderness. But for the tribes, it is very much about *manoomin*, and the threat to the plant, given its sensitivity to water-quality impacts. And it is about court recognized treaty rights of access and of management of wild rice in the ceded territories. The legal fact of off-reservation rights to rice beds downstream from the proposed sulfide ore mines is clear, but the weight of those rights in the political maelstrom has proved less clear. The three bands involved not only formally opposed the mines; they have brought their own scientific analyses to the environmental review process that challenge the optimistic premises on which rest other analyses predicting less dire consequences. Still, the final Environmental Impact Statement on the first proposed project, the PolyMet mine, effectively relegates the bands' views to an expansive appendix, taking the concerns and the science backing them up "into account" as the environmental law requires, but citing "major differences of opinion" on virtually each of the appendicized conclusions.[47]

Wild Rice Activism and Food Sovereignty

Such activism, like other *manoomin* activism of the last hundred years, is involved with a food sovereignty movement that addresses threats to the plant and food in the discourse of "bio-colonialism."[48] Sovereignty thus imagined in food sovereignty is economic, political, and physical, but as I shall indicate by way of conclusion, it is also spiritual.

Physically, it is of course a matter of indigenous health. Roughly one-third of the adult population at White Earth served by Indian Health has diabetes, a disease exacerbated if not caused by a "rapid transition from traditional foods to industrialized food."[49]

Economically, it has to do with indigenous people spending resources externally for food. LaDuke estimates that at White Earth, 7 of the 8 million dollars spent annually by tribal members on food are spent off-reservation. This is a clear drain on wealth that could better sustain the community. According to LaDuke, one-fourth of the tribal economy is lost and a major source of wealth is gone.

The political dimension of food sovereignty is not just suggestive or poetic. Sovereignty is of course not only a key concept of European-American political theory, but inflected in indigenous idioms as an organizing principle for a broad array of indigenous rights, including religious rights. The relationship between *manoomin*'s natural or environmental history and Anishinaabe political history is seen perhaps most keenly in the matter of the Upper Mississippi watershed dams. Threats to the plant (like targeted threats to Great Plains bison) were intended and felt as threats to the autonomy of the people living in relationship to *manoomin*. In this light, it should not be so surprising that *manoomin* is expressly included in the first article of the White Earth Nation's new constitution. "The White Earth Nation shall have jurisdiction over citizens, residents, visitors, altruistic relations, and the whole of the land, including transfers, conferrals, and acquisitions of land in futurity, water, wild rice, public and private property."[50]

In February of 2019, White Earth Nation's government legally adopted the *Rights of Manoomin* within its reservation boundaries, part of a global movement to ensconce rights language for nonhuman life but apparently the first to articulate the legal rights of a plant.

> Manoomin, or wild rice, within the White Earth Reservation possesses inherent rights to exist, flourish, regenerate, and evolve, as well as inherent rights to restoration, recovery, and preservation. These rights include, but are not limited to, the right to pure water and freshwater habitat; the right to a healthy climate system and a natural environment free from human-caused global warming impacts and emissions; the right to be free from patenting; as well as rights to be free from infection, infestation, or drift by any means from genetically engineered organisms, trans-genetic risk seed, or other seeds that have been developed using methods other than traditional plant breeding.[51]

Enforcement provisions of the law affirm *manoomin*'s standing to bring legal action on the plant's behalf through the White Earth government "in the name of manoomin as the real party in interest."[52]

Conclusion

We have become accustomed to understanding such assertions of rights to *manoomin*, or activism to contain the reach of genetic modification and sulfide mining, in terms of the discourses of political science, law, and economy. But as Larry Nesper has pointed out in the case of assertion of treaty rights to spear fish in northern Wisconsin, there is so much more than the legal, political, and economic goings-on in and through these facets of *manoominikewin*.[53]

The legal assertion of treaty rights to harvest wild rice, hunt, and fish in ceded lands of the 1837 and 1854 treaties, which the Supreme Court confirmed in a landmark 1999 ruling in favor of the Mille Lacs Band (*Minnesota v. Mille Lacs Band of Chippewa Indians*, 526 U.S. 1729) have been tremendously important affirmations of tribal sovereignty more generally. But their assertion in practices of *manoominikewin* have been far more than the political or legal posturing that is often assumed by non-Natives as part of a broader attempt to cast aspersions on Native presence.[54]

As necessary as it can be in legal or administrative processes to translate Anishinaabe claims into the language of resource, the translation risks obscuring the depth of the claims to Anishinaabe peoplehood and the spiritual commitments to the peoplehood of nonhuman life on Anishinaabe Akiing. The dam controversy took more than 100 years to settle (if settled it ever was), not because Anishinaabe leaders were negotiating for more cash on the logic of just compensation. It is in this rich context that Anishinaabe people relate their own peoplehood and the peoplehood of others who call Anishinaabe Akiing home. When Anishinaabeg say such things as "What happens to the land happens to us," they are offering something not so much poetic or quaint but an indigenous way of knowing and of valuing. Winona LaDuke puts it so well that I'll close, as I began, with her words.

> There is no way to set a price on this way of life. That simple truth more than anything else encapsulates the Anishinaabeg people's struggle with the federal government, the miners, and the logging companies. For the past hundred years, Native people have been saying that their way of life, their land, their trees, and their very future, cannot be quantified and are not for sale. And for that same amount of time, government and industry accountants have been picking away, trying to come up with a formula to compensate Indians for the theft of their lands and livelihoods.[55]

It seems that the story of a timeless Anishinaabe relationship to *manoomin* involving mutual obligations, together with the timely rearticulation of that relationship amid environmental, political, legal, and economic, illustrates the importance of a religious studies sensibility for understanding the spiritual depth and religious urgency of those commitments.

Notes

I thank in particular *manoomin* activists Joe Lagarde, the late Paul Schultz, former chair of the White Earth Nation Erma Vizenor, and the important written and spoken work of Winona LaDuke. I'm also grateful for Lawrence Gross's prose poem to ricing in this volume, which refreshingly speaks to Anishinaabe peoplehood.

1. Winona LaDuke, "Seeds of our Ancestors, Seeds of Life." TEDxTC talk. March, 2012, accessed November 2013, http://www.youtube.com/watch?v=pHNlel72eQc.

2. This phrase "other-than-human person" was first employed by A. Irving Hallowell. A. Irving Hallowell, "Ojibwa Ontology, Behavior, and World View," in *Teachings from the American Earth: Indian Religion and Philosophy*, eds. Dennis Tedlock and Barbara Tedlock (New York: Liveright, 1975), 171. Originally published in Stanley Diamond, ed., *Culture in History: Essays in Honor of Paul Radin* (New York: Columbia University Press, 1960).

3. See Jill Doerfler, Niiganwewidam James Sinclair, and Heidi Kiiwetinepinesiik Stark, eds., *Centering Anishinaabeg Studies: Understanding the World through Stories* (E. Lansing: Michigan State University Press, 2013).

4. Protect Our Manoomin, http://protectourmanoomin.weebly.com/protect-our-manoomin---mission-statement--declaration.html.

5. Protect Our Manoomin, http://protectourmanoomin.weebly.com/protect-our-manoomin---mission-statement--declaration.html.

6. It is considered inappropriate, even dangerous, to use the name of the Trickster except in winter when snow lay on the ground, so I will refer to him here simply as Trickster.

7. Andy Favorite, as cited in Minnesota Department of Natural Resources, "Natural Wild Rice in Minnesota: A Wild Rice Study Document," February 15, 2008.

8. For a sustained meditation on Anishinaabe teachings about plants as elders and teachers, see Robin Wall Kimmerer, *Braiding Sweetgrass: Indigenous Wisdom, Scientific Knowledge, and the Teachings of Plants* (Minneapolis: Milkweed, 2013), 156–66.

9. Tribal Adaptation Menu Team, "Dibaginjigaadeg Anishinaabe Ezhitwaad: A Tribal Climate Adaptation Menu," Great Lakes Indian Fish and Wildlife Commission, Odanah, Wisconsin, 2019.

10. Mary Black-Rogers, "Ojibwa Power Belief System," in *The Anthropology of Power*, eds. Raymond Fogelson and Richard Adams, 141–50 (New York: Academic Press, 1977).

11. Basil Johnston, *Ojibway Heritage* (Lincoln: University of Nebraska, 1990).

12. Martin Buber, *I and Thou*, trans. Walter Kaufmann (New York: Scribner's, 1970).

13. White Earth Band of Ojibwe Reservation Business Committee, *Rights of Manoomin* Resolution 1(a) (December 2018).

14. Kimmerer, *Braiding Sweetgrass*, 382.

15. Ignatia Broker, *Night Flying Woman* (St. Paul: Minnesota Historical Society Press, 1983), 55–56.

16. Broker, *Night Flying Woman*, 56.

17. Scott Richard Lyons, *X Marks: Native Signatures of Assent* (Minneapolis: University of Minnesota Press, 2010), 59.

18. A. Irving Hallowell, "Ojibwa Ontology, Behavior, and Worldview," in *Teachings from the American Earth*, 171.

19. Michael D. McNally, *Honoring Elders: Aging, Authority, and Ojibwe Religion* (New York: Columbia University Press, 2009).

20. Winona LaDuke, "Seeds of our Ancestors, Seeds of Life," TEDxTC talk. March, 2012, accessed November 1, 2013, http://www.youtube.com/watch?v=pHNlel72eQc.

21. Erma Vizenor, Chair of White Earth Nation, "Manoomin and the Anishinaabeg," submitted for International Indian Treaty Council's Shadow Report to the United Nations Committee on the Elimination of All Racial Discrimination," 2013.

22. Thomas Vennum Jr., *Wild Rice and the Ojibway People* (St. Paul: Minnesota Historical Society Press, 1988), 68.

23. For careful attention to the implications of historical trauma for the "historicity" of indigenous healing, I am indebted to Suzanne Crawford O'Brien, *Coming Full Circle: Spirituality and Wellness in Native Communities of the Pacific Northwest* (Lincoln: University of Nebraska Press, 2013), and Lawrence Gross, *Anishinaabe Ways of Knowing and Being* (London: Ashgate, 2014).

24. Catherine Bell, *Ritual Theory, Ritual Practice* (New York: Oxford University Press, 1992).

25. John Borrows. *Drawing Out Law: A Spirit's Guide* (Toronto, ON: University of Toronto Press, 2010).

26. Brenda J. Child, *Holding our World Together: Ojibwe Women and the Survival of Community* (New York: Penguin, 2012).

27. Rachel Walker and Jill Doerfler, "Wild Rice: The Minnesota Legislature, a Distinctive Crop, GMOs, and Ojibwe Perspectives, Hamline Law Review 32 (Spring 2009): 499–527.

28. "A Sister from East Lake," as cited in Endaso-Giizhik. "The Heart and Soul of Protect our Manoomin," accessed 10/20/13, http://www.protectourmanoomin.org/1/post/2011/09/the-heart-and-soul-of-protect-our-manoomin.html.

29. "A Sister from East Lake," as cited in Endaso-Giizhik, "The Heart and Soul of Protect our Manoomin," accessed 10/20/13, http://www.protectourmanoomin.org/1/post/2011/09/the-heart-and-soul-of-protect-our-manoomin.html.

30. Tim Roufs, "When Everybody Called Me *Gah-bay-bi-nayss*, "Forever-Flying-Bird": An Ethnographic Biography of Paul Peter Buffalo," accessed 10/20/13, http://www.d.umn.edu/cla/faculty/troufs/Buffalo/PB14.html.

31. Maude Kegg, "Manoonimikeng/Ricing," in John D. Nichols, editor and translator, *Portage Lake: Memories of an Ojibwe Childhood* (Edmonton: University of Alberta Press, 1991), 122–25.

32. As cited in Vennum, *Wild Rice and the Ojibway People*, 196.

33. Article V, Treaty with the Chippewa, 7 Stat. 536, July 29, 1837.

34. *Minnesota v. Mille Lacs Band of Chippewa Indians*, 526 U.S. 172 (1999).

35. Bruce White, "Criminalizing the Seasonal Round," Presented at Annual Meeting of Ethnohistory Society, 1998. See also Karl Jacoby, *Crimes Against Nature: Squatters, Poachers, Thieves, and the Hidden History of American Conservation* (Berkeley: University of California Press, 2003).

36. Albert Jenks, *The Wild Rice Gatherers of the Upper Lakes: A Study in American Primitive Economics* (Washington, DC: GPO, 1900).

37. Brenda Child, *Holding Our World Together: Ojibwe Women and the Survival of Community* (New York: Penguin, 2012), 114.

38. Child, *Holding our World Together*, 97–120.

39. See Vennum, *Wild Rice and the Ojibway People.*

40. "In the 1950s, University of Minnesota researchers decided it was time to liberate the rice from the indigenous people. So they set out to domesticate wild rice. A university scientist named Ervin Oelke began the process, using germ plasma collected from twenty-four natural stands within the 1837 treaty area. Over the years, the Minnesota Agricultural Extension office was able to 'create' several strains of 'wild' rice: Johnson in 1968, M1 in 1970, M2 in 1972, M3 in 1974, Netum in 1978, Voyager in 1983, Meter in 1985, Franklin in 1992, and Purple Petrowski in 2000." White Earth Land Recovery Project Native Harvest Website, nativeharvest.com/node/249.

41. White Earth Land Recovery Project/Native Harvest, "Patents and Biopiracy," nativeharvest.com/node/249.

42. Vennum, *Wild Rice and the Ojibway People*, 269–71.

43. White Earth's tribal government had sought unsuccessfully to persuade the University in 1998 to cease the genomic research at its School of Agriculture.

44. Joe Lagarde, "Sacred Rice Must Be Protected," *Minneapolis Star Tribune*, August 1, 2004.

45. Winona LaDuke, "Ricekeepers: A Struggle to Protect Biodiversity and a Native American Way of Life," *Orion* (July/August 2007), accessed November 2013, http://www.orionmagazine.org/index.php/articles/article/305. This perspective is surely informed by the history of genetic research involving Native American peoples. For a discussion of that history, see Kim Tallbear, *Native American DNA: Tribal Belonging and the False Promise of Genetic Science* (Minneapolis: University of Minnesota Press, 2013).

46. Article 11. "Treaty with the Chippewa." 10 Stats. 1109, September 30, 1854.

47. Final Environmental Impact Statement. PolyMet, Inc./NorthMet Project, December 2015.

48. Citing the work of Stephanie Howard, LaDuke describes the trend as follows: "The flow of genes is primarily from indigenous communities and rural communities in 'developing countries' to the Northern-based genetics industry. Ninety-seven percent of all patents are held by industrialized countries." See Steph-

anie Howard, et al., "Indigenous Peoples, Genes and Genetics: What Indigenous People Should Know about Biocolonialism," Indigenous Peoples Council on Bio-Colonialism (2000), as cited in LaDuke, "Ricekeepers."

49. LaDuke, "Seeds of our Ancestors, Seeds of Life."

50. Constitution of the White Earth Nation. chapter I: Territory and Jurisdiction.

51. White Earth Band of Ojibwe Reservation Business Committee, *Rights of Manoomin* Resolution 1(a). (December 2018).

52. White Earth Band of Ojibwe Reservation Business Committee, *Rights of Manoomin* Resolution 3(e). (December 2018).

53. Larry Nesper. *The Walleye War* (Lincoln: University of Nebraska Press, 2002).

54. This point was made by Walker and Doerfler, "Wild Rice: The Minnesota Legislature, a Distinctive Crop, GMOs, and Ojibwe Perspectives," 505.

55. Winona LaDuke, *All Our Relations: Native Struggles for Land and Life* (Boston: South End Press, 1999), 116.

Bibliography

Bell, Catherine. *Ritual Theory, Ritual Practice*. New York: Oxford University Press, 2009.

Black-Rogers, Mary. "Ojibwa Power Belief System." In *The Anthropology of Power*, edited by Raymond Fogelson and Richard Adams, 141–50. New York: Academic Press, 1977.

Borrows, John. *Drawing Out Law: A Spirit's Guide*. Toronto: University of Toronto Press, 2010.

Broker, Ignatia. *Night Flying Woman: An Ojibway Narrative*. St. Paul: Minnesota Historical Society Press, 1983.

Buber, Martin. *I and Thou*. Translated by Walter Kaufmann. New York: Scribner's, 1970.

Child, Brenda J. *Holding Our World Together: Ojibwe Women and the Survival of Community*. New York: Penguin Books, 2013.

Crawford O'Brien, Suzanne. *Coming Full Circle: Spirituality and Wellness among Native Communities in the Pacific Northwest*. University of Nebraska Press, 2016.

Doerfler, Jill, Niigannwewidam James Sinclair, and Heidi Kiiwetinepinesiik Stark, eds. *Centering Anishinaabeg Studies: Understanding the World through Stories*. E. Lansing: Michigan State University Press, 2013.

Doerfler, Jill, and Rachel Walker. "Wild Rice: The Minnesota Legislature, a Distinctive Crop, GMOs, and Ojibwe Perspectives." *Hamline Law Review* 32 (Spring 2009): 499–527.

Endaso-Giizhik. "The Heart and Soul of Protect Our Manoomin." Accessed October 20, 2013. http://www.protectourmanoomin.org/1/post/2011/09/the-heart-and-soul-of-protect-our-manoomin.html.

"Final Environmental Impact Statement." PolyMet, Inc/NorthMet Project. December 2015.

Gross, Lawrence W. *Anishinaabe Ways of Knowing and Being*. Surrey, UK: Ashgate, 2014.

Hallowell, A. Irving. "Ojibwa Ontology, Behavior, and World View." In *Teachings from the American Earth: Indian Religion and Philosophy*, edited by Dennis Tedlock and Barbara Tedlock. New York: Liveright, 1975, 141–78. Jacoby, Karl. *Crimes against Nature: Squatters, Poachers, Thieves, and the Hidden History of American Conservation*. Berkeley: University of California Press, 2014.

Jenks, Albert. *The Wild Rice Gatherers of the Upper Lakes: A Study in American Primitive Economics*. Washington, DC: GPO, 1900. http://archive.org/details/wildricegatherer00jenkuoft.

Johnston, Basil. *Ojibway Heritage*. Lincoln: University of Nebraska Press, 1990.

Kegg, Maude. "Manoonimikeng/Ricing." In *Portage Lake: Memories of an Ojibwe Childhood*, edited and translated by John D. Nichols, 122–25. Edmonton: University of Alberta Press, 1991.

Kimmerer, Robin Wall. *Braiding Sweetgrass: Indigenous Wisdom, Scientific Knowledge and the Teachings of Plants*. Minneapolis: MN: Milkweed Editions, 2015.

LaDuke, Winona. *All Our Relations: Native Struggles for Land and Life*. 2nd ed. Chicago, Ill.: Haymarket Books, 2016.

———. "Ricekeepers: A Struggle to Protect Biodiversity and a Native American Way of Life." *Orion*, July 2007. Accessed November 2013. http://www.orionmagazine.org/index.php/articles/article/305.

———. "Seeds of our Ancestors, Seeds of Life." TEDxTC talk. March, 2012. Accessed October 2013. http://www.youtube.com/watch?v=pHNlel72eQc.

Lagarde, Joe. "Sacred Rice Must Be Protected." *Minneapolis Star Tribune*, August 1, 2004.

Lyons, Scott Richard. *X-Marks: Native Signatures of Assent*. Minneapolis: University of Minnesota Press, 2010.

McNally, Michael D. *Honoring Elders: Aging, Authority, and Ojibwe Religion*. New York: Columbia University Press, 2009.

Minnesota Department of Natural Resources. "Natural Wild Rice in Minnesota: A Wild Rice Study Document." February 15, 2008.

Minnesota v. Mille Lacs Band of Chippewa Indians, 526 U.S. 172 (March 24, 1999).

Nesper, Larry. *The Walleye War: The Struggle for Ojibwe Spearfishing and Treaty Rights*. Lincoln: University of Nebraska Press, 2002.

Northwest Indian College Traditional Plants and Foods Program. "Plant Medicine." Accessed May 15, 2015. http://nwicplantsandfoods.com/plant-medicine.

"Protect Our Manoomin Mission Statement and Declaration." Accessed June 20, 2016.http://www.protectourmanoomin.org/protect-our-manoomin---mission-statement--declaration.html.

Roufs, Tim. "When Everybody Called Me *Gah-bay-bi-nayss*," Forever-Flying-Bird": An Ethnographic Biography of Paul Peter Buffalo." Accessed October 20, 2013.http://www.d.umn.edu/cla/faculty/troufs/Buffalo/PB14.html.

TallBear, Kim. *Native American DNA: Tribal Belonging and the False Promise of Genetic Science*. 1st ed. Minneapolis: University of Minnesota Press, 2013.

Treaty with the Chippewa. "Article V." 1837.

Treaty with the Chippewa. "Article 11. 10 Stats. 1109." September 30, 1854.

Tribal Adaptation Menu Team. "Dibaginjigaadeg Anishinaabe Ezhitwaad: A Tribal Climate Adaptation Menu." Odanah, WI: Great Lakes Indian Fish and Wildlife Commission, 2019.

Vennum, Thomas. *Wild Rice and the Ojibway People*. 1st ed. St. Paul: Minnesota Historical Society Press, 1988.

Vizenor, Erma. "Manoomin and the Anishinaabeg." Unpublished manuscript, 2013.

White, Bruce. "Criminalizing the Seasonal Round." Presented at Annual Meeting of Ethnohistory Society, 1998.

White Earth Land Recovery Project/Native Harvest Website. http://nativeharvest.com.

White Earth Land Recovery Project/Native Harvest. "Patents and Biopiracy." http://nativeharvest.com/node/249.

"Wild Rice Products." Native Harvest Ojibwe Products, a subdivision of White Earth Land Recovery Project. Accessed September 20, 2019. https://nativeharvest.com/collections/wild-rice-products.

4

Harvesting Wild Rice

Lawrence W. Gross

In order to better understand the importance of wild rice, or *manoomin*, to the Anishinaabeg, it is helpful to have a sense of what the act of harvesting wild rice entails. By this, I do not mean the steps involved in harvesting wild rice. Information on the process of harvesting wild rice can be found easily enough on the internet, including videos. But in my experience, even those internet videos of harvesting wild rice do not capture the essence of the effort. Instead, what I am talking about here is the bodily experience of harvesting wild rice, involving as it does not just the sights and sounds, but the smell and feel of being out on the lake. Taken together, they work to affect one's mental being, bringing about a sense of calmness and connection. The experience seeps into the soul and touches the heart. So, harvesting wild rice is not just a means for procuring food. It is an act that unites the Anishinaabe people with their environment and provides a sense of wholeness of being. It fills the heart. And, with a full heart, it is easier to live more fully as a human being on this earth. Because of the importance of the affective aspect of wild ricing, I would like to offer this piece as something of a prose poem, an ode to harvesting wild rice that attempts to convey in some small way the sensory and emotional feel of harvesting wild rice.

The season for harvesting wild rice technically begins at the end of August or the beginning of September, depending on the location and the weather. But as a point of fact, the wild rice season really begins at the start of summer when the wild rice first starts making its appearance above the waves. In driving around northern Minnesota, the roads come into close proximity to lakes on a regular basis. A person gets to know which lakes have wild rice observable from the road, and so is always on the lookout in going by those locations to monitor the progress of the rice on the lake. I think of such locations as Minnesota State Highway 200 as it curves past Roy Lake on the White Earth reservation. There on the south side of the road is a patch of wild rice right next to the road as it skirts the lake. Or, I think of the bridge on Minnesota State Highway 371, driving south from Cass Lake to Walker as it passes Kabekona Bay. Additionally, the Anishinaabeg as a group spend a good deal of time on the water fishing during the summer months. During these excursions, it is not unusual to go by stands of wild rice. For the Anishinaabeg, checking out the wild rice at these times is a matter of great interest. Observations about the nature of the crop for the year become a regular part of conversation as the people anticipate the harvest ahead.

Standing on a lake shore observing the wild rice is a rich sensory experience. The water itself can take on a variety of hues. Gray is fairly common, especially if the wind has any kick to it. On calmer days, the famous sky-blue waters of the lakes in Minnesota are a refreshing sight to behold. On other days, the water can be a pure pitch black. When the wind is calm early in the morning or at sunset, the lake can become just silver with a smooth, mirror-like finish. It almost looks like glass, it is so smooth. The sounds of the wind through the trees add to the effect, most especially the whispering of the breeze through the pine trees. Times like that are reminders of the teaching that the sound of the wind in the trees is the voice of our ancestors talking to us. At the height of summer, the warm southern breeze is comforting. After the long winter, feeling the warm touch of a summer breeze relaxes a person's spirit, even if the thought of winter is never far away. Lakes often have a smell about them as well, rich and pungent, a combination of rotting debris and moist soil. It is the smell of the earth going through its cycles. Indeed, standing on a lake shore taking in the view is an experience in and of itself. The lakes, the trees, and the sky all speak to the fact that this is home for the Anishinaabeg.

But summer does not last long in the North Country, and soon enough the northwest winds that herald the turn of the seasons start to arrive. In my experience, this usually happens right around August 11, give or take a few days. Growing up in Minnesota, I was always amazed at the regularity with which the northwest winds start blowing right around that date every year. The northwest winds are different from the summer winds. The summer winds come up from the south, bringing the warm, moist air of the Gulf of Mexico with them. Thunderstorms usually drive up from the southwest, moving northeast across the landscape, the same direction tornados follow. The northwest winds of autumn have a different feel to them. At their very first appearance, they put a chill in the air. This is well before the same winds will bite with cold as autumn turns to winter. The air brought with the northwest wind is drier as well, and it is easy to feel the difference as opposed to a warm, southern breeze. The clouds, though, most clearly signal the arrival of autumn. These are not the rain clouds of the summer months; instead the northwest winds carry puffy cumulus clouds, maybe a few at first, but growing in number until they dominate the sky. Depending on the strength of the wind, they can move at their leisure or race across the sky. But, they always move from the northwest to the southeast. Even though it is only early August and the autumn equinox is still over a month away, there can be no mistake in the message. The weather is speaking to us. The land is speaking to us. The time for harvesting wild rice is drawing near.

In the weeks before the harvest begins, it is time to start making preparations. For those who participate in the harvest on a regular basis, most of the equipment for harvesting wild rice will be at hand: the knockers, the pole, and the canoe. If not, or if equipment needs replacing, now is a good time to do so. Knockers are used to knock the wild rice from the plants into the canoe. They are usually made out of cedar wood because it is a nice, light wood with a straight grain that is easy to work. Since knocking rice can entail spending many hours in a canoe, keeping the knockers lightweight is important to cut down on fatigue. Lightweight wood is easier on the delicate wild rice plants as well. Knockers are usually around thirty inches long and about an inch around at the base, tapering to a blunt point at the end. The straight grain of cedar wood makes it easier to shave the knockers to the desired shape. When finished, the knockers will weigh less than a pound.

The pole is another matter. The pole is used to propel the canoe through the water, which would not be much of a problem, except for one thing. As I like to say, a wild rice bed is two feet of water and three feet of loon . . . let us be polite here and call them "droppings." In other words, the muck at the bottom of the lake is like some kind of supermud. Once the pole hits the lake bottom, it just keeps going into the mud, and going, and going, and going. It takes a while for the pole to stabilize enough to be able to actually push the canoe forward. And, that is just getting the pole into the mud. Once the canoe is moving forward, the fun work of pulling the pole out of the mud begins. Mud has a suction power and it refuses to let that pole go. For these reasons, the pole has to be long enough to reach the bottom of the lake, reach the bottom of the mud, and actually move the canoe forward. A good ricing pole will generally be on the order of fourteen to sixteen feet long. There is a way of attaching a section from a forked branch of a tree, which I will not go into here. Suffice it to say, the fork allows the pole to get a foothold in the mud while still making it possible for the pole to be extracted from the same.

With both the knockers and the pole, it is good to think about their respective feel in the hands. The knockers are thin, light, and smooth, and they have a comfortable feel. Also, the location of one's grip on the knockers does not move during the harvesting process. So, they are going to stay in the hands, acting as an extension of the arms in pulling the rice over the canoe for harvesting. The pole is another matter. It is not uncommon for the pole to be made out of a small tree. Tamarack works best because it is light and strong. But no matter how light tamarack may be, a fourteen- to sixteen-foot pole made out of tamarack will still carry some heft. In making the pole, the bark will be stripped off. However, the pole will still have knots in it. Also, it is not necessarily the case that the pole will be sanded to a smooth finish. Unlike the knockers, the pole will have a much rougher feel in the hand.

The canoe is the canoe. Nowadays, most people use aluminum or fiberglass canoes. But it is not unheard of for people to use flat-bottomed boats as well. However, if a boat is to be used, it is important for it to be narrow enough so the knocker—that is, the person harvesting the rice—can reach out over both sides of the boat to bring the rice over the boat for harvesting.

So, now the equipment is ready. The rice is coming ripe, and it is time to get out on the water. First off, let us keep in mind that the wild rice is growing out of the water to varying heights. On some lakes in some locations, the rice rises two or three feet above the side of the canoe. However, I remember being on Rice Lake on the White Earth reservation one year, and the rice was a good six to seven feet above the side of the canoe. The poler standing in the back could not even see above the rice. There is a reason they call it, "Rice Lake," that is for sure.

Launching the canoe is always a challenge in that it is pretty likely somebody is going to get their feet wet. It is also not unusual to scrap along the mud in the shallows near the shore before the canoe starts to float in open water. Since the rice beds are near the shore, there usually is not much of a need to paddle. Instead, the poler will guide the canoe along the shore line toward the rice. Once the ricing gets started, the experience of the knocker and the poler are quite different. We will start with the knocker close in to the rice.

The knocker cannot sit too far toward the back of the canoe since the poler usually stands in the back. For better balance, the knocker will be closer to two-thirds of the way toward the back, sometimes on a short stool, sometimes kneeling, sometimes sitting, depending on the preference of the knocker. The sights and sounds available to the knocker are more limited than for those of the poler. Sitting in the canoe, the knocker cannot see over the top of the rice. Once they are in the rice bed, the view for the knocker is pretty much limited to the wild rice and the sky. That is all the knocker needs to see, however. Reaching out with one arm holding onto the knocking stick, the knocker gathers a sheath of rice and bends it over the canoe. Then with the other knocking stick, he or she runs the stick along the stems in short, quick motions, knocking the rice into the bottom of the canoe. The stick hitting the rice makes a characteristic sound—*swish, swish*, first on one side, then *swish, swish*, on the other as the knocker alternates sides.

When first starting, the rice strikes the bottom of the canoe with a sound resembling the patter of rain, but with a crisp edge to it—*tick-a-tick tick-tick*. The rice will also lie flat in the bottom of the canoe at first. However, that does not last for long due to the shape of the raw wild rice seed. The top of the chaff extends about an inch or two beyond the seed itself. Technically, that extended growth is called an "awn." Growing out of the awn are many short, fine hairs. The awn, with its short, fine hairs, is called the "beard." The beard helps the rice anchor itself in the mud so it does not get washed away by any moving water. Once enough rice starts to accumulate in the bottom of the canoe, however, the seeds will align themselves, with the beards pointing up. The rice aligning itself in this manner is called "bearding up," and it is always a good sign to see that happen. I have also heard it called "porcupining up," an apt metaphor that is easy to imagine.

It is important to be mindful of the beards, though. Because of their nature, if they get into the eyes, they tend to get stuck. Therefore, it is always a good idea to carry a pocketknife with tweezers when harvesting wild rice, just in case. That also leads to the old story about the hippie who came down to the boat landing as some Anishinaabeg were coming off the water with their raw wild rice, beards and all. The hippie asked the Anishinaabeg what they had. When the Anishinaabeg told him it was wild rice, he said, "Let me try some." Then, before the Anishinaabeg could stop him, the hippie grabbed some wild rice and stuffed it in his mouth. That hippie had quite a time getting those beards out of his mouth (and maybe his beard, too).

Raw wild rice seeds have a distinctive color. The chaff tends to be a light brown or tan. So, as the ricing goes along, the canoe gets more and more full with the light-brown grain. The beards are black, and the bottom of the canoe looks brown with a clear hint of black. If the ricing is good, eventually the canoe will be filled to the gunwales with rice. That can weigh up to 100 pounds. Getting that much rice in a day is always a good feeling.

The experience of the poler is much different. Because he or she is standing, usually in the back, they can see above the rice. So, the poler can take in the view. Remember those cumulus clouds we talked about earlier? Well, it is pretty likely the cumulus clouds will be blowing in from the northwest. The bright white of the clouds contrasts with the blue of the sky, setting up a dramatic color difference. Still keeping our eyes to the skies, it is not unusual to see an eagle or hawk soaring above, taking in the scene. One feels blessed seeing an eagle overhead. The woods along the shore have yet to change color except for the red maples. Red maples are the first tree to turn color, and by ricing season they have already turned a bright red. Scanning the shoreline, the red maple trees will be lighting up the woods. Now the red of the maples is added to the blue of the sky and the white of the clouds. A more picturesque scene can hardly be envisioned. And yet, the picture is not complete. Usually there will be other canoes on the water as well. However, the canoes themselves cannot be seen, only the poler standing in the back. What can be seen are these other individuals gliding through a sea of grass. Their movements have a certain grace and rhythm to them.

There is no doubt that poling is physically demanding, however. As discussed above, the mud at the bottom of the lake can be quite thick, and it can take quite a bit of effort to keep the canoe moving. At this point, it might be good to recall the Anishinaabe teachings about kinesiology. I remember receiving this lesson from my Ojibwe language teacher at the University of Minnesota, the late Rose Barstow. She taught us that the Anishinaabeg were students of kinesiology and had studied closely the most efficient methods for using the body to perform work. She especially stressed the importance of using our joints to create leverage. She also told us the Anishinaabeg knew to lift with their legs, and not with their backs. She told us about how the Anishinaabeg would go help with the sugar beet harvest in the Red River Valley years ago. Part of the harvesting required picking up fifty-pound bags of beets and throwing them in the back of a truck. The Anishinaabeg would lift with their legs and use a leverage motion with their arms to throw the bags. The white men would lift with their backs and use something of a twisting motion of their torso to throw the bags. By the end of the day, the Anishinaabeg were tired, but they did not have sore backs like the white men. Too bad those white men thought the Indians were primitive savages who did not know anything. Many backs could have been saved if only white people had been able to get over their hubris, respect the Indians, and listen to what they had to say. These are the kind of thoughts that would go through my mind when I was poling. So, yes, poling is hard work. But the Anishinaabeg have their ways of lessening the burden. I would like to add here, Rose Barstow was the daughter of Tom Shingobe, who was an Anishinaabe elder from whom I also received teachings.[1] I would like to take this opportunity to acknowledge and give thanks to Tom and Rose for the teachings they gave me.

Continuing on with the harvest, there is no need to bring a smart phone and plug into its music library while on the lake. Instead, the welcoming sound of the wind through the grass greets the ricers. The knocker responds with the *swish-swish* of harvesting the rice. The poler will invariably hit the pole against the side of the canoe, making for an occasional *clunk-clunk* sound. The sounds of the harvest make their own music, which is comforting to the ears and soothing to the soul.

There are scents and sights associated with the lake as well. The wild rice puts off its own grassy odor. The moisture of the lake rises up to fill the lungs. And every now and then the pungent smell of rotting debris and the earth going through its cycles, which we discussed above, makes its presence felt as well. The lake is also full of sights that are simply pleasant to behold. Since the ricers are not operating in open water but instead keep closer to shore, there always exists the opportunity to see a variety of plants and animals. Sometimes in moving from one rice bed to another, the canoe will go by a patch of water lily plants, their broad leaves gleaming in the sun. Or, a painted turtle might be spied sunning itself on a half-submerged log. As the canoe pulls closer, the turtle might go into the water with a plop. These are all the little things about ricing that add so much to the overall experience.

The body is moving for both the knocker and the poler. It can feel very pleasant putting in the physical work of the harvest. The sights and sounds of nature envelop the effort. The perfumes of the earth and water fill the air. Truly, the experience of harvesting wild rice is a whole-body experience.

Beyond the individual, there is one other aspect of ricing that should be mentioned as well, the social dimension. Although it might be possible to harvest wild rice alone, harvesting wild rice is really a team effort. People have to work closely with their partners to have a successful harvest. The poler has to keep the canoe in the rice as much as possible, and the knocker has to keep moving to gather the rice in the canoe. Any two people can form a team, but in the past and still to this day, it is not unusual for a husband and wife to harvest wild rice together. It is not hard to imagine the ways in which working peacefully and silently together on the lake can bring two people closer together. I say "silently" because often there is very little talking that occurs on the lake. Both individuals are focused on their respective tasks, which keeps the chit-chat to a minimum. Besides, it just feels good to work together in silence. I talked about making a heart-to-heart connection working in silence elsewhere.[2] Harvesting wild rice is another way in which working together in silence can promote a heart-to-heart connection and help a person become a fulfilled human being. Not all teams are husband and wife. But even in those cases when they are not, harvesting wild rice can help people develop strong bonds with other Anishinaabe relatives and friends as well.

It is also not unusual for people in different canoes to stop and chat while out on the lake. Sometimes people will bring their lunches with them and eat while still on the lake. It is also not unusual for people to come together and eat their lunches and visit. As a result, even though ricing might seem like it has limited opportunities to socialize since people are working in their own canoes, the Anishinaabeg create the space to build social bonds on the lake as well. Having strong social bonds is a way for people to feel connected with others and thereby live life as fulfilled human beings.

So in both instances, working with a ricing partner and talking with others on the lake, there is an affective side to the social aspects of ricing as well. The total experience of ricing thus works through the body by way of the senses connecting the harvesters to nature. But it works through the heart as well by way of promoting positive emotional connections with others.

And now, the harvest is done. The visiting is over. The canoe is filled with rice. And it is time to head home. Upon reaching the shore, the wild rice is put into large bags and taken away to be processed. And with that, the appeal of harvesting wild rice becomes easier to understand. Why would I say "appeal"? In the end, we have to admit that harvesting wild rice is hard work. It is not easy to pole a canoe, especially when it is loaded down with a ricing partner and a canoe full of wild rice. Knocking the rice all day takes effort as well. With all of today's modern conveniences, the Anishinaabeg do not have to go out on the lakes. They could get their food in other ways. Yet, year after year, the lakes draw the Anishinaabeg, and they continue the ancient practice of harvesting wild rice. The appeal, then, is not just having wild rice to eat, give away as gifts, use in ceremony, or even to sell to raise some cash. Part of the appeal comes from the act of harvesting the wild rice itself. Harvesting the rice, taking in the sights and sounds, and enjoying the chance to socialize add up to an organic whole. It can ease the mind and relax the soul. The heart can become full and connected to others. A person can live as a healthy, happy human being on this blessed earth of ours and achieve the ideal of the Anishinaabeg, *mino-bimaadiziwin*—the Good Life.

Notes

1. Lawrence W. Gross, *Anishinaabe Ways of Knowing and Being* (Farnham, UK: Ashgate, 2014), 2.
2. Gross, 63–66.

Bibliography

Gross, Lawrence W. *Anishinaabe Ways of Knowing and Being*. Farnham, UK: Ashgate, 2014.

5

They Call Us "Caribou Eaters"

Negotiating Tłįchǫ Dene Relationships with Caribou

David S. Walsh

In 2013 in Yellowknife, Northwest Territories, Canada, a group of Dene and Inuit hunters and elders gathered along with Canadian government wildlife biologists for three days to discuss the decline of the Bathurst and other caribou herd populations.[1] I attended the gathering and listened as many Dene and Inuit participants spoke of the need to respect the caribou and the importance of their indigenous traditions. Many were also critical of the Government of the Northwest Territories' implementation of strict caribou hunting regulations on the caribou herds three years prior, and participants questioned the accuracy of scientific claims regarding caribou viability.

One Chipewyan Dene elder succinctly summarized indigenous understandings and perceived Western misunderstandings when he questioned the territorial government. He stated, "They call us 'Caribou Eaters,'" referring to the name given by European explorers to the first Dene they encountered; this title continues to capture a sense of Dene identity and pride.[2] He continued, "Does the government know caribou? Do they even eat caribou?" The elder questioned government and scientific responses to the caribou decline by raising the issue of what it means to know another being. The elder implied that Dene know caribou because they eat caribou; they engage caribou in a reciprocal relationship wherein Dene have learned the appropriate behavior that caribou find to be respectful and thus worthy of them, continuing to give themselves to the people for food. In this chapter I address the implications of the above elder's question and examine Tłįchǫ Dene responses to the recent caribou herd decline and the hunting restrictions that followed.[3]

The Tłįchǫ are an indigenous Dene nation who have maintained hunting lifestyles on their ancestral homeland in subarctic Canada.[4] Caribou have traditionally been a primary source of food, clothing, shelter, and material culture and have remained a central source of identity for Tłįchǫ and most northern Dene people. Dene oral narratives establish proper relations between Dene and beings in their environment, often articulated around food. One Tłįchǫ story relates animals taking pity on the first Dene peoples who could not fend for themselves. The animals held a meeting to decide who would be food for the Dene. Bear stated that its meat is good for food and medicine, but other animals asked what Dene would eat when bear is hibernating. Caribou and fish stated they would be the main food, which was agreed on, and thus established their roles in Dene lives.[5]

Stories of how animals determined their relationships with Dene, such as the above narrative, demonstrate a relational ontology wherein Dene and animals participate in social, personal relationships predicated on exchanges of food.[6] Dene actions are passive in the narrative, while animals actively decide to give their meat. Through a shared history between Dene and caribou, Dene have come to understand a respectful etiquette that entices the animals to give themselves to the people through the hunt.[7] Dene demonstrate respect to the hunted by sharing the meat with family, with the community, and with ancestors who aided the hunt. Dene also show respect to animals through proper treatment of their bodies, such as leaving their carcasses orderly and returning bones to the land so other animals may use them in a new life. "The basic rule was to take only what was needed, in a respectful way," anthropologist Joan Ryan remarks of Dene hunting. She explains that prior to Canadian conservation practices, "Dene maintained their traditional territories well because they understood the fragile balance between the life cycle and the availability of food."[8] Dene acts of respect toward food animals maintain this fragile balance of human/animal relationships. A give-and-take dynamic has governed Tłįchǫ Dene relationships with caribou since time immemorial, but the relationship has recently become more tenuous.

The primary caribou herd for Tłįchǫ hunters is the Bathurst. However, climate change and other factors have caused a rapid decline in the population of the herd since 2009. With few exceptions, all migratory tundra caribou herds in North America have exhibited a declining trend in the early 2000s, with the Bathurst caribou herd suffering the most dramatic decline from approximately 475,000 animals in the mid-1980s to just 16,000 to 22,000 animals in 2015.[9] Concern over Bathurst caribou viability prompted the Government of the Northwest Territories to enact strict hunting restrictions in 2010. The territorial government has altered the form of these restrictions as they negotiated with indigenous peoples and updated scientific data, yet the restrictions remain today.

Tłįchǫ and other Dene have responded to the hunting restrictions in complex ways. For example, in March, 2011, I cofacilitated with a Tłįchǫ researcher the community-driven workshop "Tłįchǫ Traditional Caribou Conservation: Youth and Elders Working Together," in which Tłįchǫ elders taught the youth participants about traditional means of respecting caribou.[10] Elders discussed the importance of caribou for Tłįchǫ survival and taught the importance of treating caribou properly. Tłįchǫ elders termed this education *dò nàowoò*: the living-out of Tłįchǫ culture, traditional knowledge, and way-of-life.[11] Elders demonstrated the importance of their relationships with the caribou to the youth participants, to the ethnic community at large, to non-Dene such as Canadian government, biologists and environmentalists, and most importantly, directly to the caribou. Elders stated that the caribou were listening and were pleased we spoke well of them. The workshop created a space for Tłįchǫ to communicate with the caribou and convey that they respected the animal and desired that they return and continue to give themselves. Thus, the elders demonstrated a social relationship based on cultural understandings of the nature of food.

Tłįchǫ Dene Caribou Hunting and Restrictions

Tłįchǫ hunt tundra caribou twice yearly as the animals migrate through Tłįchǫ lands. Tłįchǫ hunting practices have altered over time, particularly with the introduction of a settled lifestyle and snowmobiles, but practices have remained remarkably consistent.[12] Helm states that caribou migration fluctuates according to weather and food availability, meaning that exact times and locations for when and where a herd migrates through

Tłı̨chǫ lands varies substantially.[13] However, Tłı̨chǫ elders tell me that their knowledge of caribou movement proves accurate for each migration.

The Bathurst caribou's fall migration is south from their calving grounds near Bathurst Inlet on the arctic coast, to the tree line between the tundra and the boreal forest on the eastern edge of Tłı̨chǫ lands. In December Bathurst migrate southwest to the boreal forest near the four Tłı̨chǫ communities of Behchokǫ̀, Whatì, Gamètì, and Wekweètì, before the herd returns to the tundra in March. The Bluenose East, the secondary herd for Tłı̨chǫ hunters, travel northwest and west of the four Tłı̨chǫ communities in winter, making the Bathurst herd more convenient for hunting. Tłı̨chǫ have appropriated scientific caribou herd categorizations that distinguish between the Bathurst and the Bluenose East in order to comply with hunting restrictions. However, Tłı̨chǫ traditionally only distinguish between migratory tundra caribou, *ekwǫ̀*, and boreal woodland caribou, *tǫdzi*. The latter do not migrate, live in different ecological settings, and have morphological differences from tundra caribou. The Bluenose East and the Bathurst herds are both tundra caribou but are distinguished based on breeding lines; the herds maintain separate calving grounds in May, with the Bluenose East's calving grounds closer to the Arctic Ocean than the Bathurst's. Both herds are scientifically classified as *Rangifer tarandus groenlandicus*.

On January 1, 2010, the Government of the Northwest Territories, citing concerns over an "accelerated rate of decline," implemented a temporary hunting ban on the Bathurst herd.[14] The Bluenose East herd was originally placed under this ban, which was lifted for indigenous hunters although some hunting restrictions were later self-imposed by Dene hunters from Deline.[15] The ban consisted of a no-hunting zone for caribou stretching east and north from Great Slave Lake in the Northwest Territories to the Nunavut border, covering hunting territory of Tłı̨chǫ and Yellowknives Dene, North Slave Métis, Northwest Territories' nonindigenous resident hunters, and Northwest Territories' tourist hunting outfitters.

Tłı̨chǫ elders told me of lean times in the past without caribou. However, Environment and Natural Resources, the Government of the Northwest Territories' authority on wildlife management, found that the contemporary population decline of the Bathurst herd constituted a crisis in the species that required government intervention. In the mid-1980s, Environment and Natural Resources wildlife biologists estimated the Bathurst caribou herd population at 475,000 animals. From the late 1980s to the early 1990s, the Bathurst herd declined to 350,000 animals.

The Bathurst herd continued a steady decline to an estimated 166,000 in 2006, then plummeted to less than 32,000 animals in 2009 and remaining stable until 2012.[16] Wildlife biologists determined that reduced calf survival, compounded by reduced survival of adult females, caused the Bathurst's 5 percent annual decline.[17] They contended that reducing hunting would improve adult survival but that the herd would not recover without increased calf survival as well. In 2011 they revised the previous assessment and suggested that overhunting exacerbated the rapid decline of Bathurst caribou from 2006 to 2009.[18]

Environment and Natural Resources wildlife biologists found that, prior to the current hunting restrictions, between 6,000 and 7,000 Bathurst caribou were hunted annually. Outfitters and nonindigenous residents' hunting accounted for 500 to 600 caribou annually, with indigenous hunters claiming the rest. The majority of hunted Bathurst caribou, between 4,000 and 5,000, were female cows of breeding age. Wildlife biologists have estimated that the Bathurst herd would be extinct or near extinction in four to five years, by 2014, if cow and calf survival rates remained unchanged. They acknowledge that, due to climate factors, the herd would have declined in the early 2000s regardless of hunting, but they assert that aggressive contemporary hunting practices coupled with ease of access to the herd were detrimental to the declining Bathurst.[19]

In June 2015, Environment and Natural Resources conducted a population survey on the Bathurst herd with disheartening results. Although an official report has not been released at the time of this writing, the wildlife biologists concluded that conservation efforts have not greatly affected herd viability. They estimated that the Bathurst herd has dropped to between 16,000 and 22,000 animals, down from 32,000 estimated during the previous count of 2012 and a 96 percent decline since the 1980s. Additionally, they stated that the number of breeding cows has dropped 50 percent to approximately 8,000 animals, greatly reducing the herd's prospects for growth. The Bluenose East caribou population was in decline in the 2000s but showed signs of recovery from 66,700 animals in 2006 to 80,000 animals in 2010, and they were not placed under hunting restrictions. The Bluenose East has since declined to approximately 35,000 to 40,000 animals in 2015 with breeding cows equally plummeting by 50 percent since 2013 to only 17,000 animals, leading to renewed hunting restrictions on this herd.[20]

Several factors affect caribou viability in the Northwest Territories, including climate change, development (towns, roads, and diamond mines), wolf predation, and overhunting. Environment and Natural Resources wildlife biologists found, however, that the primary reason for the rapid Bathurst decline was environmental factors compounded by overhunting. Average temperatures in the Northwest Territories have risen two degrees centigrade since 1948, but the rapidity of weather fluctuation, with warmer summers and colder winters, poses more of a threat to caribou than temperature increases, particularly as forest fires increase and threaten lichen, the primary food source for caribou.[21] Ironically, larger caribou herds reduce the effects of climate change as caribou grazing on lichen limits plant dominance while leaving healthy roots for regrowth.[22]

Land development in northern Canada has affected caribou negatively, although to what extent is a matter of debate.[23] In 1998 the first large-scale diamond mine opened at Ekati, followed by Diavik in 2003, Snap Lake from 2008 to 2016, and Gahechokue, which began production in 2016. Canada is now a major global producer of diamonds with the majority coming from these four mines in eastern Tłı̨chǫ territory. Tłı̨chǫ are apprehensive about new mines on their lands; however, many Tłı̨chǫ have found employment opportunities with the mines.[24] Tłı̨chǫ and wildlife biologists agree that the active mines are within the Bathurst caribou fall migration zone and that these mines reduce caribou range as the animals avoid the mine areas. Biologists state, however, that the caribou simply avoid the area and thus the mines have limited impact, a contention with which many Tłı̨chǫ disagree. Mining companies consistently claim that they have no impact on caribou range, migration, or viability. My Tłı̨chǫ consultants argue that the noise and smell produced by mines drives the caribou away and that winter roads leading to the mines create a barrier the caribou do not like to cross, thereby implying that the Bathurst choose to remain inaccessible to humans in part because of the mines.

My Tłı̨chǫ consultants contend that the caribou collar monitoring used by wildlife biologists is itself disrespectful and could also drive the caribou away. Environment and Natural Resources biologists have fitted twenty Bathurst caribou with collars monitored by satellite, which is less than 1 percent of the herd. They say that collars are nonobtrusive and do not cause the caribou harm or concern. Dene elders at the Yellowknife caribou gathering cited at the beginning of this chapter stated that collaring is disrespectful to the caribou because it treats them like dogs rather than wild animals, suggesting that caribou should not be cared for and managed like dogs, but rather, respected because the caribou take care of the people who are dependent on them.[25] Similar to the Dene, Rock

Cree find caribou tagging by researchers to cause unnecessary suffering, contending that tagged caribou have been found in shock, starving, and with broken hearts.[26] Koyukon Dene are against the capture and release necessary for caribou collaring because they believe it is a spiritual affront to the caribou and that the animals will then shun the area and the people.[27]

Contemporary hunting practices and claims of overhunting or improper hunting are the most widely discussed reasons for caribou scarcity by indigenous and nonindigenous northerners alike. However, their implications differ. Tłı̨chǫ elders warn against overhunting, as it can disrupt balanced relationships and threaten survival of both the Tłı̨chǫ and the caribou.[28] My Tłı̨chǫ consultants say that, prior to modern hunting technology, caribou inaccessibility was not uncommon as smaller herds were difficult to hunt without snowmobiles, high-powered rifles, and satellite imagery. Wildlife biologists state that these declines in hunting allowed caribou to repopulate and return with stronger numbers in subsequent migrations.[29]

In the mid-2000s, the Bathurst herd migrated farther west than usual and spent the winter on the ice road near Behchokǫ̀, allowing an unprecedented ease of access for hunters, of which many took advantage. The proximity of Bathurst migrations coupled with modern technologies, including the ability to drive directly to the herd, provided easy hunting for Tłı̨chǫ, for other indigenous peoples from the Northwest Territories and northern Alberta, and for non-Natives from Yellowknife and other communities. Tłı̨chǫ consultants recalled with sadness and anger how some nonindigenous hunters filled their truck beds with choice cuts of meat and left the excess to waste. A Tłı̨chǫ community project documented non-Tłı̨chǫ hunters leaving a mess of blood on the ice road, which Dene say is disrespectful to the caribou and to other hunters.[30] This context informed both Tłı̨chǫ and biologists' assessments that hunting practices must be changed to ensure caribou viability.

In late winter 2013, I attended a caribou hunt with three Tłı̨chǫ hunters. In stark contrast to those who hunted from their trucks on the ice roads when the Bathurst migrated close to the highway and southern communities, we drove six hours to the northern community of Gamètì, stayed overnight, and then drove snowmobiles an additional four hours north before finding about 200 caribou of the Bluenose East herd. We performed established Dene practices of respectful hunting, such as killing the caribou quickly, moving the carcasses to the side of the frozen lake before field dressing them, taking nearly all the meat, and leaving the remains in neat piles for scavengers. Furthermore, we each individually offered a piece of our fresh caribou meat dinner to the fire in a feeding-the-fire ceremony of thanks. Additionally, as I had not visited that site before, my hunting partners instructed me to make an offering to the lake where the caribou had appeared to us, which I did, using a dollar coin from my pocket. In subtle ways this hunt demonstrated to me the complex social relationship many Dene hunters have with the hunted.

Dene Responses to Hunting Restrictions

Indigenous and nonindigenous hunters were shocked by the 2010 hunting ban, although they were already aware of Environment and Natural Resources reports of caribou herd declines and shared concerns about the animals' viability. In 2006 the Government of the Northwest Territories first notified the public of significant declines in caribou herd populations and of the need for urgent herd management.[31] Discussions between the Dene Nation and the territorial government concerning caribou management had stalled by the end of 2009, however. The Wek'èezhìi Renewable Resources Board, an environmental comanagement board composed equally of Tłįchǫ and territorial government members, was charged with resolving the hunting issue. Shortly before the winter hunting season began, the Wek'èezhìi Renewable Resources Board postponed their meetings until March 2010, corresponding to the end of the winter hunting season. The territorial government stated that the Wek'èezhìi Renewable Resources Board effectively abdicated their responsibility of caribou management and that therefore the government had to impose a caribou hunting ban rather than allow unrestricted hunting.[32]

Dene, non-Dene residents, and sport hunting outfitters spoke defiantly against the caribou hunting ban.[33] The Government of the Northwest Territories and representatives from Dene governments met in Behchokǫ̀ to publicly debate the hunting ban in February 2010.[34] Dene leaders questioned the accuracy of the Bathurst population survey, and some asked the government where they thought the caribou had gone. Shortly after the ban took effect, wildlife officers seized caribou meat from a Yellowknives hunting party, prompting Dene chiefs to demand that the territorial government allow Dene hunting. Bill Erasmus, Grand Chief of the Dene Nation, contended that the territorial government prematurely imposed restrictions rather than working with indigenous people.[35] Leon Lafferty, former Behchokǫ̀ chief, proclaimed that Tłı̨chǫ hunters would ignore the ban and he invited Environment and Natural Resources officers to criminally charge him.[36] Yellowknives Dene Nation chief Edward Sangris declared that the caribou hunting ban violated treaty rights and that his people would ignore the government's decision.[37] Sangris was later caught hunting and his caribou meat was confiscated by Environment and Natural Resources officers, as was that of Dene Nation Grand Chief Erasmus.[38] John B. Zoe, a prominent Tłı̨chǫ citizen, adds historical context to Tłı̨chǫ reactions to hunting restrictions by stating, "Our revered former Chief Mǫwfwi, who was a signatory to the treaty of 1921, said that he and his people would not be restricted from carrying on their nàowo [Tłı̨chǫ culture, knowledge, and way of life], and that includes hunting." Zoe explains, "So when people hear about targets on total allowable harvest and restrictions, it is perceived as an attack on who we are as a traditional hunting society."[39] Dene fought back against this perceived attack.

Jackson Lafferty, a Tłı̨chǫ member of the territorial legislative assembly, asserted that the government lacked the authority to declare a hunting ban because of nonrestrictive treaty hunting rights and he sought to bring the issue to court.[40] The territorial government argued that the rapid Bathurst population decline was an environmental emergency, one that takes precedence over indigenous hunting rights. However, in March, 2010, indigenous and territorial leaders decided to forge an agreement for management themselves and, rather than testing the limits of indigenous rights and territorial government authority, they chose not to pursue a court case. The indigenous and territorial leadership passed a motion calling for the territorial government to consult with indigenous people on managing caribou and to find a joint territorial-indigenous government alternative to the hunting ban.

In March 2010, Environment and Natural Resources held a five-day public hearing in Behchokǫ̀ on the state of the Bathurst herd and presented the "Bathurst Caribou Joint Management Proposal"; the Dene and territorial government's alternative caribou management plan.[41] The territorial government presented their case for continuing the hunting ban but stated that a limited hunt of 500 Bathurst caribou, reduced from the previous 5,500 animals hunted annually, could allow the herd to stabilize over a six-year period. The hearing was met with disbelief by the Tłı̨chǫ and the situation escalated in the news as commercial hunting outfitters, the NWT Wildlife Federation, and other parties added to the indigenous voices that questioned the accuracy of herd population estimates. Many stakeholders asserted that the caribou were not in decline. Commenting on the public debates in the national newspaper *The Globe and Mail*, Patrick White stated that unlike other discussions of Canadian caribou herds in decline, "only around Yellowknife is the political climate so combustible, and the caribou so important, that loss can undermine an entire system of government."[42]

In October, 2010, the Wek'èezhìi Renewable Resources Board, the Tłı̨chǫ Government, and the Government of the Northwest Territories reached a solution. They agreed on an indigenous hunting target of 300 Bathurst caribou for the 2011–2012 winter hunting season.[43] A target was chosen rather than a quota in order to reflect that the herd's size is an estimate and to encourage Dene hunters to take responsibility for staying within the target range rather than having to acquire tags from a governing body. The proposal was accepted after the Tłı̨chǫ government agreed to split the 300 target evenly with the Yellowknives Dene and it remained in effect until the 2014–2015 winter hunting season.[44]

As a condition of the 2010 agreement, commercial hunting remained prohibited, effectively ending outfitting in the Northwest Territories.[45] From 2000 to 2008 each outfitting company was allowed 180 caribou tags per company per hunting season before it dropped to 75, and then to a zero allotment in 2010.[46] While the outfitters' clientele were nonindigenous, some outfitters worked closely with indigenous communities, shared meat from sport hunts with them, employed Dene as hunting scouts, and created a cultural experience for tourist hunters. One outfitting company was Tłı̨chǫ owned-and-operated, yet it too was forced to close.

The Métis, a postcontact indigenous people who are sometimes referred to as Canada's forgotten indigenous people, contend that their indigenous hunting rights were ignored as they were neither consulted in Bathurst management nor granted tag allotments.[47] The North Slave Métis Alliance sued the territorial government under section 35 of the Constitution Act, which protects indigenous hunting rights. In June 2013, the Supreme Court of the Northwest Territories found that the territorial government had failed to consult the North Slave Métis Alliance.[48] The Métis victory was moot, however, as the territorial government again implemented Bathurst hunting restrictions in anticipation of 2015 population survey data projected to show a continuing decline.[49]

In January, 2015, Environment and Natural Resources replaced the limited tag system with a mobile no-hunting zone. The zone was an area around the herds' core determined by the location of 20 collared Bathurst caribou. The zone moved with the herd and hunting was prohibited within the zone while Tłįchǫ hunted Bathurst that strayed from the core of the herd beyond the mobile zone. However, hunters would have to remain apprised of zone movements based on maps updated weekly on the Environment and Natural Resources website, or risk breaking the law. In an effort to respect Dene tradition, the territorial government made an exception for one "ceremonial" hunt of up to fifteen Bathurst caribou.[50]

Many Tłįchǫ were upset with the new management strategy. They claimed that the mobile hunting zone was too complicated and that the ceremonial hunt, for which Dene would have to apply to the territorial government, was an insult. Eddie Erasmus, Tłįchǫ Grand Chief, spoke against the mobile hunting zone and ceremonial hunt provision, stating, "It is concerning that [the territorial government] will determine what is ceremonial to the Tłįchǫ and what is not."[51]

The provision demonstrated the degree to which the territorial government misunderstands Dene notions of the role of respectful hunting in species viability: a ceremonial hunt cannot repair the rapport between Tłįchǫ and the caribou. Victor Turner has argued that ceremonies provide confirmation of social roles and relationships.[52] In this case, respectful Dene hunting practices confirm social roles and relationships among the Dene and between Dene and caribou. The irony of an allowance for a fifteen-animal ceremonial hunt is that the Government of the Northwest Territories denies what is inherent in Dene hunting traditions: that every hunt should be ceremonial.

Previous Hunting Restrictions and Dene Responses

Canadian authorities have enacted hunting restrictions on caribou and other species in the past, to which Dene have responded much as they are at the time of this book's publication. In 1997, Dene elder and author George Blondin lamented that "wildlife laws and the overhunting of many animals make it hard for us to eat good, wild meat all of the time."[53] Blondin also raised the issue of replacing traditional diets with store-bought foods: "We drink coffee and eat instant food full of chemicals; many children seem to live on pop, chips, and chocolate bars."[54] Furthermore, a lack of caribou in indigenous diets as a result of the Bathurst hunting ban was expected to have detrimental impacts on health, as Blondin suggested, such as exacerbating obesity and diabetes rates.[55] Blondin claims that Dene were concerned about food security and the replacement of traditional foods with cheap and unhealthy store-bought items prior to the current hunting restrictions; the current changes to Dene diets only intensifies these worries.[56]

Since first forming ties with the Canadian government, Dene peoples' concerns have primarily been about hunting and land use rights. Roman Catholic Oblate priest and political activist Rene Fumoleau writes that Dene, who negotiated Treaty 8 in 1899 and Treaty 11 in 1921, were focused on "the protection of their freedom to hunt, trap, and fish." They would only sign Treaty 8 after the Treaty Commissioners promised said rights and also that Dene hunting rights "would be protected against the abuses of white hunters and trappers."[57] However, measures to protect animals from overhunting and trapping by non-Natives were not enforced and many species suffered. This prompted the application of game restrictions to native and non-Native hunters and trappers alike, regardless of treaty rights. The 1917 "Act respecting Game in the Northwest Territories of Canada" established closed seasons wherein hunting musk ox and other large species, including caribou, was restricted for all hunters during certain times of the year. Dene protested the 1917 Act at the 1920 Treaty Days celebration at Fort Resolution, stating that it violated Treaty 8. Two days of negotiations resulted in an agreement to reverse closed hunting seasons. However, the documents of the agreement reportedly perished in a 1928 fire.[58]

Also in 1917 a treaty between Canada, Mexico, and the United States resulted in the Migratory Birds Convention Act, which introduced restrictive hunting seasons on waterfowl and greatly impacted Dene and other indigenous peoples. John Sandlos states that this act, coupled with the establishment of twelve national parks that restricted hunting and the creation of the Advisory Board on Wildlife Protection in 1916, had "profoundly negative consequences for Native hunters." The Migratory Bird Convention Act opened season on waterfowl on September 1, after many birds like ducks and geese would have left the Canadian North for winter, effectively denying Dene hunters access to these birds.[59] Dene people continued to hunt waterfowl in secret, however, in 1964 Michael Sikyea, a Yellowknife Dene elder who had been an interpreter for a 1923 addition to Treaty 8, was caught with a single duck hunted out of season. Sikyea appealed the decision as a violation of his treaty rights. Recalling being present at treaty signing he stated that hunting rights were guaranteed to remain, "as long as the river is running and the sun is rising that's the law."[60] Sikyea's appeal was taken to the Canadian Supreme Court, who ignored a discussion of treaty rights but, after a lengthy and costly attempt to determine if the duck was wild or domestic, stated violation of the Migratory Bird Convention Act was paramount. The Sikyea case had major implications for indigenous treaty rights; for Dene it confirmed that hunting rights were not to be respected by the Canadian government.

In the 1950s Canada imposed restrictions on small game hunting and trapping, which Dene regarded as a joke and did not abide by as they did not fear penalization from the government. June Helm, who worked first with the Slavey Dene and later with the Tłı̨chǫ, suggests that Slavey did not think restrictions affected small game viability and therefore felt no moral dilemma in breaking the laws.[61] However, Slavey and Tłı̨chǫ took caribou hunting restrictions more seriously than small game restrictions. Tłı̨chǫ demonstrated this when Game Warden Gene Earl declared at the 1962 Behchokǫ̀ Treaty Days that caribou hunting would be restricted for the upcoming season. Earl stated through a Tłı̨chǫ interpreter, "The population of the caribou is still on the downgrade . . . If you kill a caribou, save the lower jaw and bring it in [for documentation] . . . [female caribou] are off-limits the year round." A discussion "verging on a hassle" followed, with Tłı̨chǫ announcing they would not follow the decree.[62] Game Warden Earl replied that Tłı̨chǫ should think of future generations. Behchokǫ̀ Chief Jimmy Bruneau answered,

> In the old days, everyone thought of caribou. Now, the young ones hang out in bars—that's all they ever think about . . . You fellows don't give us anything. . . . We are all living on the caribou . . . We haven't got any money. We get out in the bush, get a little meat, that's what we eat. You guys all got jobs. You walk in a restaurant and buy food with your money. Out there, the caribou is our money.[63]

For Chief Bruneau, speaking on behalf of the Tłı̨chǫ, the reason for caribou inaccessibility was not that Tłı̨chǫ were not thinking of future generations, but rather that young Tłı̨chǫ were not thinking of the needs of the caribou. The point was that Tłı̨chǫ must continue to rely on caribou in a positive manner by thinking of caribou rather than relying on Canadian city life. Chief Bruneau did not disagree with Game Warden Earl regarding human responsibility toward the caribou, but he fundamentally disagreed on the nature of their relationship with the caribou.

Many Dene perceive hunting restrictions as arrogant because restrictions fail to take into account the fact that caribou determine the success of a hunt, based on how respected or disrespected they feel. For example, Slavey Dene blamed caribou's disappearance during the 1951–1952 winter hunting season on "the slaying of a caribou with a stick by an Indian from a neighboring band."[64] A Tłįchǫ consultant similarly told me that caribou did not come one winter in the 1950s because a Sahtú Dene hunter hit a caribou with a stick, possibly referring to the same incident.

The notion that Dene are at the mercy of caribou was emphasized to me in August 2013, when Tłįchǫ community governments canceled their fall hunts because the Bluenose East herd did not return. My consultants stated that Tłįchǫ scout planes failed to find caribou along their usual migration route in the tundra. I was told that Tłįchǫ had never canceled a hunt prior to that fall but that the community governments did not deem it worth the financial cost to charter planes if no caribou could be found. Previously, hunters had traveled to the tundra to find that caribou had not arrived, but modern technology now allowed them to know in advance that the trip would be unproductive.

My Tłįchǫ consultants suspected that the Bluenose East did not migrate into Tłįchǫ lands in 2013, due to an incident the previous winter when fifty caribou from the herd were found slaughtered in a disrespectful manner with most of their meat left behind.[65] The Department of Environment and Natural Resources charged a Tłįchǫ elder with "meat wastage" for the incident but my consultants thought that a stranger from outside the community was responsible.[66] Once the fall hunt was canceled Tłįchǫ discussed this incident repeatedly, assuming the disrespectful hunt was responsible for the Bluenose East's disappearance and that the caribou were offended and chose not to return. This incident illustrates how Dene conceptions of the effect of hunting on animal populations contrast sharply with the conservation perspective inherent within Canadian game laws.

Dene Responses to the Caribou

At present, Dene articulate varied responses to the current state of caribou populations. Some of my Tłįchǫ consultants are persuaded by the science presented on caribou decline and agree on the need to change herd management. Other Tłįchǫ consultants, including most elders, state that caribou cannot be managed by humans. They assert that discussing the caribou as being in a state of decline is disrespectful and they prefer terminology of caribou inaccessibility, connoting caribou agency in managing themselves. As evidenced by several accounts in this chapter, Dene assert that animals know when they are disrespected and thus the animals withdraw from contact.[67] For example, Blondin relates his Sahtú Dene understanding that, "caribou think badly of people who do not treat them with respect. If the caribou don't come near some years, it is because they feel that you have not treated them properly and they avoid you."[68] Zoe, who had a primary role in drafting the Tłįchǫ perspective, states that the intent of joint Tłįchǫ and territorial government caribou management plans

> is to help Tłįchǫ relearn their traditional ways, their nàowo, and respect and relationship with ekwǫ̀ [tundra caribou]. If these traditions are renewed, ekwǫ̀ will come back . . . The elders have always believed that when ekwǫ̀ became scarce they would go away to be left alone—to recover and replenish themselves. They would then come back to offer themselves to the Tłįchǫ.[69]

Regardless of wildlife biologists' findings, Tłįchǫ have dynamic and nuanced understandings of the contemporary caribou situation and they articulate responses consistent with historical Dene responses to animal scarcity. My consultants state that hunters either need to maintain, return to, or adopt Dene respectful hunting practices.

One manner in which Tłįchǫ articulate respectful responses to caribou scarcity is through community projects. For example, the Rae-Edzo Friendship Centre of Behchokǫ̀, Northwest Territories implemented the community-led project "Keeping Our Community Healthy," a multifaceted project that addressed changes in Tłįchǫ foodways and advocated for supplementing a lack of caribou in Tłįchǫ diets with other traditional foods rather than store-bought foods. In the winter and spring of 2013, I facilitated two on-the-land trips for the project in which elders taught youth how to catch and cook traditional foods as we spent five days each trip in the bush, staying in tents and old cabins in historical communities. We trapped muskrats, snared rabbits, and ice fished with nets. The elders taught the youth how to catch animals respectfully using traditional means, such as hitting a trapped muskrat over the head with an axe handle to quicken the muskrat's death and end its suffering.

Two years earlier, in Behchokǫ̀ in 2011, I cofacilitated another Rae-Edzo Friendship Centre community-led project: "Tłı̨chǫ Traditional Caribou Conservation: Youth and Elders Working Together."[70] This workshop was coordinated in response to the Bathurst caribou herd's inaccessibility and subsequent hunting restrictions put in place the year prior. Seven Tłı̨chǫ elders and four youths discussed the historical and continued importance of caribou, predominantly in their Tłı̨chǫ Dene language. The elders spoke of surviving on caribou while living on the land before the Canadian government moved them to settled communities in the 1960s. The elders taught the youth about respectful caribou practices from their youth in the bush and how to maintain those practices today. They taught to only hunt what is needed, to share hunted meat with the community, and to return bones to the land to aid the animals' regeneration. Once again, elders' discussions revealed a different interpretation of the current state of the Bathurst herd than that of the Canadian government and biologists: one predicated on the agency of caribou.

During the workshop elders identified a primary directive to share with Dene and other hunters: when hunters kill a caribou on a frozen lake they should move the animal to land and "cut them there."[71] Furthermore, Western hunting terms are considered conceptually incorrect; Tłı̨chǫ elders prefer the terminology of *meeting* or *following* the animals rather than *stalking*, and *cutting up* is preferred to *butchering*.[72] In the Tłı̨chǫ language *yeghaegè* means to meet an animal and *niitsèt'à* means to field dress or cut meat. According to Tłı̨chǫ elders at the workshop, *niitsèt'à* is performed respectfully when done on land because (1) it shows care to the animal; (2) because it is respectful to the lake as the caribou's blood does not mix with the water when the lake thaws; and (3) because it is respectful to the ravens and bears that awaken from hibernation and eat the carcasses left in neat piles.[73]

As a result of attending the workshop, youth participants determined that the elders' message about respectfully field-dressing caribou should be shared with hunters. After the workshop the Tłı̨chǫ youth created a large road sign and placed it on the winter ice-road that leads from Behchokǫ̀ to the then-unrestricted Bluenose East caribou hunting grounds. The sign read, "Attention Hunters! Respect the Caribou: Place Them on the Land and Cut Them There." The sign's purpose is more rhetorical than informative. The sign's general message of respectful hunting is already known to Dene hunters and the specific directive is in response to sloppy field dressing of caribou on the ice road during the prior winter. The sign reminds hunters of their responsibility to caribou and also informs caribou that Tłı̨chǫ are respectful of them. Elders at the workshop asserted that it is important to tell positive stories of caribou and not focus on the Bathurst herd decline and hunting restrictions. Elders said caribou were listening and that they would be happy to hear stories about how Dene need them but they would be upset to hear us speaking of how caribou are not doing well. Thus, both the road sign and the workshop were demonstrations of respect to the caribou.

At the end of the workshop the elders asked if I had questions. I asked if speaking well of caribou will help the animals survive as a species. My question revealed the degree to which I had not understood Dene ontology and ignored the agency of the caribou. I had assumed a causal relationship, wherein our words affected caribou sustainability. The Tłı̨chǫ participants were confused by my question and answered, "No, only God can make or take away a species." Speaking well of caribou during the workshop was, I thought, a strategy for conservation. However, the term *conservation* is inadequate for expressing Dene relationships with caribou. Speaking well of caribou does not help caribou survive, nor does it improve population numbers. I had misunderstood that the elders were making an emotional appeal to persuade caribou to choose to return.

The workshop was a ceremony wherein participants demonstrated respect in order to repair the mutually beneficial relations between Dene and caribou that existed prior to the current caribou scarcity and hunting restrictions. At the workshop, elders noted that caribou knew what we were doing, what we said about caribou, and what we thought about them. Later it was explained to me that caribou could hear the workshop proceedings through a kind of telepathy. This is consistent with the Dene conception that thought is not a mental force, but a form of "communication with other thinking entities and therefore . . . [has] consequences when heard and acted upon."[74] In the Dene relational universe thought itself is communication, and workshops that consist of respectful thoughts and actions may persuade caribou to reciprocate.

On October 22, 2015, the Tłı̨chǫ government took an unprecedented step and announced they would suspend hunting of the Bathurst caribou herd for the 2015–2016 hunting season. In a press release on the Tłı̨chǫ government website, Tłı̨chǫ Nation Grand Chief Eddie Erasmus stated, "Our Government is determined to support the efforts to help the herd recover. . . . We have made this difficult choice as an investment in our future and we as a people need to do this."[75] Unlike the fall 2013 hunt,

Modeling (Yellowknife, NT: Department of Environment and Natural Resources, 2009), 2.

15. Laura Busch, "Wasted Meat Provokes Outrage: Yellowknifers Cry Foul as edible Parts of at Least 50 Caribou, Including Pregnant Cows, Found Abandoned," *Northern News Service*, May 10, 2013, http://www.nnsl.com/frames/newspapers/2013-05/may10_13waste.html.

16. Adamczewski, et al., *Decline in the Bathurst*, 2, 55.

17. John Boulanger and Anne Gunn, *Exploring Possible Mechanisms for the Decline of the Bathurst Herd of Barren-Ground Caribou Using Demographic Modeling* (Yellowknife, NT: Department of Environment and Natural Resources, Government of the Northwest Territories, 2007).

18. John Boulanger, Anne Gunn, Jan Adamczewski, and Bruno Croft, "A Data-driven Demographic Model to Explore the Decline of the Bathurst Caribou Herd," *Journal of Wildlife Management* 75, no. 4 (2011): 883–96.

19. Adamczewski, et al., *Decline in the Bathurst*, 2.

20. Livingstone, "Declines in NWT Barrenground Caribou."

21. See Weirong Chen, D. E. Russell, Anne Gunn, Bruno Croft, R. Fernandes, H. Zhao, J. Li, Y. Zhang, and K. Koehler, "Habitat Indicators for Migratory Tundra Caribou under a Changing Climate: Winter and Pre-calving Migration ranges," *Climatic Change* (2009): 1–40; Anne Gunn, "The Position of Caribou in the North: An Overview," *Northern Perspectives* 31, no. 1 (2007): 3–5; Anne Gunn and K. G. Poole, *Environmental Trends Across the Range of the Bathurst Caribou Herd and Timing of the Arrival of Cows on their Calving Ground 1996–2009* (Yellowknife, NT: Environment and Natural Resources, 2009); Brenda Parlee and Micheline Manseau, "Using Traditional Knowledge to Adapt to Ecological Change: Denésǫłiné Monitoring of Caribou Movements." *Arctic* 58, no. 1 (2005): 26–37; Clive Tesar, "What Price the Caribou?" *Northern Perspectives* 31, no. 1 (2007):1–3; Liv Solveig Vors and Mark Stephen Boyce, "Global Declines of Caribou and Reindeer," *Global Change Biology* 15, no. 11 (2009): 2626–33.

22. See Eric Post, "Erosion of Community Diversity and Stability by Herbivore Removal under Warming," *Proceedings of the Royal Society B* 280, no. 1757 (2013): 1471–2954; Tara J. Zamin and Paul Grogan, "Caribou Exclusion During a Population Low Increases Deciduous and Evergreen Shrub Species Biomass and Nitrogen Pools in Low Arctic Tundra," *Journal of Ecology* 101 (2013): 671–83.

23. See Justin Kenrick and Jerome Lewis, "On the Return of the Native," *Current Anthropology* 45, no. 2 (2004): 260–67; Parlee, "Using Traditional Knowledge," 28, 34; E. Reimers and J. E. Colman, "Reindeer and caribou (Rangifer tarandus) response towards human activities," *Rangifer* 26, no. 2 (2006): 55–71; Tesar, "What Price?"

24. On Tłįchǫ attitudes toward previous mines, specifically the Rayrock Mine, which extracted uranium from Tłįchǫ lands to be used for atomic bomb

testing in Navajo land in the United States, see Allice Legat, *Walking the Land, Feeding the Fire: Knowledge and Stewardship among the Tlicho Dene* (Tuscan: University of Arizona Press, 2012), 191.

25. See Barnaby, *Bathurst Caribou*, 14–15.

26. Robert A. Brightman, *Grateful Prey: Rock Cree Human-Animal Relationships* (Berkeley: University of California Press, 1993), 112.

27. Richard K. Nelson, *Make Prayers to the Raven: A Koyukon View of the Northern Forest* (Chicago: University Of Chicago Press, 1983), 23.

28. See Ryan, *Doing Things*, 26.

29. See Adamczewski, et al., *Decline in the Bathurst*, 3.

30. Allice Legat, Georgina Chocolate, Bobby Gon, Sally Anne Zoe, and Madelaine Chocolate, *Caribou Migration and the State of Their Habitat* (Yellowknife, NT: West Kitikmeot Slave Study Society, 2001), 66.

31. Joseph Judas and Jody Snortland, "Using Dual Knowledge Systems to Inform Management Decisions: a Wek'èezhìi Renewable Resources Board Example," *Rangifer* 32, no. 2 (2012): 47.

32. "Traditional Hunters Vow to Ignore Caribou Ban," *CBC News North*, December 21, 2009, http://www.cbc.ca/news/canada/north/traditional-hunters-vow-to-ignore-caribou-ban-1.802082.

33. Deneze Nakehk'o, "Lift N.W.T. caribou hunting ban, Dene chiefs demand," *CBC News North*, January 21, 2010, http://www.cbc.ca/news/canada/north/story/2010/01/21/dene-chiefs-caribou.html.

34. "Debate over N.W.T. caribou hunting ban goes public," *CBC News North*, February 9, 2010, http://www.cbc.ca/news/canada/north/debate-over-n-w-t-caribou-hunting-ban-goes-public-1.893827.

35. Roxanna Thompson, "Deh Cho First Nations defies North Slave caribou hunt ban," *Northern News Services*, January 28, 2010, http://www.nnsl.com/northern-news-services/stories/papers/jan28_10car.html.

36. "Traditional Hunters Vow."

37. Thompson, "Deh Cho."

38. Patrick White, "NWT Natives Fight to Hunt Dwindling Caribou," *Globe and Mail*, May 4, 2010, http://www.theglobeandmail.com/news/national/nwt-natives-fight-to-hunt-dwindling-caribou/article1557045/; Tim Querengesser, "Deer in the Headlights: Aboriginals, Whites and the Clash over Caribou," *Up Here*, June 2010.

39. Zoe, "Ekwǫ̀ and Tłı̨chǫ," 69–70.

40. "Debate over N.W.T. Caribou Hunting."

41. Andrew Livingstone, "NWT Defends Caribou Hunting Ban," *Northern News Services*, March 4, 2010, http://www.nnsl.com/frames/newspapers/2010-03/mar24_10cari.html.

42. White, "NWT Natives Fight."

43. "Bathurst Caribou Herd Protected by New Preservation Plan," *Alaska Dispatch*, October 14, 2010, http://www.alaskadispatch.com/article/bathurst-caribou-herd-protected-new-preservation-plan?page=0,0.

44. Maria Church, "Harvest Re-approved for Select Caribou, Bison Herds," *Northern Journal*, December 16, 2013.

45. "Bathurst Caribou Herd Protected."

46. "Battle over Caribou Management Heads to the Courts," *Up Here Business*, May, no. 52 (2011).

47. Lyndsay Herman, "Metis Assert Right to Caribou," *Northern News Services*, June 18, 2012, http://nnsl.com/northern-news-services/stories/papers/jun18_12car.html. On the Métis as Canada's forgotten indigenous people see Ute Lischke and David T. McNab, eds. *The Long Journey of a Forgotten People: Métis Identities and Family Histories* (Waterloo, ON: Wilfrid Laurier University Press, 2007).

48. "North Slave Métis back in Court over Bathurst Caribou," *CBC News North*, December 1, 2014, http://www.cbc.ca/news/canada/north/north-slave-métis-back-in-court-over-bathurst-caribou-1.2856517.

49. "NWT Stops Giving out Bathurst Tags," *CBC News North*, December 19, 2014, http://www.cbc.ca/news/canada/north/n-w-t-stops-issuing-remaining-bathurst-caribou-tags-1.2880037.

50. "Bathurst Caribou: Mobile Mo-hunting Zone Set Up Using Radio Collars," *CBC News North*, January 28, 2015, http://www.cbc.ca/news/canada/north/bathurst-caribou-mobile-no-hunting-zone-set-up-using-radio-collars-1.2935488.

51. "Tlicho Say They still Have 'Grave Concerns' about Caribou Plan," *CBC News North*, February 2, 2015.

52. Victor Turner, "Betwixt and Between: The Liminal Period in Rites de Passage," *Proceedings of the American Ethnological Society Symposium on New Approaches to the Study of Religion* (1964): 4–20.

53. George Blondin, *Yamoria the Lawmaker: Stories of the Dene* (Edmonton: NeWest Press, 1997), 65.

54. Blondin, *Yamoria the Lawmaker*, 65.

55. See "Caribou Hunting Ban Raises Dene Health Concerns," *Canadian Obesity Network*, February 11, 2010, http://www.con-aboriginal.ca/detail.aspx?menu=17&dt=3267&app=70&cat1=434&tp=12&lk=g.

56. See M. G. Mackey, "The Impact of Imported Foods on the Traditional Inuit Diet," *Arctic Med Res* 47, Supplement 1 (1988): 128–33; T. L. Nancarrow, H. M. Chan, A. Ing, and Harriet V. Kuhnlein, "Climate Change Impacts on Dietary Nutrient Status of Inuit in Nunavut, Canada," *The FASEB Journal* 22 (2008); Olivier Receveur, M. Boulay, and Harriet V. Kuhnlein, "Decreasing Traditional Food Use Affects Diet Quality for Adult Dene/Métis in 16 Communities of the Canadian Northwest Territories," *Science* 127, April (1997): 2179–86.

57. René Fumoleau, *As Long as This Land Shall Last: A History of Treaty 8 and Treaty 11* (Calgary: University of Calgary Press and Arctic Institute of North America, 2004), 6.

58. Fumoleau, *Long as This Land Shall Last*, 124, 130.

59. Sandlos, John, *Hunters at the Margin: Native People and Wildlife Conservation in the Northwest Territories* (Vancouver: University of British Columbia Press, 2007), 24.

60. Dorothy Harley Eber, *Images of Justice: A Legal History of the Northwest Territories and Nunavut as Traced through the Yellowknife Courthouse Collection of Inuit Sculpture* (Montreal, QC: McGill-Queen's University Press, 1997), 118.

61. Helm, *People of Denendeh*, 35.

62. Helm, *People of Denendeh*, 66.

63. Ibid.

64. June Helm Macneish, "Contemporary Folk Beliefs of a Slave Indian Band," *Journal of American Folklore* 67, no. 264 (1951): 189.

65. Busch, "Wasted Meat."

66. See Daniel Campbell, "Elder Denies Mass Meat Wastage: Johnnie Washie Pays Fine, but Says He Only Shot One Wounded Calf Near Hottah Lake," *Northern News Services*, September 9, 2013.

67. See also Robin Ridington, *Little Bit Know Something: Stories in a Language of Anthropology* (Iowa: University of Iowa Press, 1990), 89.

68. George Blondin, *Trail of the Spirit: the Mysteries of Medicine Power Revealed* (Edmonton, AB: NeWest Press, 2006), 178.

69. Zoe, "Ekwǫ̀ and Tłįchǫ," 71.

70. See Drybones and Walsh, *Tłįchǫ Traditional Caribou Conservation*.

71. Drybones and Walsh, *Tłįchǫ Traditional Caribou Conservation*, 4.

72. Allice Legat, Georgina Chocolate, and Madelaine Chocolate, *Monitoring the Relationship between People and Caribou* (Yellowknife, NT: West Kitikmeot Slave Study Society, 2008), 12.

73. Drybones and Walsh, *Tłįchǫ Traditional Caribou Conservation*, 8.

74. Marie-Francois Guédon, "Dene Ways and the Ethnographer's Culture," in Being Changed: The Anthropology of Extraordinary Experience, eds. Jean Guy Goulet and D. E. Young (Peterborough, ON: Broadview Press, 1994), 55.

75. Giselle Marion, "Tłįchǫ Government Decides to Not Harvest the Bathurst Herd," *Tłįchǫ Government*, October 22, 2015, http://tlicho.ca/news/tlicho-government-decides-not-harvest-bathurst-herd.

Bibliography

Adamczewski, Jan, John Boulanger, Bruno Croft, and Dean Cluff, *Decline in the Bathurst Caribou Herd 2006–2009: A Technical Evaluation of Field Data and Modeling* Yellowknife: Department of Environment and Natural Resources, 2009.

Andrews, Thomas D., and John B. Zoe. "The Idaà Trail: Archaeology and the Dogrib Cultural Landscape, Northwest Territories, Canada." In *At a Cross-*

roads: Archaeology and First Peoples in Canada, eds. George P. Nicholas and Thomas D. Andrews, 160–77. Vancouver: Archaeology Press, Simon Fraser University, 1997.

Astor-Aguilera, Miguel, *The Maya World of Communicating Objects: Quadripartite Crosses, Trees, and Stones*. Albuquerque: University of New Mexico Press, 2010.

Barnaby, Joanne, and Deborah Simmons, "Bathurst Caribou Harvester's Gathering." Behchokǫ̀ and Yellowknife, NT: Tłįchǫ Government and Wek'èezhìi Renewable Resources Board, 2013.

"Bathurst Caribou: Mobile No-Hunting Zone Set Up Using Radio Collars." CBC News North, January 28, 2015. http://www.cbc.ca/news/canada/north/bathurst-caribou-mobile-no-hunting-zone-set-up-using-radio-collars-1.2935488.

"Bathurst Caribou Herd Protected by New Preservation Plan." *Alaska Dispatch*, October 14, 2010. http://www.alaskadispatch.com/article/bathurst-caribou-herd-protected-new-preservation-plan?page=0,0.

"Battle over Caribou Management Heads to the Courts," *Up Here Business* 52 (May 2011).

Blondin George, *Trail of the Spirit: the Mysteries of Medicine Power Revealed*. Edmonton, AB: NeWest Press, 2006.

Blondin, George, *Yamoria the Lawmaker: Stories of the Dene*. Edmonton, AB: NeWest Press, 1997.

Boulanger, John, and Anne Gunn, *Exploring Possible Mechanisms for the Decline of the Bathurst Herd of Barren-Ground Caribou Using Demographic Modeling*. Yellowknife: Department of Environment and Natural Resources, Government of the Northwest Territories, 2007.

Boulanger, John, Anne Gunn, Jan Adamczewski, and Bruno Croft, "A Data-Driven Demographic Model to Explore the Decline of the Bathurst Caribou Herd." *Journal of Wildlife Management* 75, no. 4 (2011): 883–96.

Brightman, Robert A., *Grateful Prey: Rock Cree Human-Animal Relationships*. Berkeley: University of California Press, 1993.

Busch, Laura. "Wasted Meat Provokes Outrage: Yellowknifers Cry Foul as Edible Parts of at Least 50 Caribou, including Pregnant Cows, Found Abandoned." *Northern News Services*, May 10, 2013. http://www.nnsl.com/frames/newspapers/2013-05/may10_13waste.html.

Campbell, Daniel, "Elder Denies Mass Meat Wastage: Johnnie Washie Pays Fine, but Says He Only Shot One Wounded Calf near Hottah Lake." *Northern News Services*, September 9, 2013.

"Caribou Hunting Ban Raises Dene Health Concerns." *Canadian Obesity Network*, February 11, 2010. http://www.conaboriginal.ca/detail.aspx?menu=17&dt=3267&app=70&cat1=434&tp=12&lk=g.

Chen, Weirong, D. E. Russell, Anne Gunn, Bruno Croft, R. Fernandes, H. Zhao, J. Li, Y. Zhang, and K. Koehler. "Habitat Indicators for Migratory Tundra

Caribou under a Changing Climate: Winter and Pre-calving Migration Ranges." *Climatic Change* (2009): 1–40.

Church, Maria. "Harvest Re-approved for Select Caribou, Bison Herds." *Northern Journal*, December 16, 2013.

"Debate over N.W.T. Caribou Hunting Ban Goes Public." CBC News North, February 9, 2010. http://www.cbc.ca/news/canada/north/debate-over-n-w-t-caribou-hunting-ban-goes-public-1.893827.

Descola, Philippe. *Beyond Nature and Culture*, translated by Janet Lloyd. Chicago: University of Chicago Press, 2013.

Eber, Dorothy Harley. *Images of Justice: A Legal History of the Northwest Territories and Nunavut as Traced through the Yellowknife Courthouse Collection of Inuit Sculpture*. Montreal, QC: McGill-Queen's University Press, 1997.

Fumoleau, René. *As Long as This Land Shall Last: A History of Treaty 8 and Treaty 11*. Calgary: University of Calgary Press and Arctic Institute of North America, 2004.

Guédon, Marie-Francois. "Dene Ways and the Ethnographer's Culture." In *Being Changed: The Anthropology of Extraordinary Experience*, eds. Jean Guy Goulet and D. E. Young, 39–70. Peterborough, ON: Broadview Press, 1994.

Gunn, Anne. "The Position of Caribou in the North: An Overview." *Northern Perspectives* 31, no. 1 (2007): 3–5.

Gunn, Anne, and K. G. Poole. *Environmental Trends across the Range of the Bathurst Caribou Herd and Timing of the Arrival of Cows on their Calving Ground 1996–2009*. Yellowknife, NT: Environment and Natural Resources, 2009.

Hallowell, A. Irving. "Ojibwa Ontology, Behavior, and World View." In *Teachings from the American Earth: Indian Religion and Philosophy*, eds. Dennis Tedlock and Barbara Tedlock, 141–78. New York: Liveright, (1960) 1975.

Harvey, Graham. *Animism: Respecting the Living World*. London: Hurst and Company, 2005.

Helm, June. *The People of Denendeh: Ethnohistory of the Indians of Canada's Northwest Territories*. Iowa City: University of Iowa Press, 2000.

Herman, Lyndsay, "Metis Assert Right to Caribou." *Northern News Services*, June 18, 2012. http://nnsl.com/northern-news-services/stories/papers/jun18_12car.html.

Ingold, Tim. *The Perception of the Environment: Essays on Livelihood, Dwelling and Skill*. London and New York: Routledge, 2000.

Judas, Joseph, and Jody Snortland. "Using Dual Knowledge Systems to Inform Management Decisions: A Wek'èezhìi Renewable Resources Board Example." *Rangifer* 32, no. 2 (March 2012): 47.

Kenrick, Justin, and Jerome Lewis. "On the Return of the Native." *Current Anthropology* 45, no. 2 (2004): 260–67.

de Laguna, Frederica, and Dale DeArmond. *Tales From the Dena: Indian Stories from the Tanana, Koyukuk and Yukon Rivers*. Seattle: University of Washington Press, 1995.

Legat, Allice. *Walking the Land, Feeding the Fire: Knowledge and Stewardship among the Tlicho Dene.* Tucson: University of Arizona Press, 2012.

Legat, Allice, Georgina Chocolate, and Madelaine Chocolate, *Monitoring the Relationship between People and Caribou.* Yellowknife, NT: West Kitikmeot Slave Study Society, 2008.

Legat, Allice, Georgina Chocolate, Bobby Gon, Sally Anne Zoe, and Madelaine Chocolate. *Caribou Migration and the State of Their Habitat.* Yellowknife, NT: West Kitikmeot Slave Study Society, 2001.

Lischke, Ute, and David T. McNab, eds. *The Long Journey of a Forgotten People: Métis Identities and Family Histories.* Waterloo, ON: Wilfrid Laurier University Press, 2007.

Livingstone, Andrew. "NWT Defends Caribou Hunting Ban." *Northern News Services,* March 4, 2010. http://www.nnsl.com/frames/newspapers/2010-03/mar24_10cari.html.

Mackey, M. G., "The impact of imported foods on the traditional Inuit diet." *Arctic Med Res* 47, Supplement 1 (1988): 128–33.

MacNeish, June Helm. "Contemporary Folk Beliefs of a Slave Indian Band." *Journal of American Folklore* 67, no. 264 (April–June 1954): 185–98.

Marion, Giselle. "Tłı̨chǫ Government Decides to Not Harvest the Bathurst Herd." Tłı̨chǫ Government, October 22, 2015. http://tlicho.ca/news/tlicho-government-decides-not-harvest-bathurst-herd.

Morrison, Kenneth M. The Solidarity of Kin*: Ethnohistory, Religious Studies, and the Algonkain-French Religious Encounter.* Albany: State University of New York Press, 2002.

Nakehk'o, Deneze. "Lift N.W.T. Caribou Hunting Ban, Dene Chiefs Demand." CBC News North, January 21, 2010. http://www.cbc.ca/news/canada/north/story/2010/01/21/dene-chiefs-caribou.html.

Nancarrow, T. L., H. M. Chan, A. Ing, and Harriet V. Kuhnlein. "Climate Change Impacts on Dietary Nutrient Status of Inuit in Nunavut, Canada." *The FASEB Journal* 22 (March 2008).

Nelson, Richard K. *Make Prayers to the Raven: A Koyukon View of the Northern Forest.* Chicago: University of Chicago Press, 1983.

"North Slave Métis Back in Court over Bathurst Caribou." CBC News North, December 1, 2014. http://www.cbc.ca/news/canada/north/north-slave-métis-back-in-court-over-bathurst-caribou-1.2856517.

"NWT stops giving out Bathurst tags." CBC News North, December 19, 2014. http://www.cbc.ca/news/canada/north/n-w-t-stops-issuing-remaining-bathurst-caribou-tags-1.2880037.

Parlee, Brenda, and Micheline Manseau. "Using Traditional Knowledge to Adapt to Ecological Change: Denésǫ̨łiné Monitoring of Caribou Movements." *Arctic* 58, no. 1 (March 2005): 26–37.

Post, Eric. "Erosion of Community Diversity and Stability by Herbivore Removal Under Warming." *Proceedings of the Royal Society* B 280, no. 1757 (2013): 1471–2954.

Querengesser, Tim. "Deer in the Headlights: Aboriginals, Whites and the Clash over Caribou." *Up Here*, June 2010.

Receveur, Olivier, M. Boulay, and Harriet V. Kuhnlein. "Decreasing Traditional Food Use Affects Diet Quality for Adult Dene/Métis in 16 Communities of the Canadian Northwest Territories." *Science* 127 (April 1997): 2179–86.

Reimers, E., and J. E. Colman. "Reindeer and Caribou (Rangifer tarandus) Response towards Human Activities." *Rangifer* 26, no. 2 (January 2006): 55–71.

Ridington, Robin. *Little Bit Know Something: Stories in a Language of Anthropology.* Iowa: University of Iowa Press, 1990.

Russell, Frank. *Explorations in the Far North: Being the Report of an Expedition Under the Auspices of the University of Iowa during the Years of 1892, '93, and '94.* Iowa: University of Iowa Press, 1898.

Sandlos, John, *Hunters at the Margin: Native People and Wildlife Conservation in the Northwest Territories.* Vancouver: University of British Colombia Press, 2007.

Shorter, David Delgado. *We Will Dance Our Truth: Yaqui History in Yoeme Performances.* Lincoln: University of Nebraska Press, 2009.

Tesar, Clive. "What Price the Caribou?" *Northern Perspectives* 31, no. 1 (2007): 1–3.

Thompson, Roxanna. "Deh Cho First Nations Defies North Slave Caribou Hunt Ban." *Northern News Services*, January 28, 2010. http://www.nnsl.com/northern-news-services/stories/papers/jan28_10car.html.

Tłı̨chǫ Government. *Gonàowo t'a Nàts'etso; Ełets'àts'edi t'a Nats'etso: Tłı̨chǫ Language, Culture and Way of Life: A Report from the Cultural Coordinator 2010–2013.* Behchokǫ̀, NT: Office of the Cultural Coordinator, 2013.

"Tlicho Say They Still Have 'Grave Concerns' about Caribou Plan." CBC News North, February 2, 2015.

"Traditional Hunters Vow to Ignore Caribou Ban." CBC News North, December 21, 2009. http://www.cbc.ca/news/canada/north/traditional-hunters-vow-to-ignore-caribou-ban-1.802082.

Turner, Victor. "Betwixt and Between: The Liminal Period in Rites de Passage." *Proceedings of the American Ethnological Society Symposium on New Approaches to the Study of Religion* (1964): 4–20.

Viveiros de Castro, Eduardo. "Cosmological Deixis and Amerindian Perspectivism." *Journal of the Royal Anthropological Institute* 4, no. 3 (September 1998): 469–88.

Vors, Liv Solveig, and Mark Stephen Boyce. "Global Declines of Caribou and Reindeer." *Global Change Biology* 15, no. 11 (May 2009): 2626–33.

Walsh, David. "The Nature of Food: Indigenous Dene Foodways and Ontologies in the Era of Climate Change." *Scripta Instituti Donneriani Aboensis* 26 (April 2015): 225–49.

White, Patrick. "NWT natives fight to hunt dwindling caribou." *Globe and Mail.* May 4, 2010. http://www.theglobeandmail.com/news/national/nwt-natives-fight-to-hunt-dwindling-caribou/article1557045/.

Zamin, Tara J., and Paul Grogan. "Caribou Exclusion during a Population Low Increases Deciduous and Evergreen Shrub Species Biomass and Nitrogen Pools in Low Arctic Tundra." *Journal of Ecology* 101 (2013): 671–83.

Zoe, John B. "Ekwǫ̀ and Tłı̨chǫ Nàowo/Caribou and Tłı̨chǫ Language, Culture and Way of Life: An Evolving Relationship and Shared History." *Rangifer* 32, no. 2 (2012): 69–74.

6

Bringing a Berry Back from the Land of the Dead

Coast Salish Huckleberry Cultivation and Food Sovereignty

Suzanne Crawford O'Brien
and Kimberly Wogahn

> If you get sick, eat your traditional foods. You have to feed your Indian. Native foods feed your body, but they also feed your spirit.
>
> —Hank Gobin, Tulalip

Swədaʔx̌ali: The Place of Mountain Huckleberry

It is August 2015, and a group of eleven middle school students from the Tulalip Indian reservation are spending five nights in the mountains of the Mount Baker–Snoqualmie National Forest. This time has been set aside so that young people have an opportunity to learn from their elders about camping, gathering, tribal history, treaty rights, costewardship of their traditional territories, and the role these mountains historically played in traditional culture and spirituality. The location of the camp is a special one: it is known in Lushootseed Coast Salish as *Swədaʔx̌ali*, or the Place of Mountain Huckleberries.

The Tulalip Tribes are part of the broader Coast Salish community, which today includes nearly 50,000 enrolled tribal members living in reservation communities and reserves throughout western Washington and southwest British Columbia. The Tulalip Tribes comprise those Coast Salish bands and villages who were successors to the signatories of the 1855 Treaty of Point Elliot, including members of the Snohomish, Snoqualmie, Skykomish, and other allied tribes and bands. The treaty ensured these communities a reservation home and it guaranteed them the rights to fish, hunt, and gather in their usual and accustomed places. But of course the present-day reservation encompasses only a small part of the traditional resource territories inhabited by these central Coast Salish communities, which ranged west from the coast and extended east deep into the Cascade Mountains and beyond. With the signing of treaties and the loss of access to some of the families' ancestral gathering sites, the forests were no longer managed as they once had been.

Despite these major historical shifts in land ownership patterns and access, treaty tribes reserved their gathering rights, and huckleberries remain a staple food for Coast Salish people. With over fourteen different varieties, huckleberries come in red and blue and grow at low and high elevations. They are eaten fresh, dried in cakes, canned, frozen, and some leaves can be made into tea.[1] Black huckleberries (also known as big huckleberry or mountain huckleberry), in particular, were a historically prized trading commodity throughout Puget Sound and along the Columbia River.[2] They were so valuable, in fact, that much of the summer season was devoted to their harvest, as families spent weeks or even months in the mountains, gathering at their traditional sites.[3] As Warren King George explains,

> Our beloved Mother Nature provides us Salish Sea Natives with an array of precious traditional food gifts . . . Of all the gifts there is one that can be assured to be coveted by all Salish Sea Natives . . . the precious Huckleberry or *s.weda'x* in Southern Puget Sound language. Some individuals use specific indicators in the lower elevations of their villages to signify when it is time to make the annual pilgrimage to their favorite harvesting site, or as I like to refer to it, their very own "Huckleberry Heaven" which can be located anywhere between 3,500 to 6,000 feet above sea level. Indicators vary and will depend upon the individual. Some use the call of the Red Winged Flicker or some use the Fireweed plant to

> notify them that it is time to pull their baskets out of storage and prepare for approximately three weeks of gathering one of mother nature's most delectable and nutritious treats. The berry to this day is considered by some to be worth its weight in gold. The nutritional value alone places this food gift in a very unique category, the medicinal properties of which can address some extremely serious health issues among Native Communities in the 21st century.[4]

Indeed, the health benefits of huckleberries are highly praised. Ethnobotanists, archaeologists, and contemporary nutritionists agree that huckleberries provide a key component of the healthy Coast Salish diet. As Valerie Segrest (Muckleshoot tribal nutritionist) and ethnobotanist and herbalist Elise Krohn have argued,

> Huckleberries are one of the healthiest traditional foods, and quite possibly the reason that many Native elders lived to be over 100 years old. They are considered an anti-aging food . . . Antioxidants within the plant protect body tissue from damage by "free radicals" within the cell wall. They prevent inflammation and increase tissue strength. Additionally, huckleberries are one of the only fruits that does not raise blood sugar. All fruits contain natural sugars, but huckleberries have a compound that actually lowers blood sugar . . . making them a perfect food for diabetics.[5]

Tulalip Forestry Manager Jason Gobin explained the rationale for the proposed 2015 youth camp at *Swədaʔx̌ali*: "One of the most important things about Mountain Camp is getting our youth back into their mountain areas, and educating them, so they understand they have treaty rights there."[6] Working with huckleberries means learning their stories and songs. It means learning how to make the traditional baskets used for harvesting. It means bringing young people and elders out of the relatively urbanized context of the reservation and its surrounding cities. And it means reminding the Tulalip people that they are also people of the mountains.

Huckleberry cultivation also occurs within Coast Salish tribal gardens around the region. While mountain huckleberries can only be grown at high altitudes above three thousand feet, other varieties grow well at lower elevations, and are featured prominently in community gardens such as those at Tulalip, Muckleshoot, and Nisqually.

The Nisqually community garden was purchased by the tribe over fifteen years ago as part of a restoration project for salmon habitat on the Nisqually River. In addition to growing food and medicine for those living on the reservation, the garden also serves as an educational facility, offering instruction in harvesting and preparing traditional foods. It is adjacent to a ceremonial longhouse, where community members gather for meals and events. The garden currently grows three-quarters of an acre of vegetables, with an additional one-half an acre of traditional medicines, as well as a grove of berries and fruit trees.[7] During a visit, the Nisqually Community Garden program supervisor was asked about her favorite plant. She gestured toward the huckleberries. "The berries," she said. "Because [unlike the annuals] they're here year after year, growing and changing. I love seeing people coming up here every season, every year, working with the plants and seeing how they change. And besides, everyone loves berries."[8]

The past decade has seen a virtual explosion in tribal community gardening projects throughout Puget Sound, inspired in part by Northwest Indian College's remarkable Traditional Plants and Foods Program, which supports food sovereignty initiatives around Coast Salish territory. These initiatives include community gardens, kitchen gardens, classes, workshops, and symposia.[9] The Native Berry Garden at the Northwest Indian Drug and Alcohol Treatment Center is one such project, where patients have the opportunity to grow, harvest, and prepare huckleberries. As Traditional Foods Educator Elise Krohn, argues, "If you want people to heal, you have to treat them within their own culture, and a part of that culture is the use of native plants. If people can remember where they come from and what traditions are a part of their culture, that is where the healing begins."[10]

Huckleberries in Coast Salish Religious Traditions

In addition to their obvious health benefits, huckleberries also play an important role within Coast Salish religion and culture. The berries themselves have traditionally been honored in a Huckleberry Feast every summer. Culture bearer and ceremonial leader *Subiyay* (Gerald Bruce Miller) described four ceremonies necessary to maintain the balance of the Coast Salish world: the Huckleberry Feast, First Salmon Feast, Elk

Ceremony, and Cedar Ceremony. These ceremonies ensured that the people cultivated a spirit of humility and gratitude, and helped people maintain a harmonious relationship with the plant and animal people.[11] These first foods ceremonies were given after a time of great conflict, when human beings were nearly wiped out by their greed, violence, and jealousy. In the midst of a time of great famine, the human people and the animal people played a gambling game (in Coast Salish, *sləhal*), to determine who would live. With help from spirit songs of the more charitable plant and animal people, the human beings won. Thereafter, the plant and animal people would consent to become food. Monica Charles, Lower Elwha Klallam, explains the significance of the story this way: "Every day something gives up life so you might live. They all do it knowingly . . . We must give them thanks. This is why we do the traditional first foods ceremony."[12] In 1953, eighty-year-old Chehalis elder Silas Heck described a huckleberry ceremony, in which prayers of gratitude were offered to the Creator "for making these hills, for planting these berries." Only after offering the prayer were the people permitted to begin harvesting berries.[13]

Huckleberries also play an important role within one of the most sacred Coast Salish rites: the Soul Retrieval Ceremony, or *spəłtəʼdaq*. Within traditional Coast Salish worldviews, each individual is comprised of multiple aspects of the self: mind, spirit, shadow, soul, and guardian spirit power. Prompted by shock, grief, trauma, or loss, any one of these might depart from an individual and begin its journey to the land of the dead, threatening the life of the individual in question. If this were determined to be the case, a *spəłtəʼdaq* might be held.[14] Within the ceremony, a spiritual leader and his assistants would travel to the land of the dead, battle against dangerous obstacles, and return with the patient's lost soul. The rite could take several days, and was one of the most complex and dangerous ceremonies in the Coast Salish tradition. While the ceremony does not appear to have been held for nearly a century, it remains a powerful presence in Coast Salish memory, art, and story, and some spiritual leaders are working to bring it back.[15] Huckleberries were an important part of this soul retrieval ceremony: they were the only food carried by the practitioners on their journey. Sprigs of huckleberries adorned the carvings of the spirit helpers that would accompany the medicine men. And, should one of the healers manage to bring back a berry from the land of the dead, it ensured both well-being for the patient and the promise of a good berry harvest for the coming year.[16] Huckleberries thus take on a powerful symbolic resonance as plants that ensure health, long life, and spiritual rebirth and renewal. The Coast Salish are not alone in ascribing particular value and wisdom to Huckleberry. The Yakima, their neighbors to the east, explain that huckleberries, "have great power in the high country. They are the same as good words from the other world. They know everything. They do nothing wrong. They are very wise."[17]

"Listening to the Plant People": Relationships with Plants in Coast Salish Cultures

In order to better understand the significance of huckleberries within Coast Salish traditional cultures, it is necessary to remember that plants are not merely resources, but relatives and ancestors. The Tulalip are not simply picking berries. They are maintaining millennia-old *relationships with plant people*. In mythic times, plants were people, to whom Transformer (*Dukwibał*) assigned a task: to hold the earth together, to provide food, and to store up wisdom. The plant people were the people's first teachers, *Subiyay* explains, containers of wisdom and memory.

> [The plant people] were the first created in our oral tradition, before the animals, before the fish, before the birds, and their duty was to hold the earth together and live their life as a teaching for those who would be created in the future. The plants left many things to us as human beings. They left the ones who would be our food, they left the ones that would be our medicine, they left the ones that would be our building material, they left the ones that would be our basketry material, they left the ones that would be the scent and fragrance of the sacred in this universe, they left beauty and they dressed the earth. The earth was bare before the plant people were created.[18]

Coast Salish foodscapes reflect an edible and simultaneously relational landscape, populated with different peoples—plants, animals, and natural features that themselves have spirits and agency in the world. Plant and animal peoples are integral in the origin stories of many Coast Salish groups, where various bands and tribes are descended from particular plant and animal people.[19] "The tree people," describes Upper Skagit elder *Taqʷšəblu* (Vi Hilbert), "are our elders."[20]

For all of these reasons, plant medicine has as much to do with the prayerful process of gathering as it does with biochemistry. An herbalist at a south Puget Sound Native women and girls' gathering had this to say about working with medicinal plants: "Medicines are prayed for, and they reveal themselves to a person's spirit. It's their spirit that makes them effective. It's the relationship with the plant that makes them work . . . I thought that was just an old bush, a shrub, that that plant over there was just a weed. But no, I learned, Creator put spirit in everything, and it's the spirit that heals."[21]

Another way to explain this sense of kinship with huckleberries and other plant people is to consider the idea of *shxwelí*. The Coast Salish of the Fraser River Valley use the term *shxwelí* to explain their kinship relationship with the plant and animal people. In the era of the mythic Transformer, all persons were assigned tasks: some to be plants, some to be animals, some to be mountains or powerful rock formations. All things that were originally "persons" share in this spirit or life force or *shxwelí*. From this perspective, plants and animals are not "simply regarded as food and a resource," but instead "like an ancestor." Sto:lo elder Rosaleen George puts it this way.

> *Shxwelí* is inside us . . . it is in your parents . . . then your grandparents, your great grandparents, it's in your great-great-grandparents. It's in the rocks, it's in the trees, it's in the grass, it's in the ground. *Shxwelí* is everywhere. What ties us? . . . It's the shxweli. . . . So our resources are more than just resources, they are our extended family. They are our ancestors, our shxwelí . . . Our Elders tell us everyone has a spirit. So when we use a resource . . . we have to thank our ancestors who were transformed into those things.[22]

Within the Coast Salish worldview such notions of relationship and responsibility do not end with the human community. The idea of *shxwelí* requires that all spirits be treated with utmost respect, and encompasses the reciprocal relationship that exists between human people and plant people. The plant people who give themselves up so that the Coast Salish may eat do so out of compassion for the needs of the human people. "Such a view demands that one show reverence, care and respect when harvesting food and disposing of waste, taking care so that the plant or animal in question will be able to renew its life, providing food for future generations."[23] This sense of interconnection with all things raises the obligation to interact respectfully with food resources so as to properly honor the lives they have given up. The act of eating for Coast Salish people thus evokes and makes visceral those relationships that define one's life.

At the Nisqually community garden, one Nisqually tribal member shared her views on the spiritual practices associated with gathering food, which included praying, giving offerings, and properly preparing before gathering. They emphasized that the Nisqually are "people of the grasslands, people of the river"—that is, quite literally, descended from the grasslands and the river—and as such, have a responsibility to tend to their relations on the prairies and in the waters.[24] This individual explained that while many of the plants she harvests are for eating, such as wild strawberry, salmonberry, licorice roots, camas bulbs, and nettles, many are for making baskets or for medicines, such as cedar bark, cherry bark, black moss, and devil's club—and that all are sacred. To such participants, the act of gathering and cultivating traditional plants is a religious activity, explaining their relationship to resources in the following way:

> When you go gathering, you want to be in a good way—never angry, never upset—but it's hard to stay upset with plants, you know, because they sure have a way of taking it—that—out of you. They give you oxygen, they make you feel good, they bring you life . . . So you give an offering, whether it's water, tobacco, food. Sometimes if you don't give an offering, you know, you can get, you can a little bit get hurt, and that's just their way of taking the offering. Just a little scratch . . . When I gathered cedar, I went in a good way, and I gathered and I found a deer antler in the woods. And just this last week, I was gathering nettles in a patch, and I found another deer antler . . . You go gather these things, gifts are given.[25]

Here, gathering food at the farm is as much a spiritual experience as gathering in the woods; the plants she interacts with in both settings are sentient beings that must be treated with respect so that the gatherer may receive sustenance in turn. When one forgets the proper behavior for interacting with plant people, the result is physical injury, the plants' own way of "taking the offering." However, when the reciprocal nature of *shxwelí* is observed, "gifts are given." The Nisqually community garden is thus not only providing culturally appropriate foods that the tribe does not have access to or that are in diminishing supply, but it is also providing a spiritual outlet through the foods it grows and the opportunities for harvesting those foods.

Traditional Coast Salish elders still educate young people by encouraging them to spend time with the plant people, to seek spiritual growth "in the vast expanse of old-growth forest, gathering plants and preparing medicine."[26] And this is one reason why protecting and restoring habitats such as *Swədaʔx̌ ali* is so important. As *Subiyay* goes on to say, "Protecting the environment is essential, because the Skokomish spiritual philosophy focuses not on events but on relationships with entities like the earth, water, air, animals, and plant people. Maintaining this symbolic connection is important to the survival of our traditional culture, because a spiritual relationship with other life forms pervades all aspects of our life."[27]

Valerie Segrest, Muckleshoot Food Sovereignty project coordinator, explains that one of her primary goals is to help the community gain access to "the cultural teachings of our most revered traditional foods."[28] It is important to note that she does not say teachings *about* the foods, but the teachings *of* the foods. The foods *themselves* have wisdom to convey. As she writes elsewhere, learning these lessons can change lives. "Every plant and animal is thought to carry its own spiritual gifts, and the methods to honor these with prayers, songs and ceremonies are passed down through the generations. When young people become the caretakers of this knowledge, it gives them an important role and purpose in society."[29]

Not Your Hipster's Huckleberry: Food Sovereignty and the Alternative Food Movement

Having discussed the importance of huckleberries and other plants within the revitalization of Coast Salish foodways, we would like to pause a moment to consider how this case study sheds light on broader ethical issues within the predominately Euro-American alternative food movement (AFM). In their article "Environmental and Food Justice: Toward Local, Slow, and Deep Food Systems," Teresa Mares and Devon Peña begin by discussing a recent conversation between Peña and a friend. The friend, a vegan activist committed to "slow food," explained her personal food philosophy as a series of intimate connections between her plate, local farmers, and the land. She ate only local, organic, plant-based foods like grains, vegetables, fruits, and nuts from farmers or gatherers she knew personally, and every meal she ate was cooked from scratch. She prided herself on avoiding not only the animal suffering prevalent in the industrial food system, but also much of the human suffering caused by both animal food production and low-quality farmworker conditions in the United States. However, when asked about local Native American foodways, she drew a blank.

Mares and Peña argue that the way their vegan friend constructs ethical food consumption is shallow, overestimating and simplifying the impact she has had on her own ecological "footprint" and ignoring her very privileged position to make such consumption choices. Her narrative omits the fact that she, and the mostly white farmers in the Skagit Valley that she takes pride in buying from, are benefiting from a long history of colonial and structural violence against Native peoples. Her idealization of an agricultural past of slow meals and local foods in the United States is not accessible to everyone, and in fact for many may signify histories of displacement, indentured servitude, and slavery. "Should we not also," Mares and Peña question, "consider how a call to eat locally invokes spaces that have been settled, colonized, ruptured, and remade through complex processes of human movement and environmental history making?"[30]

The (predominantly Euro-American) alternative food movement is represented by such diverse organizations as farmers markets, Community Supported Agriculture (CSA), food co-ops, urban garden projects, and organic farms and farmers, and can be characterized by three values. One of the core values of the movement is a "back-to-the-land" rhetoric that celebrates a simpler style of living. This involves preparing meals from whole food ingredients and having either a physical or interpersonal relationship with local foodways. Second, the AFM employs a universal rhetoric, which maintains that the values it supports, specifically with regards to consuming local, organic, and natural foods, will benefit the health, social well-being, and environmental safety of everyone.[31]

Such an approach, however, with its emphasis on individualism and individual choice, can serve to occlude collective responsibility and the need for systemic change. Indeed, a third value the AFM emphasizes is personal change in consumption habits in order to live out the values it advocates. Advocates of alternative food argue that by buying socially and environmentally responsible food, this food is made more accessible to others; as Michael Pollan says in his book *In Defense of Food: An Eater's Manifesto*, "Not everyone can afford to eat high-quality food in America and that is shameful; however, those of us who can, should."[32] By contrast, the Indigenous food sovereignty movement supports a broader definition of the human "right to food," one that is informed by the history of colonialism, demands tribal sovereignty, and recognizes the importance of food in cultural, spiritual, and community revitalization.

Back to Whose Land?

Cultural Geographer Julie Guthman has argued that the alternative food movement, especially farmers markets and CSAs, are fueled by what she calls "whitened cultural histories" that place an emphasis on individual ethical food choices as a mechanism for change. Such an approach not only assumes a universalization of these "whitened" values and ideals, but ignores the larger structural and historical biases that have prevented Indigenous people from having control over their food choices. One of the most salient discourses in the alternative food movement is the idea of going "back to the land," expressing a desire to reconnect to an agrarian past, and idealizing those who have managed to do so (i.e., small-scale, local farmers). In her article "Unsettling Ecocriticism: Rethinking Agrarianism, Place, and Citizenship," Janet Fiskio discusses the tenets of what she terms the "agrarian myth," an idea that upholds the cultivation of an intimate relationship with the land and a sense of place through long-term habitation and physical labor.[33] Fiskio argues that the agrarian myth and the desire to have a connection with land have a long cultural history in the United States. For example, many of the European immigrants to the Americas came because of restrictive land-holding practices in Europe. For them, owning one's own land held a mythic power that bespoke individualism, frontierism, and the American Dream. Thomas Jefferson himself believed that farmers make the best citizens, an idea later echoed by sustainable farming advocate Wendell Berry in the 1970s, who emphasized working the land not only as a form of environmental political statement, but also as a resistance to what he saw as the loss of a "sense of place" among U.S. citizens.[34]

Barbara Kingsolver's best-selling book, *Animal, Vegetable, Miracle: A Year of Food Life*, provides an example of this back to the land ideal. Kingsolver chronicles her and her family's decision to eschew industrial foodways for one year in favor of eating only what they can grow, gather, or buy from local sources within a 100-mile radius of their rural farm. "We wanted to live in a place that could feed us," she says, "where rain falls, crops grow, and drinking water bubbles right up out of the ground."[35] Kingsolver is a success story of the agrarian myth, someone who forged her own relationship with food by returning to a simpler style of living and a more aesthetic understanding of what good food is.

However, the agrarian myth of a common agriculture background that we must return to is in itself highly problematic and exclusionary of Native people. Wendell Berry, Michael Pollan, Barbara Kingsolver, and others like them, all appear to overlook an important part of United States history. Historically, land ownership was limited to whites, while Native people were excluded from access to arable land. Under the Homestead Act, for instance, non-Native settlers could petition for 160 acres per person. Native people were excluded from the Act, and only eligible for 80 acres under the Dawes Severalty Act. According to Julie Guthman, "Land was virtually given away to whites at the same time that reconstruction failed in the South, Native American lands were appropriated, Chinese and Japanese were precluded from land ownership, and the Spanish-speaking *Californios* were disenfranchised of their ranches."[36] At other times reservation communities were coerced into farming, despite its incompatibility with their local ecosystem. Or, when Native people did show signs of success at agriculture, those lands were often lost as legislation, outright theft, or sharing the land among subsequent generations reduced their holdings to parcels too small to support growing families.[37] The fact that returning to traditional ways of working the land is lauded in environmental circles is ironic when one considers that many Native American populations are still unable to access their traditional hunting and gathering territories, and that Native populations espoused these goals long before any food activists did.[38] Guthman further argues that the assumption that returning to agricultural roots is a goal accessible to all races shows a lack of cultural competency and historical knowledge, which necessarily, if unintentionally, excludes non-Euro-Americans from the alternative food conversation.[39]

The alternative food movement is also dominated by a second narrative that is likewise tied to the agrarian myth: the nutritional and aesthetic superiority of organic and "natural" foods. "Organic" is held up as an idealized state of being in food discourse, synonymous with environmental responsibility, human health, and purity. It is also, for many, a status symbol—a way someone can "perform" their social class and standing through the food they consume. Because "organic" is often culturally associated with "expensive" and "white," it can have connotations of elitism and privilege along with its environmental and activist roots.[40] While shifting toward an organic food system is undeniably vital for a sustainable future on our planet, it is also the reality that ideas about organic food are tied up in a history of racism and classism.[41] In the alternative foodscape today, organic food can serve to differentiate those who have "good" taste from those who do not. It can also very easily serve as a recolonizing gesture, where Native people are "rescued" by well-meaning outsiders who appear to once again be making decisions on behalf of Native people.

But, one might argue, don't the goals of the alternative food movement align with those of tribal community gardens and Indigenous food advocates? In many ways, yes. But the problem is that many of these well-intentioned organizations don't stop at assuming a universally held (and non-Native) narrative will draw Native and other minority consumers. Instead, their discourse can focus with almost missionary zeal on converting perceived "others" to the local and sustainable food movements, disregarding the distinct histories and cultures of the people they are supposedly serving. This is problematic because such an approach ends up emphasizing personal responsibility for good food practices and preparation instead of seeking systematic change.

Guthman supports this claim, noting that because these organizations promote individual improvement and consumer responsibility to change the market, they also support a system of ideas that has historically disenfranchised Native people.[42] A fundamental tenet of the alternative food movement is that if just enough people make a commitment to "go local" or "go organic," the entire industrial system will be flipped on its head. When writers such as Pollan claim that those of us who can afford to buy high-quality food should, he puts those who can't afford high-quality food (regardless of the social phenomena that cause this) into the category of "other," outside of our moral consideration.[43] By emphasizing that individual changes in eating are solely responsible for changes in the food system, the alternative food movement operates within the framework of neoliberal values and goals, supporting a capitalist system that commodifies both food and people, the very issue their discourse seeks to address. A 2004–2005 study by Julie Guthman confirmed the racial disparity among customers of farmer's markets and CSAs. When asked to account for this, CSA and market managers all pointed to issues related to individual choice, claiming that those who chose to frequent these markets showed "more concern about food quality," were "more health conscious," and had "more time."[44] They resisted her suggestion that there might be a causal relationship between such racial disparity and issues of race or ethnicity, saying that targeting nonwhite or low-income consumers would compromise the color-blindness they were aiming for in their business.[45] Such strategies of "color-blindness" serve to further alienate those who do not accept the narratives implicit in the movement, and further occlude the structural, rather than personal inequalities that account for such disparities.

And, perhaps most important, it is this emphasis on the individual as the locus of reform that most distinguishes the predominately Euro-American alternative food movement from similar tribally led efforts.

The construct of a back-to-the-land rhetoric, the belief in the universal superiority of natural and organic foods, and the emphasis on individual mechanisms of change in the alternative food discourse serve to mark alternative food spaces such as farmers markets and CSAs as colonial spaces. Although certainly many Euro-American food activists are aware of neocolonial tensions in food discourse, racial and historical environmental injustice are not always prioritized in the discourse of alternative foodscapes, leading to the marginalization of Indigenous people within "sustainable food" conversations.[46]

Indigenous Food Sovereignty: Regaining the Right to Native Foods

While sharing many of the same goals and values as the alternative food movement, the Indigenous food sovereignty movement works toward those goals in very different ways. The Indigenous food sovereignty movement is made up of diverse groups ranging from local tribal food sovereignty projects and community gardens, to multinational peasant rights organizations. It differentiates itself from the alternative food movement by means of differing narratives and goals regarding food and the right to food. First, the Indigenous food sovereignty movement is characterized by a recognition of historic and current inequalities in Indigenous communities as the root cause of environmental and food injustice today, especially with regard to colonization, slavery, and commodification inherent in particular economic systems.[47] Second, the Indigenous food sovereignty movement embraces a diversity of definitions as to what constitutes "good food." What counts as good food is not necessarily what is organic or local or vegetarian, although it can encompass any of these things; rather, it depends on the stated goals of the community with regard to the food they wish to eat. This movement seeks to restore community sovereignty over their food consumption habits and methods, and emphasizes that "good" food is that which is culturally appropriate to the community.[48] Finally, the Indigenous food sovereignty movement argues that change is not about individual consumer choices, but requires a fundamental challenge to—even as they sometimes work in cooperation with—existing hegemonic power structures in order to more adequately transform them.[49]

Indigenous food sovereignty advocates emphasize *historical and current racial inequalities* as a main cause of community food insecurity and incorporate a broader definition of the right to food that includes both spiritual foodways and community agency. In contrast to the agrarian myth of the alternative food movement, the Indigenous food sovereignty movement approaches food justice by first acknowledging histories of oppression and racism that have resulted in disparate access to food in Indigenous communities. This puts the environmental concern of food access into a broader, historicized social context that ties it to the lived experiences of marginalized populations.[50] In their article "Breaking the Food Chains: An Investigation of Food Justice Activism," Alison Alkon and Kari Norgaard conducted an eighteen-month study of the Karuk Tribe's efforts to regain access to traditional fishing grounds on the Klamath River in northern California.[51] In opposition to what Julie Guthman encountered studying farmers market and CSA managers in California, Alkon and Norgaard found that tribal activists almost universally spoke of systematic and racial inequalities rather than poor individual food choices when discussing the primary causes of food insecurity and high rates of diet-related diseases. Norgaard asserts: "The Karuk tribe articulates their right to traditional foods not only as an issue of food insecurity but of food justice. They locate their current food needs in the history of genocide, lack of land rights, and forced assimilation that have so devastated this and other Native American communities. These processes have prevented tribal members from carrying out land management techniques necessary to food attainment."[52] Her interviews with tribal members particularly emphasized assimilation to a Western diet as marking the advent of many food access issues. They also associated health issues within the tribe with environmental degradation and racist practices that disproportionately degraded traditional Karuk fishing areas on the Klamath River. One tribal member explained, "A healthy riverine system has a profound effect on the people of the river . . . all the fishing community is devastated by the unhealthy riverine system."[53] This environmental degradation stems not only from Western interventions in the form of dams, deforestation, and development, but from the disruption of traditional Native land management, something that Norgaard admits is hard for non-Indians to appreciate.[54] "Institutionalized racism," Norgaard argues, "manifests not only as a disproportionate burden of exposure to environmental hazards, but also in denied access to decision-making and control over resources."[55] For the Karuk Tribe of California, the primary goals of their food sovereignty efforts are not limited to supporting sustainability efforts, but rather focus on mitigating a history of environmental violence that has resulted in a lack of food access.

The back-to-the-land rhetoric of the predominantly Euro-American alternative food movement implicitly denies another historical reality—that the Indigenous people of this place had a long history of land management and cultivation that looked very different from intensive European agriculture. In their book *Keeping It Living: Traditions of Plant Use and Cultivation on the Northwest Coast of North America*, Douglas Deur and Nancy Turner argue that anthropological scholarship has largely misrepresented Native land management practices, first denying their existence, and where admitting they exist, placing these cultivation practices on the "backward, less-developed side of the imaginary evolutionary scale."[56]

Turner and Deur point out that Coast Salish peoples used varying management techniques that, while unrecognizable to European settlers, maintained impressively large stores of over 300 plant species for food, materials, and medicine.[57] As the late Hank Gobin, Tulalip elder and former director of the Tulalip Tribes' Hibulb Cultural Center and Natural History Preserve argued, "For thousands of years, tribes nurtured the landscapes they depended upon for their health and survival. . . . That included land-management practices to maintain a diversity of plant and animal populations, like burning for wildlife forage, and pruning or burning for huckleberry."[58] Likewise, in contrast to Euro-American assumptions that the land was unclaimed and so free for the taking, Coast Salish communities had extensive and complex notions of ownership. However, unlike the extraction and commodification model favored by Euro-Americans, Coast Salish notions instead emphasized a reciprocal relationship with the place that entailed responsibilities to manage and care for the site, to ensure a respectful harvest, and to share those resources within ones' community.[59] "Wealth" in Coast Salish cultures had less do with private property, and far more to do with hereditary rights to knowledge, gathering sites, and the ability to share food with others.[60]

Tribal gardeners, along with Segrest, emphasize that food insecurity is tied to structural inequalities rather than personal choices, and that a legitimate history of land management contradicts colonial settler mythologies. Of particular concern for the Indigenous food sovereignty movement is the historic erasure of Native cultures. At the outset of a tour of the Nisqually Community Garden, the director began by acknowledging its Westernized layout, explaining the necessity for such a design, even though the Nisqually tribe's historical practices of prairie management functioned long before European settlement.

> You know, [the Nisqually] did practice agriculture—there was all sorts of cultivation—but the thing is that, the way we're growing here—tilling, growing row-crops—that's not traditional. There was a natural abundance, but that habitat has been largely destroyed. . . . and even in places where it still exists, it was banned to do things like burning and tending the prairies for a long time, and so access to those most traditional resources is just broken and doesn't exist anymore.[61]

Here, lack of access to traditional management techniques, environmental degradation, and histories of suppressing Native knowledge of the land are situated as key components in the Nisqually's food sovereignty story. When asked to characterize the causes of food insecurity in a community, the garden director spoke to a lack of financial resources, a lack of food providers (grocery stores, farmers markets, etc.), and in particular a lack of access to traditional foods and knowledge around harvesting and preparing those foods, again rejecting the idea that individual choice dictates who has access to what foods. "I think even if there is money and if there is a grocery store and if you do have access to things, if you don't have access to [traditional knowledge] . . . it's a big deal."[62] Segrest, director of the Muckleshoot food sovereignty program agrees: "We're dealing with healing from historical trauma . . . where our communities were told that the knowledge we carry was not important and was not heard."[63]

The same sentiment is reiterated at She Nah Nam Seafood, a Native-run seafood processing company that seeks to help tribal fishermen and women earn a living wage. Three men involved with the company shared their perspectives on what food sovereignty means in Puget Sound. Throughout the interview two men, one a Nisqually tribal member and the other from the nearby Quinault tribe, repeatedly attributed food insecurity in Coast Salish communities to fish mismanagement practices, lack of government adherence to treaty fishing rights, and environmental degradation. They explained that one of the main goals of their organization was to preserve the right to traditional fishing locations and techniques, the same rights that Nisqually fishing rights activist and environmentalist Billy Frank Jr. fought for his whole life.[64] However, while all three men emphasized the importance of sharing their knowledge and pride of fishing traditions, they recognized that many of the struggles Native communities face in obtaining both knowledge and resources is largely due to an economic and political system that has historically disenfranchised them. "This food and the food we have access to is a lot healthier than going around the corner to the next McDonald's. But they just keep shoving [that food] down these young people's throats." The third man, also a Nisqually tribal member added, "We just don't have as deep pockets as they do."[65]

The view of food sovereignty exemplified by activists of the Karuk tribe, the Nisqually community garden, and She Nah Nam Seafood implicitly rejects the "color-blindness" of the white alternative food movement, asserting the historical realities of genocide, displacement, forced assimilation, and devaluation of Native foodways and food knowledge. Although environmental issues are prioritized, they are seen in a colonial context where the degradation and domination of the land is intimately connected with the oppression faced by its people. Native food activist Alysha Waters makes clear that many contemporary health crises in Native communities are directly tied to this history of colonialism and displacement.

> Only a hundred and fifty years ago, the ancestors of this region were the healthiest of any group of peoples living upon the earth. Cancer was very rare and diabetes and heart disease were virtually unknown. For thousands of years Pacific Northwest tribes had food production systems that sustained healthy communities. These foods systems were rich in tradition and ceremony while connecting integrally to trade commerce and sound environmental practices. . . . The health and nutrition of Indian peoples has been greatly affected by the destruction of sustainable Native American food production systems. . . . Recent research and traditional ways and knowledge both indicate that where native peoples live, eating local indigenous foods is better for our bodies, our communities, our economies and the land itself.[66]

Such arguments make clear that narratives regarding food and spiritual foodways in the Indigenous food sovereignty movement inform a different understanding of environmental injustice and the human "right to food" than is found in the alternative food movement. While a growing number of non-Native organizations—such as Seattle Tilth—have grown sensitive to these concerns, and are working to become allies with Native communities, more work needs to be done. Emphasis on previously devalued knowledge of the land and historical oppression serves to reject the color-blind assertions of many white food activists, redirecting one's focus toward tribal sovereignty and the history of colonialism instead of seeing individual choice as a main player in food insecurity.

Food Sovereignty versus Food Security: Moving toward a Coast Salish Ethos

While NGOs and other food rights organizations emphasize the challenge of *food scarcity*, tribal communities point to a historic degradation of Native land and foodways as a rationale for *food sovereignty*. The United Nations Food and Agriculture Association (FAO) includes three concepts in its definition of food security: physical availability of food; physical and economic ability to access food; and nutritional adequacy of food. The Indigenous food sovereignty movement argues instead for several new rights, including the "right to produce food" and "the right of peoples to food sovereignty," wherein local communities can claim a more active role in food policy.[67] The European Food Sovereignty Movement and the United Nations define food sovereignty as "the right to sufficient, healthy, and culturally appropriate food for all individuals, peoples and communities," as well as local agency over managing and protecting Indigenous resources.[68] For Coast Salish communities, local agency over food resources means the formation of both intertribal alliances (like the Northwest Indian Fisheries Commission, the South Puget Intertribal Planning Agency, or Northwest Indian College's Traditional Foods Program) and tribally based programs like community gardens, cooking and preserving classes, and first food ceremonies. And, it means working collaboratively with public lands management agencies like the United States Forest Service to develop ways to comanage their traditional territories—as the Tulalip are doing at *Swədaʔx̌ ali*.

Such efforts are giving rise to a distinctly Coast Salish perspective on food sovereignty and what it means for the Native people of this bioregion. Tulalip elder Inez Bill leads the Rediscovery Program based out of the Tulalip tribe's Hibulb Cultural Center, and has thought at great length about what it means for her Tulalip people to be in relationship with their ancestral foods. As she explains, "Our [particular] teachings and values for preparing food and meals are unique to our people . . . To prepare food in our traditional way is to share a part of ourselves with our people . . . I teach the youth workers not to harvest the whole plant, to make it like we were never here, and to thank the plant . . . there's respect in every aspect of our way of life."[69] Bill proposes several traditional values that should guide those gathering traditional foods like huckleberries. These include taking only what you need; remembering not to waste any traditional foods; sharing what you gather with family, friends, and elders; praying and giving thanks when gathering; and preparing local Native food for gatherings. She also notes that the people should prepare food "with a good heart and mind," because "the feelings of those who prepare the meal are equally important." Doing so, she explains, provides "nourishment for our people and their spirits," and even more, it also nourishes "the spirits of our ancestors."[70]

After a series of workshops and interviews with primarily Coast Salish people around Puget Sound, Segrest and Krohn also compiled a list of what they termed "Traditional Food Principles" that inform and inspire tribal food sovereignty projects in the region:

1. Food is at the center of culture. When people harvest, prepare, and share food together, it changes the way they see their landscape and their community.
2. Honor the food web. "Everything is connected," and all actions should be undertaken with that in mind.
3. Eat with the seasons. The people with whom Segrest and Krohn spoke emphasized "the power of being in the moment, and harvesting what is available," which works both to strengthen relationships with the plant and animal people, and also ensures future biodiversity.
4. Eat a variety of foods.
5. Traditional foods are whole foods.
6. Eat local.
7. Wild and organic are better for health.
8. Cook and eat with good intention. Harvesting, preparing and eating food can and should be a spiritual practice,

> one that ties you to your place, your ancestors, and your community. "Cooking is a time to honor the foods we eat. It is a time to pay respect to the life that has been given to nourish our bodies. The food we consume ties us into our place and our purpose in that place . . . thank the plants and animals that gave their lives to sustain yours."[71]

Interviews at She Nah Nam Seafood revealed similar ideas about the importance of food and community. The men spoke to a feeling of rightness with the world when they went fishing, and one consistently referred to the act of fishing or hunting as a relationship one has with a specific animal. They emphasized the importance of catching the first salmon of the season and of sharing the first salmon with the larger community, particularly elders. Generosity has always defined ideal Coast Salish kinship relations, where food, considered a gift from a spiritual being, was to be shared freely not only within tribes, but within an extended kinship network. This notion of sharing was emphasized several times in these conversations. "I'm providing for my family, taking care of my elders," one explained. "You're doing something you're supposed to be doing."

"Every Time I Pick a Berry I Remember My Ancestors"

When Tulalip youth head up to the huckleberry fields at *Swədaʔx̌ ali* for a weeklong camp, they'll be doing more than harvesting these highly valued berries. They'll also be cultivating their cultural memory. As young people gather the huckleberries, gathering them into traditionally made baskets, they'll be learning the stories that go along with that harvest, the songs, and the prayers. They'll be learning who they are, who their ancestors were. They'll be remembering that they are people of the salt water, and also people of the mountains. Segrest emphasizes this connection between food, memory, and identity in her work: "That's what people are craving—more than carbohydrates and protein. They want a connection with food, with the environment, with community. These foods help us remember who we are."[72] Picking a huckleberry is no simple act. It is a radical gesture that weaves one's identity back into one's culture, reinvigorating relationships with the spirits of the surrounding landscape and the spirits of one's ancestors. Segrest concludes, "I often say that I don't think I'm really teaching anything. I'm helping people remember what they already know. . . . Put a traditional food on a plate, and people start to remember."[73]

Harvesting traditional foods thus provides a primary means of connecting Coast Salish individuals with their ancestors, their families, and their communities. Harvesting, preparing, serving, and celebrating traditional foods binds tribal communities together.[74] It is a collective healing from a history of structural and systemic violence and oppression, a reclaiming of culture and an affirmation of ancient spiritual values. As Segrest and Krohn observe, "There is a sense of vitality and belonging that comes with eating the foods that gave your ancestors health and longevity for thousands of years."[75] Charlene Krise, director of the Squaxin Island tribe's museum and cultural center provides a final powerful example the place of plants in memory, identity, and community.

> Memories of my grandmother, Annie Jackson Krise, and grand-aunt Elvina are easily awakened by the sight, smell, touch, and taste of traditional plants. I remember as a child being taught about the importance of traditional plants, which ones were used for food. The traditional way of gathering as a group has continued through the generations of my grandparents, parents, aunts, uncles, cousins, siblings, and myself. . . . I remember my uncle and the strong smell of yarrow. . . . My dad gathered wild roses. . . . I still gather food and medicines from the forest. Gathering reminds me of my loved ones who have passed. Every time I pick a berry, I remember my ancestors. Every time I smell yarrow, I remember by grandmother. Every time I drink Indian tea, I remember by uncle. The activity of gathering keeps these memories alive.[76]

Notes

1. Nancy Chapman Turner and Marcus A. M. Bell, "The Ethnobotany of the Coast Salish Indians of Vancouver Island," *Economic Botany* 25, no. 1 (1971): 63–104. See also Leo Hitchcock and Arthur Cronquist, *Flora of the Pacific Northwest* (Seattle: University of Washington Pres, 1973).

2. Nancy Turner and Dawn Loewen, "The Original 'Free Trade': Exchange of Botanical Products and Associated Plant Knowledge in Northwestern America," *Ethnobiology* (1998): 49–70/54.

3. Ella Clark, Indian Thanksgiving in the Pacific Northwest, *Oregon Historical Quarterly* 61, no. 4 (1960): 445.

4. Warren King George, "Traditional Foods, Huckleberry Heaven and Restoration," *Feeding the People*: 68. "Oral tradition tells us that families took care of certain harvest grounds in a variety of ways including pruning, caring for the soil, and weeding out unwanted species" (*Feeding the People*, 7).

5. Krohn and Segrest, *Feeding the People*, 67.

6. http://www.tulalipnews.com/wp/2015/03/20/nurturing-connections-coast-salish-culture-and-the-natural-world/. See also Andrew Gobin, "Swedax'ali: Huckleberry Hill," *Tulalip News* (August 27, 2013). http://www.tulalipnews.com/wp/2013/08/27/swədxali-huckleberry-hill/.

7. Personal communication, Nisqually Community Garden, March 2014.

8. Personal communication, Nisqually Community Garden, April 11, 2015.

9. http://nwicplantsandfoods.com.

10. Brandi Montruel, "Hibulb Cultural Center Features Author Elise Krohn," *Tulalip News* (November 21, 2012): http://www.tulalipnews.com/wp/2012/11/21/hibulb-cultural-center-features-author-elise-krohn/ (accessed May 29, 2015).

11. Bruce Subiyay Miller, "Seeds of Our Ancestors," in *Spirit of the First People: Native American Music Traditions of Washington* State, eds. Willie Smyth and Esme Ryan (University of Washington Press, 1999), 41–42.

12. Krohn and Segrest, *Feeding the People*, 10.

13. Clark, "Indian Thanksgiving," 456.

14. See Jay Miller, *Lushootseed Culture and the Shamanic Odyssey: An Anchored Radiance* (Lincoln, University of Nebraska Press, 1999).

15. http://www1.seattleartmuseum.org/exhibit/interactives/sabadeb/flash/index.html.

16. See Suzanne Crawford O'Brien, *Coming Full Circle: Spirituality and Wellness among Native Communities in the Pacific Northwest* (University of Nebraska Press, 2014): 305–9.

17. Clark, "Indian Thanksgiving," 440.

18. NWIC Plants and Foods, Northwest Indian College, April 4, 2015. http://nwicplantsandfoods.com/plant-medicine.

19. Suzanne Crawford O'Brien, "Salmon as Sacrament: First Salmon Ceremonies in the Pacific Northwest," *Religion, Food and Eating in North America*, eds. Benjamin Zeller, Marie Dallam, Reid Neilson and Nora Rubel (New York: Columbia University Press, 2014), 8.

20. *Teachings of the Tree People: The Work of Bruce Subiyay Miller*, Islandwood Films, 2006.

21. Crawford O'Brien, *Coming Full Circle*, 183.

22. Albert McHalsie, "We Have to Take Care of Everything That Belongs to Us," in *Be of Good Mind: Essays on the Coast Salish*, ed. Bruce Granville Miller (Vancouver: University of British Columbia Press, 2007), 104.

23. Crawford O'Brien, "Salmon as Sacrament," 12.

24. Personal communication, Nisqually Community Garden (April 2, 2014).

25. Personal communication, Nisqually Community Garden (April 2, 2014).

26. Gerald B. Miller, D. Michael Pavel, and Mary J. Pavel, "Too Long, Too Silent: The Threat to Cedar and the Sacred Ways of the Skokomish," *American Indian Culture and Research Journal* 17, no. 3 (1993): 54.

27. Miller, Pavel, and Pavel, "Too Long, Too Silent," 55.

28. "Muckleshoot," *Northwest Indian College Traditional Plants and Foods Program* http://nwicplantsandfoods.com/muckleshoot (accessed May 10, 2015).

29. *Feeding the People*, 9.

30. Teresa Mares and Devon Peña, "Environmental and Food Justice: Toward Local, Slow, and Deep Food Systems," in *Cultivating Food Justice: Race, Class, and Sustainability*, edited by Alison Alkon and Julian Agyeman (Cambridge, MA: MIT Press, 2011): 198.

31. Julie Guthman, "Bringing Good Food to Others: Investigating the Subjects of Alternative Food Practice," *Cultural Geographies* 15 (2008): 435.

32. Michael Pollan, *In Defense of Food: An Eater's Manifesto* (New York: Penguin Press, 2008): 241.

33. Janet Fiskio, "Unsettling Ecocriticsm: Rethinking Agrarianism, Place, and Citizenship," *American Literature* 84, no. 2 (2012): 302.

34. Fiskio, "Unsettling Ecocriticism," 303–4.

35. Barbara Kingsolver, Steven Hopp, and Camille Kingsolver, *Animal, Vegetable, Miracle: A Year of Food Life* (New York: HarperCollins Publishers, 2007), 3.

36. Julie Guthman, "'If They Only Knew': The Unbearable Whiteness of Alternative Food," in *Cultivating Food Justice: Race Class, and Sustainability*, eds. Alison Alkon and Julian Agyeman (Cambridge, MA: MIT Press, 2011), 276.

37. See Janet McDonnell, *The Dispossession of the American Indian* (Indianapolis: Indiana University Press, 1991).

38. Mares and Peña, "Environmental and Food Justice," 201.

39. Guthman, "If They Only Knew," 276.

40. Josée Johnston and Shyon Bumann, *Foodies: Democracy and Distinction in the Gourmet Foodscape* (New York: Routledge, 2010), 22.

41. Guthman, "Bringing Good Food," 435.

42. Guthman, "Bringing Good Food," 437.

43. Guthman, "If They Only Knew," 276.

44. Guthman, "If They Only Knew," 268.

45. Guthman, "If They Only Knew," 270.

46. See also R. Panelli and G. Tipa, "Beyond Foodscapes: Considering Geographies of Indigenous Well-Being," *Health & Place* 15, no. 2 (2009): 455–65.

47. Alison Alkon, and Kari Norgaard, "Breaking the Food Chains: An Investigation of Food Justice Activism," *Sociological Inquiry* 79, no. 3 (2009): 295–97.

48. Priscilla Claeys, "The Creation of New Rights by the Food Sovereignty Movement: The Challenge of Institutionalizing Subversion," *Sociology* 46, no. 5 (2012): 850.

49. Claeys, "The Creation of New Rights," 850.

50. Alkon and Norgaard, "Breaking the Food Chains," 294.

51. Alkon and Norgaard, "Breaking the Food Chains," 293–300.

52. Alkon and Norgaard, "Breaking the Food Chains," 289, 297.

53. Alkon and Norgaard, "Breaking the Food Chains," 297.

54. Kari Marie Norgaard, Ron Reed, and Carolina Van Horn, "A Continuing Legacy: Institutional Racism, Hunger, and Nutritional Justice on the Klamath," in Alison Hope Alkon and Julian Agyeman, *Cultivating Food Justice: Race, Class and Sustainability* (Cambridge: MIT Press, 2011), 29.

55. Norgaard, Reed, and Van Horn, 28.

56. Douglas Deur and Nancy Turner, *Keeping It Living: Traditions of Plant Use and Cultivation on the Northwest Coast of North America* (Seattle: University of Washington Press, 2005), viii.

57. Deur and Turner, *Keeping It Living*, 11–13.

58. Kari Neumeyer, "Tulalip Tribes Replenish Huckleberry Gathering Areas," Northwest Indian Fisheries Commission (December 8, 2011), http://nwifc.org/2011/12/tulalip-tribes-replenish-huckleberry-gathering-areas/. See also Dana Lepofsky, Douglas Hallett, Ken Lertzman, Rolf Mathewes, Albert (Sonny) McHalsie, and Kevin Washbrook, "Documenting Precontact Plant Management on the Northwest Coast: An Example of Prescribed Burning in the Central and Upper Fraser Valley, British Columbia," in *Keeping It Living: Traditions of Plant Use and Cultivation on the Northwest Coast of North America*, eds. Douglas Deur and Nancy Turner (Seattle: University of Washington Press, 2005). See also Leslie Johnson Gottesfeld, "Aboriginal Burning for Vegetation Management in Northwestern British Columbia," *Human Ecology* 22, no. 2 (1994): 171–88. Likewise, Trusler and Johnson make a compelling case that any assessment of ideal sites for indigenous plants must take into account their engagement with Indigenous human populations. Plants were traditionally managed by Native communities, and evolved in relationship with them. Understanding Native plants, they argue "requires an enhanced appreciation for the sophistication of the strategies and techniques employed in their management and utilization." Scott Trusler and Leslie Main Johnson, "'Berry Patch' as a Kind of Place: The Ethnoecology of Black Huckleberry in Northwestern Canada," *Human Ecology* 36 (2008): 553–68.

59. Nancy J. Turner, Robin Smith, and James T. Jones, "'A Fine Line Between Two Nations': Ownership Patterns for Plant Resources among Northwest Coast Indigenous Peoples," in *Keeping It Living: Traditions of Plant Use and Cultivation on the Northwest Coast of North America*, eds. Douglas Deur and Nancy Turner (Seattle: University of Washington Press, 2005).

60. Crawford O'Brien, *Coming Full Circle*, 252.

61. Personal Communication, April 2, 2014.

62. Personal Communication, April 2, 2014.

63. Valerie Segrest, "Food and Diversity," Panel Discussion, Symposium on Food Justice, Pacific Lutheran University, April 3, 2014.

64. See Charles Wilkinson, *Messages From Frank's Landing: A Story of Salmon, Treaties and the Indian Way* (Seattle: University of Washington Press, 2006).

65. Personal Communication, April 2, 2014.

66. Alysha Waters, "Native American Food Production Systems, a Historic Perspective: Their Link to Healthy Communities," *Native Women's Wellness Newsletter* (Summer 2001): 6–7.

67. Claeys, "The Creation of New Rights," 848–49.

68. https://nyelenieurope.net/food-sovereignty, accessed November 25, 2017.

69. Kari Neumeyer, "Tulalip Tribes Harvest Highly Nutritious Stinging Nettles," *Northwest Coast Indian Fisheries Commission* (May 13, 2014): http://nwifc.org/2014/05/tulalip-tribes-harvest-highly-nutritious-stinging-nettles/.

70. Both, Krohn and Segrest, *Feeding the People*, 42.

71. Krohn and Segrest, *Feeding the People*, 33–37.

72. Kim Ekhart, "Traditional Foods Help Remind Us Who We Are," *Yes! Magazine*, October 30, 2012, http://www.yesmagazine.org/issues/its-your-body/tribe-revives-traditional-diet.

73. Ekhart, "Traditional Foods."

74. Elaine Power, Conceptualizing Food Security for Aboriginal People in Canada," *Canadian Journal of Public Health*, 2008, 95–97.

75. Krohn and Segrest, *Feeding the People*, 9.

76. Charlene Krise, "Memories of Gathering," *Native Women's Wellness Newsletter* (Summer 2001): 1–3.

Bibliography

Alkon, Alison, and Kari Norgaard. "Breaking the Food Chains: An Investigation of Food Justice Activism." *Sociological Inquiry* 79, no. 3 (2009): 289–305.

Claeys, Priscilla. "The Creation of New Rights by the Food Sovereignty Movement: The Challenge of Institutionalizing Subversion," *Sociology* 46, no. 5 (2012): 844–60.

Clark, Ella. "Indian Thanksgiving in the Pacific Northwest." *Oregon Historical Quarterly* 61, no. 4 (1960): 437–56.

Crawford O'Brien, Suzanne. "Salmon as Sacrament: First Salmon Ceremonies in the Pacific Northwest." In *Religion, Food and Eating in North America*, edited by Benjamin Zeller, Marie Dallam, Reid Neilson, and Nora Rubel. New York: Columbia University Press, 2014, 114–33.

Crawford O'Brien, Suzanne. *Coming Full Circle: Spirituality and Wellness among Native Communities in the Pacific Northwest.* Lincoln: University of Nebraska Press, 2014.

Deur, Douglas, and Nancy Turner. *Keeping It Living: Traditions of Plant Use and Cultivation on the Northwest Coast of North America.* Seattle: University of Washington Press, 2005.

Ekhart, Kim. "Traditional Foods Help Remind Us Who We Are," *Yes! Magazine.* October 30, 2012. http://www.yesmagazine.org/issues/its-your-body/tribe-revives-traditional-diet.

Fiskio, Janet. "Unsettling Ecocriticsm: Rethinking Agrarianism, Place, and Citizenship." *American Literature* 84, no. 2 (2012): 301–25.

Food and Agricultural Organization of the United Nations. *An Introduction to the Basic Concepts of Food Security*, 2013. Accessed May 20, 2015. http://www.fao.org/docrep/013/al936e/al936e00.pdf.

Gobin, Andrew. "Swedax'ali: Huckleberry Hill." *Tulalip News*, August 27, 2013. Accessed May 29, 2015. http://www.tulalipnews.com/wp/2013/08/27/swədxali-huckleberry-hill/.

Gobin, Jason, and Libby Nelson: "Enhancing Tulalip Treaty Gathering on Ancestral Lands." Presented at The Living Breath of *Wəɬəbʔaltxʷ*: Indigenous Ways of Knowing, Cultural Food Practices and Ecological Knowledge Symposium, University of Washington, May 1–2, 2013.

Gottesfeld, Leslie Johnson. "Aboriginal Burning for Vegetation Management in Northwestern British Columbia." *Human Ecology* 22, no. 2 (1994): 171–88.

Guthman, Julie. "Bringing Good Food to Others: Investigating the Subjects of Alternative Food Practice." *Cultural Geographies* 15 (2008): 421–37.

Guthman, Julie. " 'If They Only Knew': The Unbearable Whiteness of Alternative Food." In *Cultivating Food Justice: Race Class, and Sustainability*, edited by Alison Alkon and Julian Agyeman. Cambridge, MA: MIT Press, 2011, 263–82.

Hillary, Francesca. "Nurturing Connections: Coast Salish Culture and the Natural World." *Tulalip News*, March 20, 2015. Accessed May 29, 2015. http://www.tulalipnews.com/wp/2015/03/20/nurturing-connections-coast-salish-culture-and-the-natural-world/.

Jennings, Katie (director). *Teachings of the Tree People: The Work of Bruce Miller.* Islandwood Media, 2006.

Johnston, Josée, and Shyon Bumann. *Foodies: Democracy and Distinction in the Gourmet Foodscape.* New York: Routledge, 2010.

Kerns, Becky, Susan Alexander, and John Bailey. "Huckleberry Abundance, Stand Conditions, and Use in Western Oregon: Evaluating the Role of Forest Management." *Economic Botany* 58, no. 4 (2004): 668–78.

Kingsolver, Barbara, Steven Hopp, and Camille Kingsolver. *Animal, Vegetable, Miracle: A Year of Food Life.* New York: Harper Collins Publishers, 2007.

Krise, Charlene. "Memories of Gathering," *Native Women's Wellness Newsletter* (Summer 2001): 1–3.

Krohn, Elise, and Valerie Segrest. *Feeding the People, Feeding the Spirit: Revitalizing Northwest Coastal Indian Food Culture*. Centralia, WA: Gorham Publishing, 2010.

Mares, Teresa, and Devon Peña. "Environmental and Food Justice: Toward Local, Slow, and Deep Food Systems." *Cultivating Food Justice: Race, Class, and Sustainability*, edited by Alison Alkon and Julian Agyeman. Cambridge, MA: MIT Press, 2011, 197–220.

McHalsie, Albert. "We Have to Take Care of Everything That Belongs to Us." In *Be of Good Mind: Essays on the Coast Salish*, edited by Bruce Granville Miller. Vancouver: University of British Columbia Press, 2007.

Lepofsky, Dana, Douglas Hallett, Ken Lertzman, Rolf Mathewes, Albert (Sonny) McHalsie, and Kevin Washbrook. "Documenting Precontact Plant Management on the Northwest Coast: An Example of Prescribed Burning in the Central and Upper Fraser Valley, British Columbia." In *Keeping it Living: Traditions of Plant Use and Cultivation on the Northwest Coast of North America*, edited by Douglas Deur and Nancy Turner. Seattle: University of Washington Press, 2005.

McMillan, Tracie. *The American Way of Eating*. New York: Scribner, 2012.

Miller, Jay. *Lushootseed Culture and the Shamanic Odyssey: An Anchored Radiance*. Lincoln: University of Nebraska Press, 1999.

Miller, Gerald Bruce (Subiyay). "Seeds of Our Ancestors." In *Spirit of the First People: Native American Music Traditions of Washington* State, edited by Willie Smyth and Esme Ryan. Seattle: University of Washington Press, 1999, 37–43.

Miller, Gerald Bruce, D. Michael Pavel, and Mary J. Pavel. "Too Long Too Silent: The Threat to Cedar and the Sacred Ways of the Skokomish." *American Indian Culture and Research Journal* 17, no. 3 (1993): 53–80.

Montruel, Brandi. "Hibulb Cultural Center Features Author Elise Krohn." *Tulalip News*, November 21, 2012. Accessed May 29, 2015. http://www.tulalipnews.com/wp/2012/11/21/hibulb-cultural-center-features-author-elise-krohn/.

Neff, Roni, Cindy Parker, Frederick Kirschenmann, Jennifer Tinch, and Robert Lawrence. "Peak Oil, Food Systems, and Public Health." *American Journal of Public Health* 101, no. 9 (2011): 1587–98.

Neumeyer, Kari. "Tulalip Tribes Harvest Highly Nutritious Stinging Nettles." *Northwest Coast Indian Fisheries Commission* (May 13, 2014). http://nwifc.org/2014/05/tulalip-tribes-harvest-highly-nutritious-stinging-nettles/.

Norgaard, Kari Marie, Ron Reed, and Carolina Van Horn. "A Continuing Legacy: Institutional Racism, Hunger, and Nutritional Justice on the Klamath." In Alison Hope Alkon and Julian Agyeman, *Cultivating Food Justice: Race, Class and Sustainability* (Cambridge, MA: MIT Press, 2011), 23–46.

Northwest Indian College Traditional Plants and Foods Program. "Muckleshoot." Accessed May 10, 2015. http://nwicplantsandfoods.com/muckleshoot.

Northwest Indian College Traditional Plants and Foods Program. Accessed May 15, 2015 "Plant Medicine." http://nwicplantsandfoods.com/plant-medicine.

Personal interviews. Nisqually Community Garden. April 2, 2014 and April 11, 2015.

Personal interviews. She Nah Nam Seafood. April 11, 2014.

Pollan, Michael. "An Open Letter to the Next Farmer-in-Chief." *New York Times*, October 12, 2008.

Pollan, Michael. *In Defense of Food: An Eater's Manifesto*. New York: Penguin Press, 2008.

Power, Elaine. "Conceptualizing Food Security for Aboriginal People in Canada." *Canadian Journal of Public Health* (2008): 95–97.

Rios, Michael. "Seventh Annual Tulalip Tribes and U.S. Forest Service Meeting." *Tulalip News*, January 21, 2015. Accessed May 29, 2015 http://www.tulalipnews.com/wp/2015/01/21/7th-annual-tulalip-tribes-and-u-s-forest-service-moa-meeting/.

Nyéléni Forum for Food Sovereignty. *Synthesis Report*, 2007. Accessed May 20, 2015. http://www.nyeleni.org/spip.php?rubrique2.

Turner, Nancy Chapman, and Marcus A. M. Bell. "The Ethnobotany of the Coast Salish Indians of Vancouver Island." *Economic Botany* 25, no. 1 (1971): 63–104.

Turner, Nancy, and Dawn Loewen. "The Original 'Free Trade': Exchange of Botanical Products and Associated Plant Knowledge in Northwestern America." *Ethnobiology* (1998): 49–70.

Turner, Nancy J., Robin Smith, and James T. Jones. " 'A Fine Line between Two Nations': Ownership Patterns for Plant Resources among Northwest Coast Indigenous Peoples." In *Keeping It Living: Traditions of Plant Use and Cultivation on the Northwest Coast of North America*, edited by Douglas Deur and Nancy Turner. Seattle: University of Washington Press, 2005.

Waters, Alysha. "Native American Food Production Systems, a Historic Perspective: Their Link to Healthy Communities." *Native Women's Wellness Newsletter* (Summer 2001): 6–7.

Weis, Tony. "The Accelerating Biophysical Contradictions of Industrial Capitalist Agriculture." *Journal of Agrarian Change* 10, no. 3 (2010): 315–41.

Wilkinson, Charles. *Messages From Frank's Landing: A Story of Salmon, Treaties and the Indian Way*. Seattle: University of Washington Press, 2006.

7

The Black Drink throughout Cherokee History

R. Alfred Vick

Introduction

Prior to European contact with the indigenous cultures of southeastern North America, a particular beverage occupied an important place in the ceremonial, social, and medicinal aspects of Indian communities. The Black Drink, as it came to be known, was a ubiquitous part of aboriginal life in a similar manner as coffee or tea today, although its consumption was not as casual. Black Drink is a tea derived from the leaves and small twigs of yaupon holly (*Ilex vomitoria* Ait.), a native North American holly species. This tea has also been known as Asi, Cassina, South Sea Tea, Yaupon Tea, and other names. Yaupon holly is the only North American plant that contains significant amounts of the familiar stimulant, caffeine. In many indigenous communities Black Drink was consumed on a daily basis as a stimulating social beverage, often associated with a morning gathering of men to discuss important issues and politics. Its use often took on a more ceremonial formality as a way to welcome guests, engage in treaty negotiations or as a part of ceremonies such as the Creek Busk or the Cherokee Green Corn Ceremony. The Black Drink was used to promote benevolence, friendship, and peace within the town and with visitors.[1] These functions, along with others, including use as a medicine, are all derived from Black Drink's overarching usage as a powerful means to attain ritual purity.[2]

Descriptions of Black Drink pervade the historical literature, however its usage seems to have relatively abruptly ceased at some point after European contact. Substantial historical accounts have documented the importance of Black Drink in Creek ceremonial life up until the period of Removal. However, the Cherokee Indians have had a particularly perplexing history with Black Drink. Some historical accounts parallel the religious importance of the Muskogean people, while other notable sources barely mention the drink's former existence in the culture. This chapter explores the history and significance of Black Drink among the Cherokee, and other Southeastern Indians, and documents several factors that contributed to the abandonment of Black Drink (brewed with yaupon holly) as a culturally significant beverage.

Yaupon Holly Botany

Yaupon holly is an evergreen shrub found throughout the Atlantic and Gulf Coastal Plain of the southeastern United States. Its natural range extends from the northern coast of Virginia to central Florida, and west to Oklahoma and eastern Texas.[3] It is typically found growing in the coastal dunes, maritime forests, upland woodlands and pine flatwoods of these coastal areas.[4] It is also found in wetter areas such as floodplains, stream banks and wet woodlands, although it does best in well-drained soils. Other plant species often associated with yaupon in these environments include: wax myrtle, saw palmetto, yucca, live oak, longleaf pine, partridge berry, and bracken fern.[5] Many species of wildlife use yaupon for food or shelter. Yaupon leaves are browsed by white-tailed deer, and the fruits are eaten by a variety of mammals, including raccoons, skunks, foxes, armadillos, squirrels, and wild hogs.[6] Several species of birds also consume the fruits, including wild turkeys, cedar waxwings, northern bobwhites, eastern bluebirds, brown thrashers, American robins, hermit thrushes, red-bellied woodpeckers, northern mockingbirds, eastern towhees, and blue jays.[7] The dense evergreen foliage provides important cover for a wide variety of wildlife.

Yaupon is an attractive small tree or large shrub, generally growing fifteen to thirty feet tall but occasionally reaching heights of over thirty feet It has smooth whitish-gray bark that stands in noticeable contrast to the lustrous dark green leaves. The leaves are small (one-half to one and a half inches long by one-quarter to three-quarter inches wide), arranged alternately on the stems of the plant, and leathery with crenate margins and a whitish midrib on the upper surface. Small white flowers appear in clusters in March to May, flowed by small (one-quarter-inch diameter) round scarlet-red fruits (drupes) in October to November that persist into spring.[8] The species can survive cold temperatures into the single digits, but will be damaged or killed if temperatures drop below five degrees Fahrenheit.[9]

Yaupon holly has suffered a confusing history of botanical nomenclature, with at least sixteen different botanical names attributed to the species by different authors throughout the last three hundred years.[10] Shiu Ying Hu established the correct scientific name for yaupon holly as *Ilex vomitoria* Ait., in his exhaustive review of yaupon nomenclature. In addition to the numerous scientific names, yaupon holly has also been referred to by over twenty different common names.[11] Early Spanish colonists referred to it as *té del indio* or *chocolate del indio*; in England it was referred to as South Sea tea; in the Carolinas it was referred to as yaupon tea, Appalachian tea, Carolina tea and cassina; and in France it was referred to as *Apalachine* or *Apalachina.*[12] Other synonyms for yaupon in the US include: cassine, cassena, evergreen cassena, evergreen holly, Indian Black Drink, and Christmas berry. At least thirty-one cultivated varieties of yaupon have been selected for landscape purposes, and it has been widely planted outside its natural range as a hedge or foundation planting.[13] Yaupon has naturalized throughout much of the southeastern piedmont.

From an early date, yaupon was known to be a native source of caffeine in the North America. In an 1847 compendium of the history and properties of plants used in medicine, R. Eglesfeld Griffith describes *Ilex vomitoria* and its use as a diuretic among the southeastern Indians. He also notes the "slightly stimulating and tonic" properties of the closely related *Ilex paraguariensis*, the botanical source of *Maté* or Paraguay Tea, a native caffeinated beverage that is still widely consumed in South America today.[14] In 1891, Edwin Hale published a fascinating report on yaupon holly and its potential for revived consumption in North America. By that time, chemical analysis by Henry M. Smith in 1872 and F. P. Venable at the University of North Carolina in 1883 and 1885 had established that *Ilex vomitoria* (referred to as *Ilex cassine* in the report) did, in fact, contain caffeine.[15] This finding was more formally analyzed and reported by Power and Chestnut in 1919, in response to a request to investigate "the possibility of increasing the present production of caffeine, and the utilization of other sources than tea" in connection with the war activities of the National Research Council.[16] In numerous samples of air dried and parched leaves, they found a range of caffeine content from 0.35 percent to 1.67 percent. More recent studies have confirmed caffeine concentrations in yaupon similar to those found in yerba maté.[17]

Traditional consumption of Black Drink is generally attributed to the stimulant properties of the xanthine alkaloids (caffeine and theobromine) present in yaupon holly. Although recognized as a diuretic, and used as a means to achieve ritual purity, Euro-American interpretations of Native traditions rarely ascribe any outright medicinal (in the modern sense) usage to the plant. Contemporary research, however, has shown that yaupon holly foliage possesses a high antioxidant capacity.[18] The phenolic acid and flavanols present in the plant possess anti-inflammatory properties shown to have potential to inhibit colorectal cancer and inflammatory bowel disease (IBD).[19]

Black Drink History

Black Drink has a long and well-documented place in the indigenous communities of the Southeast. Historical accounts from early Europeans suggest that all Southeastern Indian tribes used Black Drink at one time.[20] Southeastern Indian cultures have undergone significant cultural transformations throughout history, resulting in significant alterations in their religious formation, which made each transformation distinct from preceding conditions yet consistent in symbols, rites, and values. Joel Martin describes the four major religious transformations of Creek history (which generally parallel Cherokee history) that provide a useful organization for understanding the Southeastern Indian usage of yaupon holly in the Black Drink: the Woodland period (3,000 years ago until 1,000 years ago); the Mississippian period (1,000 years ago until 1540); the Classic Creek period from 1540 to 1812; and the Modern Creek period from 1812 to 1838.[21]

The Woodland period represents the beginnings of garden horticulture; cultivation of native species such as sunflower, sumpweed, chenopodium, knotweed, pigweed, giant ragweed, and maygrass; semipermanent residences; and new religious practices marked by burial mounds and effigy mounds. The use of Black Drink during the Woodland Period is likely, although unproven. It is difficult to pinpoint exactly when yaupon became a significant part of Southeastern Indian culture, although archeological evidence of black organic residue in shell cups associated with ceremonial events is the best link established to date. Early Indians consumed ceremonial beverages, and perhaps Black Drink, from shell cups made from the lightning whelk, emperor helmet, or horse conch. These drinking vessels have been linked to Black Drink ceremonialism in historic times, and their usage was widespread throughout the Southeast. Archeological evidence, such as black organic residue found in these ceremonial shell cups, suggests that the use of Black Drink preceded the Mississippian era and extends as far back as Hopewellian times (BC 200–AD 500).[22]

The Mississippian period emerged with the introduction of corn and was marked by the following: intensified cultivation; a new range of iconographic and mythological symbols—in particular, the emergence of the "corn mother" as a central belief (Selu, for the Cherokee); the establishment of a hierarchical society with a priestly class at the top; and a multidimensional presence of cultural and material innovation as well as material and practical change. The earliest documented use of Black Drink is from this time period.

Recent chemical analysis of ceramics from Cahokia establishes the use of Black Drink to a time-depth of AD 1050.[23] The distinctive combination of theobromine, caffeine, and ursolic acid detected in analysis confirm the presence of *Ilex vomitoria* (with a possibility that it was mixed with *Ilex cassine*). Cahokia is approximately 500 kilometers away from the nearest natural range of *Ilex vomitoria*, demonstrating the need to transport the dried leaves far north of the plant's natural distribution. To meet the demand of the Cahokia population, large amounts of *Ilex* leaves would have been transported through trade networks from groups to the south and east that had access to the resource. As an imported luxury, and the only available source of caffeine found in North America, Black Drink was likely interwoven into the spiritual and political life of Cahokians in much the same way as was witnessed by early European explorers among the Southeastern Indians in the sixteenth century. The ceramic beakers in which the Black Drink residue was detected may have been produced specifically for the ritual consumption of the beverage.

During the postcontact period, from 1540 until the forced removal from the Southeast (what Martin refers to as the Classic Creek period in reference to Creek religious transformations), Cherokees and their southeastern neighbors were participants in a rapidly evolving political, cultural, and economic order.[24] The hierarchical Mississippian religious complex collapsed and new communal religious forms emphasizing balance and wholeness of the town and clan, as well the individual, came to the fore. Great lengths were taken, particularly by men, to maintain ritual purity in order to be sure that things "went well in human affairs."[25] The careful observance of specific rules organized behavior by maintaining order and integrity of actions—specific foods were avoided that were seen to be unfit for people through association with animals or witches and men believed that contact with a menstruating woman would likely cause them to become impure.[26] Black Drink was seen as an important component to the achievement of purity and balance.

Several well-known accounts describe the ritual consumption of Black Drink at important meetings and ceremonies, such as the Cherokee Green Corn Ceremony and the Creek Busk. French explorers in Florida made contact with the Timicuan groups residing near the mouth of the St. Johns River in 1564, and recorded their observations of an assembly of men consuming Black Drink from shell cups. A rich written and engraved depiction of the event is provided by Jacques Le Moyne.

> The chief and his nobles are accustomed during certain days of the year to meet early every morning for this express purpose in a public place, in which a long bench is constructed, having at the middle of it a projecting part laid with nine round trunks of trees, for the chief's seat. On this he sits by himself, for distinction's sake; and here the rest come to salute him, one at a time, the oldest first, by lifting both hands twice to the height of the head, and saying, "Ha, he, ya, ha, ha." To this the rest answer, "Ha, ha." Each, as he completes his salutation, takes his seat on the bench. If any question of importance is to be discussed, the chief calls upon his laUas (that is, his priests) and upon the elders, one at a time, to deliver their opinions. They decide upon nothing until they have held a number of councils over it, and they deliberate very sagely before deciding. Meanwhile the chief orders the women to boil some casina; which is a drink prepared from the leaves of a certain root, and which they afterwards pass through a strainer. The chief and his councilors being now seated in their places, one stands before him, and, spreading forth his hands wide open, asks a blessing upon the chief and the others who are to drink. Then

> the cupbearer brings the hot drink in a capacious shell, first to the chief, and then, as the chief directs, to the rest in their order, in the same shell. They esteem this drink so highly, that no one is allowed to drink it in council unless he has proved himself a brave warrior. Moreover, this drink has the quality of at once throwing into a sweat whoever drinks it. On this account those who cannot keep it down, but whose stomachs reject it, are not entrusted with any difficult commission, or any military responsibility, being considered unfit, for they often have to go three or four days without food; but one who can drink this liquor can go for twenty-four hours afterwards without eating or drinking.[27]

Le Moyne observed emetic and diaphoretic effects of Black Drink, although he possibly misinterpreted the meaning of the vomiting that he witnessed.

Ritual purging, or vomiting, often accompanied ceremonial Black Drink consumption as an additional method of attaining purity. Early observers assumed that this response was caused by emetic qualities of *Ilex vomitoria*, although extensive research contradicts that belief. Unfortunately, this confusion has been perpetuated by the botanical name ascribed by William Aiton in 1789.[28] Ritual vomiting was either induced by consuming large quantities of the beverage after fasting, by adding other herbs or substances that possessed greater emetic qualities, or by other means.[29] Consumption of moderate quantities of Black Drink does not produce any emetic reaction, indeed the Southeastern Indians and European settlers consumed it regularly in less ceremonial occasions with no adverse effect.

According to William C. Sturtevant, the Spanish that settled St. Augustine, Florida in 1565, soon thereafter adopted the use of tea brewed from yaupon holly leaves, which they learned from the nearby Timicua Indians, and before long became addicted to its beneficial effect. He quotes Father Francisco Ximenez as stating, in 1615, that "any day that a Spaniard does not drink it, he feels that he is going to die."[30]

John Lawson extolled the virtues of yaupon holly in his journal, describing the process for preparing the leaves as follows:

> This Plant is the Indian Tea, us'd and approv'd by all the Savages on the Coast of Carolina, and from them sent to the Westward Indians, and sold at a considerable Price. All which they cure after the same way, as they do for themselves; which is thus:

> They take this Plant (not only the Leaves, but the smaller Twigs along with them) and bruise it in a Mortar, till it becomes blackish, the Leaf being wholly defaced: Then they take it out, put it into one of their earthen Pots which is over the Fire, till it smoaks; stirring it all the time, till it is cur'd. Others take it, after it is bruis'd, and put it into a Bowl, to which they put live Coals, and cover them with the Yaupon, till they have done smoaking, often turning them over. After all, they spread it upon their Mats, and dry it in the Sun to keep it for Use. The Spaniards in New-Spain have this Plant very plentifully on the Coast of Florida, and hold it in great Esteem. Sometimes they cure it as the Indians do; or else beat it to a Powder, so mix it, as Coffee; yet before they drink it, they filter the same. They prefer it above all Liquids, to drink with Physick, to carry the same safely and speedily thro' the Passages, for which it is admirable, as I myself have experimented.[31]

As noted by Lawson, Cherokees relied primarily on trade with coastal tribes to obtain yaupon holly leaves for preparation of the Black Drink, and to a lesser degree transplanting and management of groves near their towns. Cherokee towns were remote to the first Europeans, they were mountain dwellers, and separated from the coast by other tribes such as the Creek and Yamasee. The Cherokees were, however, not isolated. Their towns were located along major rivers, the highways of the time, and they were connected to the west, north and south by the Tennessee, Kanawah, and Savannah Rivers. The area that they occupied was a central location that connected to a network of water and land routes throughout the South and the Ohio Valley. Within a three- to four-week journey, the Cherokees could reach either the confluence of the Mississippi and Missouri Rivers to the west, or Charlestown to the southeast by dugout canoe.[32] This was a desirable position for commerce and prior to European contact these trade routes were active in connecting coastal resources, such as yaupon holly, to the mountains and other inland locations. Mark Catesby, the prominent botanist, remarked on this trade, as summarized by Tom Hatley.

> The "sower faces" of the Cherokee and other tribespeople when deprived of daily yaupon suggested to Mark Catesby that the "paines and expenses they are in procuring it from remote

> distances does not proceed from luxure (as with from China) but from its virtue and the benefit they receive from it." While the tribespeople in the "Maritime parts" supplied the "Mountain Indians" with it, the Cherokees themselves seemed to have used their central position in the trading system to broker it, for, Catesby continued "the inhabitants of the north and west are supplied with it by the mountain Indians in exchange for other commodities."[33]

While the Cherokee had more direct interaction (and conflict) with the French who had established settlements in the interior of the country, they remained buffered from early English settlement and trade along the Atlantic coast by coastal Indians who served as brokers for European goods such as firearms, iron pots, axes, peach trees, and watermelon vines. Cherokee resources that were exchanged for these exotic goods included deerskin, medicinal herbs, chestnuts, rivercane mats, and baskets. This brokered trading situation changed after the Yamasee War (1715–1718) which destroyed the Fall Line trading network and rekindled an older pattern of conflict between the Cherokees and Creeks, which would continue for the next thirty years. Thus began the disappearance of a reliable supply of coastal yaupon leaves.

By the 1730s, the Cherokees had assumed a much more important and direct position in the English trade network as gatekeepers to western territory and the Mississippi River. Their reliance on Creek middlemen was gone, and the former indigenous trading network was dismantled. In addition to the failing trade relations between the Cherokee and Creek, beginning in 1733 the Creek Indians were displaced from their coastal territory through a series of land cessions. Treaties with England, Georgia, and the United States ceded land that included the native range of *Ilex vomitoria*, and by 1814 the Creeks were no longer in control of any land on which yaupon holly was naturally occurring. Native traditions were being disrupted throughout the continent and the commodities being exchanged kept pace with the changing demand in inland territory—yaupon holly leaves were no longer a valued trade item.

Manufactured European goods were incorporated into Cherokee culture, often in direct substitution for a traditional item due to the technical advantages of the novel object—guns substituted for bows and arrows, for example. However, items were often incorporated in ways that deviated from the intended use. For example, iron pots were broken up and the fragments used as hoes, and mirror and glass fragments were substituted for the magic crystals of the medicine men.[34]

Some novel goods were considered exotic objects—they were often presented as gifts from European diplomats or colonial traders that, like other objects of foreign or mysterious origins, imbued them with spiritual power. Cherokee towns were considered a sacred circle, and balanced with the realms outside of the circle. Items originating outside the sacred circle represented a source of spiritual power. Their value was not measured solely in material terms, but was attributed esoteric meaning by the headmen of Cherokee towns.[35] Alcohol, introduced by Europeans, may have had a particular impact on the place of the Black Drink in ceremonial life.

Rum was introduced to Cherokees through the deerskin trade in the seventeenth century. Similar to yaupon holly, whose range was beyond Cherokee territory, this exotic beverage could only be obtained through trade, and was treated early on as an object possessing spiritual power. Black Drink was consumed by Cherokees in highly ritualized ceremonial settings and, along with other medicines, was used to attain physical and spiritual purity. "Early use of alcohol among the Cherokees almost always took place in a similar ritual context, and liquor became a corollary to Black Drink and other spiritual medicines. The terms for 'alcohol' and 'medicine' in colonial Cherokee society linguistically overlapped, and the word *nawohti*, meaning 'medicine,' came to signify alcohol as well."[36]

In Cherokee and Creek towns, the townhouse and town square or plaza served as the center of religious and community life. Men frequently gathered at the square or townhouse to consume Black Drink, promote brotherhood, and conduct economic and political business. These gatherings were important as a way to bond socially and maintain solidarity among men of different clans and lineages within the matrilineal Cherokee society.[37] The consumption of rum began to play a role similar to the Black Drink in the social bonding of men.[38]

Alcohol distribution in Cherokee country was initially restricted due to various regulatory efforts to limit or control the sale of alcohol to Indians, as well as disruptions to the Indian trade network that provided the conduit to the mountains. Consequently, alcohol usage by the Cherokees remained limited to ceremonial contexts for many years. That changed in 1721, when private trade entirely replace the government monopoly controlled by South Carolina, and unscrupulous traders began to bring rum into Cherokee territory. Eventually, excessive alcohol consumption began to threaten the internal harmony of Cherokee communities by disrupting traditional ceremonial feasts and dances, among other things. Although alcohol came to represent Cherokee vulnerability, its adoption into existing ceremonial practices can be seen as a symbol of Cherokee cultural adaptability.[39]

As access to a reliable supply of coastal yaupon leaves disappeared, ample evidence suggests that Cherokees, and other southeastern tribes, transplanted yaupon holly to inland areas closer to their own settlements. They managed these groves as a local supply of fresh yaupon leaves, which would have been critical as indigenous trade networks eroded. On September 19, 1765, a day after leaving Augusta, Georgia, on his way to Savannah, John Bartram made the following observation near a picturesque spring at the head of Beaverdam Creek:

> I found here A piece of an indian pot & many flints of ye same kind mentioned at flint hill. These ye indians brought here. I saw here several of true evergreen casseena which ye creek indians generally plant in all thair settlements, making much use of it dayly. I thought it would not grow [away?] from ye salts; but ye indians plants it several hundredred miles from ye coast. is very wholesom & far more salutary then any from ye east indies. its pitty it was not more used.[40]

The location of John Bartram's observation was revisited by his son, William, in 1773 and again in 1776, where he also noted the presence of yaupon holly.[41] Francis Harper visited the same location in 1936 and was not able to locate the yaupon holly, which led him to speculate that "it may have died out when no longer tended by the Indians.[42]

William Bartram famously observed "a little grove of the Casine yapon" near the Cherokee town of Jore, "which was the only place I had seen it grow in the Cherokee country, the Indians call it the beloved tree, and are very careful to keep them pruned and cultivated, they drink a very strong infusion of the leaves, buds and tender branches of the plant, which is so celebrated, indeed venerated by the Creeks, and all the Southern maritime nations of Indians."[43] This location has been determined to be near the present-day town of Burningtown, NC, well outside the natural range of yaupon holly. It is not clear whom within the Cherokee town had the responsibility to "prune and cultivate" the transplanted yaupon. Some contemporary sources have suggested that the Cherokee Holly Clan or

Blue Holly Clan performed this role—this is a logical and attractive theory, however, research has yet to provide historical evidence to confirm it.

James Adair also recognized the importance of yaupon, noting in 1775: "There is a species of tea, that grows spontaneously, and in great plenty, along the sea-coast of the two Carolinas, Georgia, and East and West-Florida, which we call *Yopon*, or *Cusseena*: the Indians transplant, and are extremely fond of it; they drink it on certain stated occasions, and in their most religious solemnities."[44] His observations of Creek ceremony describe the Black Drink song that accompanied the beverage.

> When this beloved liquid, or supposed holy drink-offering, is fully prepared, and fit to be drank, one of their Magi brings two old consecrated, large conch-shells, out of a place appropriated for containing the holy things, and delivers them into the hands of two religious attendants, who, after a wild ceremony, fill them with the supposed sanctifying, bitter liquid: then they approach near to the two central red and white seats, (which the traders call the war, and beloved cabbins) stooping with their heads and bodies pretty low; advancing a few steps in this posture, they carry their shells with both hands, at an instant, to one of the most principal men on those red and white seats, saying, on a bass key, Y'ah, quite short: then, in like manner, they retreat backward, facing each other, with their heads bowing forward, their arms across, rather below their breast, and their eyes half shut; thus, in a very grave, solemn manner, they sing on a strong bass key, the awful monosyllable, O, for the space of a minute: then they strike up majestic He, on the treble, with a very intent voice, as long as their breath allows them; and on a bass key, with a bold voice, and short accent, they at last utter the strong mysterious sound, Wah, and thus finish the great song, or most solemn invocation of the divine essence. The notes together compose their sacred, mysterious name, Y-O-He-Wah.[45]

While the value of the Black Drink as a general tonic to improve physiological and psychological well-being was universally recognized among the Southeastern Indians, yaupon holly does not appear to have had any specific medicinal uses related to treatment of ailments. In a letter to Benjamin Smith Barton in 1792, William Bartram states,

> I do not know what particular remedy they use against each disorder, but I believe that most, if not all of their Remedies are Vegetables, applied in various ways, particularly, Emetics, Cathartics, Suforificks, & Diureticks; The Infusion or decoction of the leaves & tender young shoots of *Ilex Cassine* is perhaps the most powerful & efficacious vegetable Diuretick yet known, for its effects are almost instantanious after the Draught; which I have experienced, often; This famous decoction (call'd Black Drink) is consider'd rather as a preventative, than a Medicine, & I do not recollect that it is properly amongst their Physick Plants, Yet held in divine estimation, supposed to be ordained for the preservation of their health.[46]

This is also illustrated in the description of its general medical virtues by Adair,

> The Yopon, or Cusseena, is very plenty, as far as the salt air reaches over the lowlands. It is well tasted, and very agreeable to those who accustom themselves to use it: instead of having any noxious quality, according to what many have experienced of the East-India insipid and costly tea, it is friendly to the human system, enters into a contest with the peccant humours, and expels them through the various channels of nature: it perfectly cures a tremor in the nerves.[47]

In Swanton's *Creek Medicine*, he states that yaupon holly has no strictly medicinal purpose, although *asi* "was daily employed by the old people in the early days to clear out the system and produce ceremonial purity."[48] In Creek towns a daily call brought the men of the community to the town square to drink *asi* and discuss matters of community and political importance. Despite the importance of the daily *asi* drinking, the practice was suspended if a death or war upset the balance of the town. Only once balance was restored would the *asi* drinking return to the square. The same disruption affected the Busk ceremony, in which *asi* figured prominently. Historically, the Creek Busk ceremony incorporated many different medicines that had been given to the people by *Ibofanga* (The-One-Above), including: *miko hoyanidja*, *pasa*, and *asi*. *Miko hoyanidja*, also known as redroot and Prairie Willow, is *Salix humilus*. It was one of the two great busk medicines, and likely the most important. *Pasa*, the other

Indians altered the religious formation again, making it "distinct from what had preceded it, yet clearly dependent on the past for key symbols, rites, and values."[55]

Swanton describes the different combinations of medicines used by various Indian communities, and provides some evidence of the evolving practice of ceremonial medicine consumption, stating the Mikasuki used *pasa*, *miko hoyanidja*, and *asi*, "but when their square ground in Florida was destroyed by the Whites and Coweta they gave up the last."[56] It is likely that this event occurred during the First Seminole War (1817–1818). In March through April of 1818, General Andrew Jackson led a force made up of US Army regulars, Tennessee volunteers, Georgia militia, and Lower Creek warriors (under the command of Creek Chief William McIntosh) into North Florida, destroying several Mikasuki villages along the way.[57] This is the only evidence of direct and intentional abandonment of Black Drink that I have found. Why was *asi*, in particular, abandoned? Perhaps the tradition of suspending *asi* consumption if death or war upset the town turned out to be permanent in this situation.

Western Cherokees

After the forced removal from the Southeast, the Cherokees struggled to establish a new livelihood and community in Indian Territory. The disruption of traditional town layout, clan structure, gender roles, and religious practices that had begun with European contact 300 years earlier were amplified by new layers of strain on the culture related to removal. The significant loss of life along the Trail of Tears included many of the elders, keepers of traditional knowledge and oral histories. The novel landscape of Indian Territory differed from the Cherokee homeland in climate, soils, topography, and vegetation. One-third of the plant species that had been utilized in the East were not present in the western lands.[58] It took years for Cherokees to adapt their farming practices to the new landscape and begin to effectively cultivate small subsistence family farmsteads.[59]

During the years immediately following the Trail of Tears, most Cherokees in Indian Territory were focused on surviving in the new land, and political efforts were focused on reestablishing the Nation and reconciling political differences that lingered between Old Settlers, the Treaty Party, and the National Party. There was neither the time, energy, nor heart to reinstate the traditional ceremonies in those early years.[60] The Baptist

Church became the center of the religious life for rural Indians, taking on the role traditionally associated with the town square. These churches incorporated much of the symbolism of town squares and stomp grounds, providing another example of the dynamic relationship between tradition and new ideas adopted by the southeastern Indians.[61] Stomp dances in the Cherokee Nation had dwindled away by the 1890s.[62]

Despite these changes, there remained individuals, families, and small groups of rural Indians who held to the traditional religious beliefs and practices from the Southeast. By 1859, the Keetoowah Society had formed in order to organize efforts to preserve and adhere to these traditions. Redbird Smith eventually came to lead the effort to rekindle traditional ceremonies, and the first stomp dance in years occurred in 1896. In addition to Cherokee individuals, Creek and Natchez traditionalists participated in this revitalization effort. Their efforts were successful, and the Fire was revived at the Creek grounds on Greenleaf Mountain, which Redbird Smith regularly attended. A few elders remembered the dances and taught the others, many of whom had never seen a stomp dance before.[63]

While yaupon holly was not readily available within the Cherokee or Creek territory in the West, participation by Creeks in this revitalization provided alternatives for the Black Drink as ceremonial medicine. As stated earlier, the Creek Busk ceremony incorporated redroot and button snakeroot in addition to yaupon holly. In John Swanton's 1928 book he states that his informant, Jackson Lewis, pronounced "that formerly the black drink (asi) was taken at the same time as the busk medicines, though it has now long been abandoned."[64] Several sources provide evidence that button snakeroot and redroot have continued to be employed as important medicines at Creek and Cherokee stomp grounds in Oklahoma.[65]

Eastern Cherokees

A small number of Cherokees remained in North Carolina after the Trail of Tears and are now recognized as the Eastern Band of Cherokees Indians. Despite the fact that they remained in the Cherokee homeland, the disruption and fragmentation of the removal efforts had a profound impact on community life for years to come. As many traditional rituals were lost from the public venue of ceremonial gatherings, some traditional rituals such as the annual rekindling of the new fire continued to persist in the homes of older individuals, taking on a private significance rather than a communal one.[66] Fieldwork conducted in 1932 by Gilbert found that a version of the Green Corn ceremony was still practiced by the Eastern Band of Cherokee Indians in Big Cove.[67] At that time, The Green Corn Dance was an all-day dance, culminating in a feast where the community could celebrate the great harvest. The inclusion of specific medicine prepared for purification appears to have been abandoned by this point, which Gilbert equates with the loss of the Medicine Dance not long before the time of his fieldwork, noting that "the modes of ritual cleansing having lapsed and the use of Native medicine and conjuring having fallen into evil days, there is little use for the dances. Spontaneous revivals have occurred from time to time in several of the villages, but the enthusiasm for the old things has lagged."[68]

Coffee had been introduced to the Cherokees in the eighteenth century and eventually supplanted Black Drink as the caffeinated beverage served to guests and during social situations.[69] An anthropologist working in North Carolina in 1892 noted that guests at Cherokee households would typically be served "hoe-cakes, greens dipped in grease, and black coffee" by their hosts.[70] If there was no coffee, sassafras tea sweetened with sorghum was a likely substitute. Today, coffee remains the caffeinated beverage of choice.[71]

Conclusion

By 1887 when James Mooney began his residency with the Eastern Band of Cherokee Indians, the Black Drink was relegated to ancient history. Mooney only mentions Black Drink in reference to Bartram's observations of the Creek Indians, and he does not record any observations of yaupon holly at all. It has been confounding that a transition of this magnitude would go unrecognized, that a daily staple in social and ceremonial life would become a vague memory of a tradition of the elders. The evidence provided in this chapter helps to offer some insight into the slow, steady aggradations of cultural change and constraints that affected the Cherokee Indians after European contact. As recognized by Gilbert, "Everything in the ancient culture has suffered diminution or abbreviation and removal from its original matrix of events. Artifacts that were once in common use, such as the flute, trumpet, blowgun, and bow, are now made in small-sized toys for children to play with. Instead of completely singing all of the songs of the dances, only the first and last and perhaps one or two of the others are now sung."[72]

Interestingly, Mooney did record the Cherokee story of Yahula, which he recognized to be a reference to the word *yoholo*, the song sung by the Creek Indians during their Black Drink ceremonies. As with all Cherokee stories, there is a deeper truth behind the narrative. Mooney may have unknowingly recorded the story of the loss of the Black Drink. Perhaps in this story, Yahula the trader represents the Black Drink itself.

Here is "Yahula," as recorded by James Mooney.

> Yahoola creek, which flows by Dahlonega, in Lumpkin county, Georgia, is called Yahulâ'ï (Yahula place) by the Cherokees, and this is the story of the name: Years ago, long before the Revolution, Yahula was a prosperous stock trader among the Cherokee, and the tinkling of the bells hung around the necks of his ponies could be heard on every mountain trail. Once there was a great hunt and all the warriors were out, but when it was over and they were ready to return to the settlement Yahula was not with them. They waited and searched, but he could not be found, and at last they went back without him, and his friends grieved for him as for one dead. Some time after his people were surprised and delighted to have him walk in among them and sit down as they were at supper in the evening. To their questions he told them that he had been lost in the mountains, and that the Nûñnë'hï, the Immortals, had found him and brought him to their town, where he had been kept ever since, with the kindest care and treatment, until the longing to see his old friends had brought him back. To the invitation of his friends to join them at supper he said that it was now too late—he had tasted the fairy food and could never again eat with human kind, and for the same reason he could not stay with his family, but must go back to the Nûñnë'hï. His wife and children and brother begged him to stay, but he said that he could not; it was either life with the Immortals or death with his own people—and after some further talk he rose to go. They saw him as he sat talking to them and as he stood up, but the moment he stepped out the doorway he vanished as if he had never been.

After that he came back often to visit his people. They would see him first as he entered the house, and while he sat and talked he was his old self in every way, but the instant he stepped across the threshold he was gone, though a hundred eyes might be watching. He came often, but at last their entreaties grew so urgent that the Nûñnë'hï must have been offended, and he came no more. On the mountain at the head of the, creek, about 10 miles above the present Dahlonega, is a small square inclosure of uncut stone, without roof or entrance. Here it was said that he lived, so the Cherokee called it Yahulâ'ï and called the stream by the same name. Often at night a belated traveler coming along the trail by the creek would hear the voice of Yahula singing certain favorite old songs that he used to like to sing as he drove his pack of horses across the mountain, the sound of a voice urging them on, and the crack of a whip and the tinkling of bells went with the song, but neither driver nor horses could be seen, although the sounds passed close by. The songs and the bells were heard only at night.

There was one man who had been his friend, who sang the same songs for a time after Yahula had disappeared, but he died suddenly, and then the Cherokee were afraid to sing these songs any more until it was so long since anyone had heard the sounds on the mountain that they thought Yahula must be gone away, perhaps to the West, where others of the tribe had already gone. It is so long ago now that even the stone house may have been destroyed by this time, but more than one old man's father saw it and heard the songs and the bell, a hundred years ago. When the Cherokee, went from Georgia to Indian Territory in 1838 some of them said, "Maybe Yahula has gone there and we shall hear him," but they have never heard him again.[73]

Black Drink brewed from yaupon holly was once a ubiquitous presence in Southeastern Indian culture. Early European settlers quickly recognized that virtues of the brewed tea, and adopted it into their daily lives as well.[74] The Black Drink was abandoned by the Cherokee due to a loss of access to the resource, the introduction and substitution of novel alternative beverages, the disruption of traditional ceremonies and cultural practices, and the eventual loss of the traditional ecological knowledge necessary to sustain its usage. Its use by white settlers declined similarly (primarily due to competition from coffee and Chinese tea). Yaupon tea was the subject of some commercial interest in the eighteenth and nineteenth centuries, and has shown great potential for wider usage.[75] Interestingly, yaupon is experiencing a resurgence in its use today.[76] Commercial producers and distributors of yaupon tea are currently present in Florida, Georgia, and Texas. If yaupon tea is to finally experience a renewed popularity, it will be due to its virtues as an enjoyable, restorative, and local drink—the same characteristics that made it popular among Southeastern Indian communities for so long.

Notes

1. Charles H. Fairbanks, "The Function of Black Drink among the Creeks," in *Black Drink: A Native American Tea*, ed. Charles M. Hudson (Athens: University of Georgia Press, 1979), 141.

2. Charles M. Hudson, "Introduction," in *Black Drink: A Native American Tea*, ed. Charles M. Hudson (Athens: University of Georgia Press, 1979), 2.

3. Wilbur H. Duncan, and Marion B. Duncan, *Trees of the Southeastern United States* (Athens: University of Georgia Press, 1998), 217.

4. Duncan and Duncan, *Trees*, 217.

5. Leslie Edwards, Jonathan Ambrose, and L. Katherine Kirkman, *The Natural Communities of Georgia* (Athens: University of Georgia Press, 2013), 553–55.

6. Milo Coladonato, "*Ilex vomitoria*," *Fire Effects Information System* (US Department of Agriculture, Forest Service, 1991), http://www.fs.fed.us/database/feis/plants/shrub/ilevom/all.html#21; Robert Shadow, *2011 Plant fact sheet for Yaupon, Ilex vomitoria* (Nacogdoches: USDA-Natural Resources Conservation Service, East Texas Plant Materials Center, 2011), 1.

7. James H. Miller and Karl V. Miller, *Forest Plants of the Southeast and Their Wildlife Uses* (Athens: University of Georgia Press, 2005), 350–51.

8. Michael A. Dirr, *Manual of Woody Landscape Plants: Their Identification, Ornamental Characteristics, Culture, Propogation and Uses* (Champaign, IL: Stipes Publishing, 1998), 487; Miller, *Forest Plants*, 350–51.

9. Dirr, *Manual*, 487.

10. Shiu Ying Hu, "The Botany of Yaupon" in *Black Drink: A Native American Tea*, ed. Charles M. Hudson (Athens: University of Georgia Press, 1979), 21.

11. Hu, "Botany of Yaupon," 22.

12. Hudson, "Introduction," 6.

13. Dirr, *Manual*, 487–89.

14. R. Eglesfeld Griffith, *Medical Botany: Or Descriptions of the More Important Plants Used in Medicine with Their History, Properties, and Mode of Administration* (Philadelphia: Lea and Blanchard, 1847), 433.

15. H. M. Smith, "Yaupon" in *American Journal of Pharmacy* XLIV, Fourth Series, no. 11 (1872): 216–17; Edwin M. Hale, *Ilex cassine: The Aboriginal North American Tea* (Washington DC: USDA Division of Botany, 1891), 9–10.

16. Frederick B. Power and Victor K. Chestnut, "Ilex Vomitoria as a Native Source of Caffeine," *Journal of the American Chemical Society* 41 (1919): 1310.

17. Matthew J. Palumbo, Stephen T. Talcott, and Francis E. Putz, "Ilex Vomitoria Ait. (Yaupon): A Native North American Source of a Caffeinated and Antioxidant-Rich Tea." *Economic Botany* 63 (2009): 135.

18. Palumbo, "Ilex," 133–35.

19. G. D. Noratto, Y. Kim, S. T. Talcott, and S. U. Mertens-Talcott, "Flavonol-rich Fractions of Yaupon Holly Leaves (Ilex vomitoria, Aquifoliaceae) Induce MicroRNA-146a and Have Anti-inflammatory and Chemopreventive Effects in Intestinal Myofibroblast CCD-18Co Cells," *Fitoterapia* 82 (2011): 557–58.

20. Hudson, "Introduction," 2.

21. Joel Martin, "Rebalancing the World in the Contradictions of History: Creek/Muskogee," in *Native Religions and Cultures of North America: Anthropology of the Sacred*, ed. Lawrence E. Sullivan (London: Continuum, 2000), 87.

22. Jerald T. Milanich, "Origins and Prehistoric Distributions of Black Drink," in *Black Drink: A Native American Tea*, ed. Charles M. Hudson (Athens: University of Georgia Press, 1979), 83–104.

23. Patricia L. Crown et al., "Ritual Black Drink Consumption at Cahokia," *Proceedings of the National Academy of the Sciences of the United States of America* 109, no. 35 (2012): 13947–48.

24. Martin, "Rebalancing," 92–100.

25. Charles M. Hudson, *The Southeastern Indians* (Knoxville: University of Tennessee Press, 1976), 336.

26. Hudson, "Introduction," 3.

27. Jacques Le Moyne, *Narrative of Le Moyne, An Artist Who Accompanied the Fench Expedition to Florida Under Laudonniére, 1564* (Boston, MA: James R. Osgood, 1875): 11–12.

28. Hu, "Botany of Yaupon," 27.

29. Hudson, "Introduction," 4.

30. William C. Sturtevant, "Black Drink and Other Caffeine-Containing Beverages among Non-Indians," in *Black Drink: A Native American Tea*, ed. Charles M. Hudson (Athens: University of Georgia Press, 1979), 150.

31. John Lawson, *A New Voyage to Carolina; Containing the Exact Description and Natural History of That Country: Together with the Present State Thereof. And a Journal of a Thousand Miles, Travel'd Thro' Several Nations of Indians* (London, 1709), 91.

32. Tom Hatley, *The Dividing Paths: Cherokees and South Carolinians through the Era of Revolution* (New York: Oxford University Press, 1993), 14.

33. Hatley, *Dividing*, 14.

34. Izumi Ishii, *Bad Fruits of the Civilized Tree: Alcohol and the Sovereignty of the Cherokee Nation* (Lincoln: University of Nebraska Press, 2008), 165.

35. Ishii, *Bad Fruits*, 14.

36. Ishii, *Bad Fruits*, 16.

37. Fairbanks, "Function," 141.

38. Ishii, *Bad Fruits*, 35.

39. Ishii, *Bad Fruits*, 19.

40. John Bartram and Francis Harper, "Diary of a Journey through the Carolinas, Georgia, and Florida from July 1, 1765, to April 10, 1766," *Transactions of the American Philosophical Society* 33, no. 1 (December 1942): 27.

41. William Bartram, *The Travels of William Bartram: Francis Harper's Naturalist Edition*, ed. Francis Harper (New Haven: Yale University Press, 1958), 291–92.

42. Bartram, "Diary," 65.

43. Bartram, *Travels*, 227.

44. James Adair, *The History of the American Indians; Particularly Those Nations* adjoining *to the Mississippi, East and West Florida, Georgia, South and North Carolina, and Virginia* (London: Edward and Charles Dilly, 1775), 46.

45. Adair, *History*, 46–47.

46. William Bartram, "William Bartram to Benjamin Smith Barton; December 29, 1792," in *William Bartram: The Search for Nature's Design*, eds. Thomas Hallock and Nancy E. Hoffman (Athens: University of Georgia Press, 2010), 167.

47. Adair, *History*, 361.

48. John R. Swanton, "Religious Beliefs and Medicinal Pracices of the Creek Indian," in *Bureau of American Ethnology Annual Report 42* (Washington, DC: Smithsonian Institution, 1928), 666.

49. Martin, "Rebalancing," 95.

50. Duane H. King, *The Memoirs of Lt. Henry Timberlake: The Story of a Soldier, Adventurer, and Emissary to the Cherokees, 1756–1765* (Cherokee: Museum of the Cherokee Indian Press, 2007), 38.

51. William Harlen Gilbert, *The Eastern Cherokee* (Washington, DC: Smithsonian Institution, Bureau of American Ethnology, 1943), 331.

52. J. P. Evans, "Sketches of Cherokee Characteristics," *Journal of Cherokee Studies* 4, no. 1 (1979): 20.

53. Gilbert, *Eastern Cherokee*, 367.

54. William C. Sturtevant, "John Ridge on Cherokee Civilization in 1826," *Journal of Cherokee Studies* 6, no. 2 (1981): 86.

55. Martin, "Rebalancing," 87.

56. Swanton, "Religious," 608.

57. John Missall and Mary Lou Missall, *The Seminole Wars: America's Longest Indian Conflict* (Gainesville: University Press of Florida, 2004), 39–43.

58. R. Alfred Vick, "Cherokee Adaptation to the Landscape fo the West and Overcoming the Loss of Culturally Significant Plants," *American Indian Quarterly* 35, no. 3 (2011): 399.

59. William G. McLoughlin, *After the Trail of Tears: The Cherokees' Struggle for Sovereignty, 1839–1880* (Chapel Hill: University of North Carolina Press, 1993), 38.

60. Janey B. Hendrix, "Redbird Smith and the Nighthawk Keetoowahs, Part I," *Journal of Cherokee Studies* 8, no. 1 (Spring 1983): 22.

61. Martin, "Rebalancing," 102.

62. Janey B. Hendrix, "Redbird Smith and the Nighthawk Keetoowahs, Part II," *Journal of Cherokee Studies* 6, no. 2 (Fall 1983): 76.

63. Hendrix, "Redbird," 76.

64. Swanton, "Religious," 549.

65. Jason Baird Jackson, *Yuchi Folklore: Cultural Expression in a Southeastern Native American Community* (Norman: University of Oklahoma Press, 2013), 229; Martin, "Rebalancing," 86; Swanton, "Religious," 607.

66. Gilbert, *Eastern Cherokee*, 369–70.

67. Gilbert, *Eastern Cherokee*, 367.

68. Gilbert, *Eastern Cherokee*, 367.

69. Gilbert, *Eastern Cherokee*, 360.

70. Frederick Starr, "Measuring Cherokees" *The Christian Union* (October 1892): 587.

71. Gina Smith, "Yaupon Takes the Stage as a Regionally Grown Source of Caffeine," *Mountain Xpress*, February 24, 2016, https://mountainx.com/food/yaupon-takes-the-asheville-stage-as-a-regionally-grown-source-of-caffeine/.

72. Gilbert, *Eastern Cherokee*, 371.

73. James Mooney, "Myths of the Cherokee," in *Nineteenth Annual Report of the Bureau of American Ethnology, 1897–98* (Washington, DC: Government Printing Office, 1900): 347–49.

74. Sturtevant, "Non-Indians," 150–53.

75. Hale, *Ilex*, 51–52.

76. B. Koslow, "Edgewater tea maker in talks with national distributor," *Daytona News-Journal*, July 7, 2014.

Bibliography

Adair, James. *The History of the American Indians; Particularly Those Nations adjoining to the Mississippi, East and West Florida, Georgia, South and North Carolina, and Virginina*. London: Edward and Charles Dilly, 1775.

Bartram, John and Francis Harper. "Diary of a Journey through the Carolinas, Georgia, and Florida from July 1, 1765, to April 10, 1766." *Transactions of the American Philosophical Society* 33, No. 1 (December 1942), i–iv; 1–120.

Bartram, William. *The Travels of William Bartram: Francis Harper's Naturalist Edition.* Edited by Francis Harper. New Haven: Yale University Press, 1958.

Bartram, William. "William Bartram to Benjamin Smith Barton; December 29, 1792." In *William Bartram: The Search for Nature's Design*, by Thomas Hallock and Nancy E. Hoffman, 166–70. Athens: University of Georgia Press, 2010.

Coladonato, Milo. "Ilex vomitoria." In *Fire Effects Informaation System*, by Forest Service US Department of Agriculture. Rocky Mountain Research Station, 1992. Accessed June 24, 2016. http://www.fs.fed.us/database/feis/plants/shrub/ilevom/all.html#21.

Crown, Patricia L., Thomas E. Emerson, Jiyan Gu, Jeffrey Hurst, Timothy R. Paauketat, and Timothy Ward. "Ritual Black Drink Consumption at Cahokia." *Proceedings of the National Academy of the Sciences of the United States of America* 109, no. 35 (August 2012): 13944–49.

Dirr, Michael A. *Manual of Woody Landscape Plants.* Champaign, IL: Stipes Publishing LLC, 1998.

Duncan, Wilbur H., and Marion B. Duncan. *Trees of the Southeastern United States.* Athens: University of Georgia Press, 1998.

Edwards, Leslie, Jonathan Ambrose, and L. Katherine Kirkman. *The Natural Communities of Georgia.* Athens: University of Georgia Press, 2013.

Evans, J. P. "Sketches of Cherokee Characteristics." *Journal of Cherokee Studies* 4, no. 1 (1979): 10–20.

Fairbanks, Charles H. "The Function of Black Drink Among the Creeks." In *Black Drink: A Native American Tea*, by Charles M. Hudson. 120–50. Athens, GA: University of Georgia Press, 1979.

Gilbert, William Harlen. *The Eastern Cherokee.* Washington, DC: Smithsonian Institution, Bureau of American Ethnology, 1943.

Griffith, R. Eglesfeld. *Medical Botany: Or Descriptions of the More Important Plants Used in Medicine with Their History, Properties, and Mode of Administration.* Philadelphia, PA: Lea and Blanchard, 1847.

Hale, Edwin M. *Ilex cassine: The Aboriginal North American Tea.* Washington DC: USDA Division of Botany, 1891.

Hatley, Tom. *The Dividing Paths: Cherokees and South Carolinians through the Era of Revolution.* New York: Oxford University Press, 1993.

Hendrix, Janey B. "Redbird Smith and the Nighthawk Keetoowahs, Part I." *Journal of Cherokee Studies* 8, no. 1 (Spring 1983): 22–39.

Hendrix, Janey B. "Redbird Smith and the Nighthawk Keetoowahs, Part II." *Journal of Cherokee Studies* 8, no. 2 (Fall 1983): 73–86.

Hu, Shiu Ying. "The Botany of Yaupon." In *Black Drink: A Native American Tea*, by Charles M. Hudson, 10–39. Athens: University of Georgia Press, 1979.

Hudson, Charles M. "Introduction." In *Black Drink: A Native American Tea*, by Harles M Hudson, 1–10. Athens: University of Georgia Press, 1979.

———. *The Southeastern Indians.* Knoxville, TN: University of Tennessee Press, 1976.

Ishii, Izumi. *Bad Fruits of the Civilized Tree: Alcohol and the Sovereignty of the Cherokee Nation.* Lincoln: University of Nebraska Press, 2008.

Jackson, Jason Baird. *Yuchi Folklore: Cultural Expression in a Southeastern Native American Community.* Norman, OK: University of Oklahoma Press, 2013.

King, Duane H. *The Memoirs of Lt. Henry Timberlake: The Story of a Soldier, Adventurer, and Emissary to the Cherokees, 1756–1765.* Cherokee, NC: Museum of the Cherokee Indian Press, 2007.

Koslow, B. "Edgewater Tea Maker in Talks with National Distributor." *Daytona News-Journal*, July 7, 2014.

Lawson, John. *A New Voyage to Carolina; Containing the Exact Description and Natural History of That Country: Together with the Present State Thereof. And a Journal of a Thousand Miles, Travel'd Thro' Several Nations of Indians.* London: n.p., 1709.

Le Moyne, Jacues. *Narrative of Le Moyne, An Artist Who Accompanied the Fench Expedition to Florida Under Laudonniére, 1564.* Boston, MA: James R. Osgood, 1875.

Martin, Joel. "Rebalancing the World in the Contradictions of History: Creek/Muskogee." In *Native Religions and Cultures of North America: Anthropology of the Sacred*, edited by Lawrence E. Sullivan, 85–103. London: Continuum, 2000.

McLoughlin, William G. *After the Trail of Tears: The Cherokees' Struggle for Sovereignty, 1839–1880.* Chapel Hill: University of North Carolina Press, 1993.

Milanich, Jerald T. "Origins and Prehistoric Distributions of Black Drink." In *Black Drink: A Native American Tea*, edited by Charles M. Hudson, 83–119. Athens: University of Georgia Press, 1979.

Miller, James H., and Karl V. Miller. *Forest Plants of the Southeast and Their Wildlife Uses.* Athens: University of Georgia Press, 2005.

Missall, John, and Mary Lou Missall. *The Seminole Wars: America's Longest Indian Conflict.* Gainesville: The University Press of Florida, 2004.

Mooney, James. "Myths of the Cherokee." In *Nineteenth Annual Report of the Bureau of American Ethnology, 1897–98.* Washington, DC: Government Printing Office, 1900.

Noratto, G. D., Y. Kim, S. T. Talcott, and S. U. Mertens-Talcott. "Flavonol-rich Fractions of Yaupon Holly Leaves (Ilex vomitoria, Aquifoliaceae) Induce MicroRNA-146a and Have Anti-inflammatory and Chemopreventive Effects in Intestinal Myofibroblast CCD-18Co Cells." *Fitoterapia* 82, no. 4 (June 2011): 577–69.

Palumbo, Matthew J., Stephen T. Talcott, and Francis E. Putz. "Ilex Vomitoria Ait. (Yaupon): A Native North American Source of a Caffeinated and Antioxidant-Rich Tea." *Economic Botany* 63 (June 2009): 130–37.

Power, Frederick B., and Victor K. Chestnut. "Ilex vomitoria as a Native Source of Caffeine." *Journal of the American Chemical Society* 41, no. 8 (1919): 1307–12.

Shadow, Robert, A. *2011Plant Fact Sheet for Yaupon, Ilex vomitoria.* Nacogdoches, TX: USDA-Natural Resources Conservation Service, East Texas Plant Materials Center, 2011.

Smith, Gina. "Yaupon Takes the Asheville Stage as a Regionally-Grown Source of Caffeine." *Mountain Xpress* (February 24, 2016): Accessed July 21, 2016. https://mountainx.com/food/yaupon-takes-the-asheville-stage-as-a-regionally-grown-source-of-caffeine/.

Smith, Henry M. "Yaupon." *American Journal of Pharmacy* XLIV, Fourth Series, no. 11 (1872): 216–17.

Starr, Frederick. "Measuring Cherokees." *The Christian Union* (October 1, 1892): 586–88.

Sturtevant, William C. "Black Drink and Other Caffeine-Containing Beverages among Non-Indians." In *Black Drink: A Native American Tea*, edited by Charles M. Hudson, 150–165. Athens: University of Georgia Press, 1979.

Sturtevant, William C. 1981. "John Ridge on Cherokee Civilization in 1826." *Journal of Cherokee Studies* 6, no. 2: 79–91.

Swanton, John R. "Religious Beliefs and Medicinal Pracices of the Creek Indians." In *Bureau of American Ethnology Annual Report* 42, 473–672. Washington DC: Smithsonian Institution, 1928.

Vick, R. Alfred. "Cherokee Adaptation to the Landscape fo the West and Overcoming the Loss of Culturally Significant Plants." *American Indian Quarterly* 35, no. 3 (Summer 2011): 394–417.

8

The Semiotics of Resistance

On the Power of Frybread

Dennis Kelley

> ". . . a good piece of frybread can turn any meal into a feast."
>
> —Thomas Builds-the-Fire in *Smoke Signals*

> If frybread were a movie, it would be hard-core porn. No redeeming qualities. Zero nutrition.
>
> —Susan Shown Harjo (Cheyenne/Hodulgee Muscogee)

For anyone who has ever gone to a powwow, Indian fair, Native arts festival, or indeed any public-access event in Indian Country, frybread is a known quantity. The flat bread—fried disks of white flour dough, not quite like a donut, funnel cake, or any other vendor fare found at such events—with either honey and powdered sugar or the full ground beef, lettuce, cheese, and salsa of the "Navajo Taco" is as much part of the festivities as the dancing or crafts. What many non-Natives don't know is the history and significance of this "traditional" Native staple. For starters, is it *actually* "traditional?"

What is certain is that many if not indeed most of the various communities that make up Indian Country are not only familiar with frybread, it is as much a part of their food culture as tortillas are for Latinx communities, or pasta for Italians. However, unlike those foods and many other "ethnic" foods like them, frybread has come to symbolize both the pan-tribal identity associated with indigenous North Americans, and the oppression experienced by the various tribes, clans, and bands that made up this continent's population prior to the arrival of Europeans. While frybread itself is an imposed food, it has become symbolic of the resilience of American Indians and First Nations people and their continued connections to their indigenous identities.

This chapter will turn on that seeming contradiction: a traditional Native food that was imposed on Native people within the last 150 or so years. But therein lies the bigger issue that goes to the theme of this book. Frybread has become one of the symbolic touchstones that connects American Indian communities to both their discrete ethnic identities and traditions, and to the reality of their colonized status. And it is this aspect, I will argue, that gives frybread its power and significance.

Food and Tradition

When I teach my Introduction to American Indian Religious Traditions course, I will often spend time discussing the US holiday known as Thanksgiving with them, their experiences growing up, school pageants, family traditions, and especially the role American Indians played in those experiences. Invariably, the role played by the typical American Thanksgiving foods and their origins comes up in these conversations. The turkey, pumpkins, cranberries, and corn are all known to be indigenous to the Americas, and for many tribes throughout the continent, corn has risen to the position of "key symbol" among tribes as varied as the Haudenosaunee, the Diné, and the Rarámuri.[1] Salmon and bison are also staple foods that have attained key symbolic status, in the Pacific Northwest and Great Plains, respectively, but with the possible exception of corn, no food associated with American Indians has the broad appeal and ubiquity as the most recent entry into the traditional foods category, frybread.

Susan Shown Harjo reminds us that bread in general is often emblematic of home, family, and health, and that Native communities have truly traditional breads such as piki for the Hopi and sofkee for the Muscogee.[2] These corn-based breads are also evidence of the long relationship indigenous Americans have had with that food resource. However, though Harjo is adamant about the need to jettison frybread from the contemporary American Indian diet, she also points to the persistent presence of this dish in two key ways: (1) the connection that frybread has to a shared identity across tribal divisions; and (2) the desire of the immigrant culture to essentialize the various tribes, bands, confederacies, and clans into one ethnic group. Frybread is now popular outside of Indian Country, often due to its characterization as "traditional American Indian food" in the diversity-obsessed contemporary social climate.

I am absolutely sympathetic to the spirit of Harjo's desire to decouple frybread from tradition due to the obvious health concerns to which frybread contributes, especially in reservation-based communities, as well as the desire to elevate foods and their connected lifeways that truly *are* traditional. However, the blowback she received to her 2005 essay is telling in that abandoning frybread entirely may be a very tough sell. The confection simply holds too much meaning, and though "commodity foods" in general continue to signify the marginalized nature of Native communities, they are also a powerful reminder of the persistence of American Indians and First Nations cultures in the face of concerted efforts to eradicate them. Frybread holds a particularly powerful place in that narrative of resistance.

Frybread: One Very Brief History

Also known as bannock among the northern tribes and in First Nation communities, the disks of fried dough are found in most regions of Indigenous North America, from central Canada to northern Mexico. What I will show is that the reasons for both the ubiquity and symbolic heft of frybread can be traced to the fact that it is a product of Euro-American staples (bleached white flour, salt, powdered milk, lard, etc.) that were provided to Native people by agents of colonial governments, in particular the United States. A simple dough made with very little leavening and fried in hot grease, the bread is used much in the way tortillas are in Latinx households. However, it is the presence of frybread at specific events such as powwows that has added to the bread's allure as a unique element of Native American cuisine.

While there are several stories of origins, each emphasizing the role of frybread in the local tribes of the storytellers, each tells the true story of colonial government attempts to provide a modicum of support for

Indigenous nations that had been displaced and/or confined to reserves, reservations, and rancherías. The early nature of the attempts by the US government to deal with the devastation created by its treatment of the Apache (N'dee) and the Navajo (Diné) under Abraham Lincoln makes this a suitable exemplar for the innovation of frybread.

In 1862, the US government moved to rid the Arizona Territory of Native people. Abraham Lincoln endorsed a "scorched earth" policy wherein Native corn, bean, and squash crops were burned, sheep and goats killed, and irrigation systems destroyed. A reservation was established at Ft. Sumner, New Mexico, with the plan being to remove thousands of N'dee and Diné via several forced marches the Diné refer to as the "Long Walk." Once established, it quickly became clear that water was scarce, and conditions poor for establishing crops or grazing land completely inadequate. Starvation and disease spread and opposition to the policy grew. After the possibility of actually massacring all the Indians, whose number had risen to around 9,000, was thankfully abandoned, the Lincoln administration developed a system of staple delivery along with a set of clothes for each person. The foodstuffs included the aforementioned flour, salt, and lard, as well as canned meats, which were often too rancid to eat once opened.[3] The Diné made the best use of these staple products that they could and were able to survive until their return to a substantially smaller portion of their original territory. However, the relationship with the Bureau of Indian Affairs continued to include some provisions, and frybread traveled back to their homelands with them.

This very simplified overview nonetheless contains the basic elements of the frybread story, repeated as it was in other tribal contexts throughout the US, as well as a brief look at the template for the commodities program still in effect in Indian Country.[4] The significance of frybread as a symbolic element of culture for contemporary Native communities draws, then, from its role as substandard replacement for traditional foods, as well as a reminder of the harsh treatment by the US Federal Government, and the continued nature of the colonial control of Native lands.

Frybread as Sign

The central puzzle in the frybread tale is how it fits into the current discourse on food sovereignty, health, and wellness programs in Indian Country, and concerted efforts to regain traditional food gathering and preparation techniques as acts of cultural revitalization. It would seem as though the arguably least healthy and certainly least "traditional" food item would be abandoned in favor of ancestral foodways. So why does frybread persist? I think the answer lies in two key overlapping factors: the reservation/reserve versus "urban Indian" divide, on the one hand, and the development of pan-Indian or pan-tribal signification systems, on the other.[5] While some of the Native people I have interacted with over the years bristle at the concept "pan-Indian," particularly if their tribal heritage originated on the Great Plains, it is nevertheless a key component in the development of contemporary American Indian identity in both positive and negative ways, and the symbolic power of frybread is located in a sense of collective indigeneity and common experiences relevant to Native Americans and First Nations people.

A key feature of the development of individual tribal responses to modernity, pan-Indianism is also a factor in the creation of what I have been referring to as "Indian Country." The historical realities surrounding the steady transformation from multiple and distinct tribal cultures to a broadly defined ethnic reality that can be termed "Native America," must include a discussion of the processes responsible for knitting together these various cultures into one common set of issues, concerns, and outlook called "Indian Country." This reality, both a feature of colonialism and a method of resistance to it, is a complex one that needs much more space than I am providing it here. However, after a brief overview of the discourse on this phenomenon, I will discuss the development of pan-tribal networks in education, politics, and activism, including the modern "powwow." It is this process of connecting to one's own Indian heritage utilizing "pan-Indian" practices in the absence of traditional communal paradigms, and the realization of American indigenousness as a cultural value, that inform the discussion of tribal identity in extra-tribal circumstances, forging a common experience from the multiplicity of tribal experiences.

In his insightful book *The Return of the Native: American Indian Political Resurgence*, Stephen Cornell uses the concept "supratribal" to refer to the practice of some American Indians, in some contexts, to express an all-encompassing "Indian" identity irrespective of individual tribal differences.[6] The term *supratribal* is helpful in that it doesn't imply a negation of important connections to specific tribal contexts that "pan-Indian" sometimes can, but nonetheless points to the permeability of those boundaries in modern circumstances. A key feature of the historical expression of this identification is the view of many non-Indians during the colonial period that any "supratribal" activities indicated assimilation.[7] This view, that "supratribal," pan-Indian identity represented a transitional stage or phase in the process of eliminating Indianness altogether, masked what may have been the more important aspect of this development: a tool for the resistance to assimilation. Supratribal interaction between Indians during the colonial period laid the groundwork for future collaborations that effectively resisted assimilation, setting the stage for more severe attempts by the nascent US government to force the issue through removal, boarding schools, and disenrollment.[8] As has been shown by several political scientists, the expected response to violent suppression of a people is most often a solidification of their collective identity, and the continued growth of adaptive mechanisms for the assertion of that identity.[9] Thus, it is possible to conceptualize the development of pan-Indian, supratribal practices as a response to the continued effort by the US government to erase Native American identity, leading to the practical tools for its maintenance. What I am suggesting is that it is this toolkit, comprised of practices and ideologies appropriate to the supratribal/pan-Indian context, that provides much of the foundation for an eventual return to *tribal-specific* religious identity by keeping the possibilities of Indianness in the modern Native American consciousness. The supratribal practices available to people who identify as American Indian, therefore, provide the foundation for the revitalization of religious practices and ideas in particular tribal contexts.

While this process is generally limited to non-reservation-based Indian communities, this pattern on US reservations and Canadian reserves where tribal traditions have lapsed is also a key factor in those communities. The key issue for my purposes here is that this revitalization, which I have elsewhere referred to as a "reprise" of American Indian identity, most often begins with culturally specific practices: practices seen as being uniquely located in the cultural histories of indigenous Americans, and providing the framework on which a viable and coherent system of beliefs and values can be reconstructed.[10] The cultural specificity of the practices ranges from those generally understood as aspects of Indianness to those with specific tribal connotations. The canoe culture revival in the Pacific Northwest contexts is one example of this latter type. For urbanized communities far removed from the lands of their tribal origins, however, opportunities to exercise their Indianness in overt ways can be limited to ceremonial gatherings, urban American Indian resource centers, or powwows. It is the contemporary intertribal powwow, in fact, where many nonreservation/reserve Native people get their frybread fix. As powwows both represent the pan-Indian context and are inexorably linked to the topic of this chapter, a brief treatment of the contemporary intertribal powwow may be helpful.

Fancy Dancing and "Navajo Tacos"

The powwow as an event varies from small and local private events to very large and very public ones. The community-based powwow is generally found in Plains Indian regions both here in the US and in Canada, where the dances and ceremonies associated with powwows have their origins. The dances, music, and regalia are steeped in the tribal traditions of the Great Plains, and, indeed, the "Fancy Dance" styles have taken on a life of their own in terms of interpreting the movements of Plains dances and the rendering of the regalia appropriate to those dances.[11]

Begun as an attempt to keep Native American youth from losing touch with traditional community values in the early twentieth century, the powwow derives from traditional seasonal gatherings, typical of Plains nations, prior to colonization. The powwow maintains the flavor of these events, even though they often occur outside of Plains regions and with non-Plains communities. In addition, the "contest" powwow (where dancers compete against each other for prizes) is a fairly common event throughout the US and Canada, and one that is often open to non-Native audiences. The intertribal contest powwows, especially large annual ones, are able to pay for the events by renting space in the powwow grounds for vendors of various kinds, from finished arts and crafts, to crafting supplies, to T-shirts and posters. Frybread vendors are ubiquitous at these powwows, and sell frybread plain, drizzled with honey and/or powdered sugar, or as the base for the "Navajo Taco," frybread with ground beef, lettuce, cheese, and salsa.

The powwow is a unique interaction between the worlds of Indian Country and the settler communities, in that Native people are interacting with each other in a way that for many Indians, especially in urbanized areas, represents an opportunity to visit with family and friends, introduce young people to other Native youth, and teach lessons about community values such as honoring elders, giving gifts, and self-discipline that may not be available in day-to-day urban life. But Native people are also in a way performing indigeneity for non-Indian spectators who may not know the complex history of pan-Indianism, attributing the dances, songs, and regalia styles to *all* American Indians and First Nations people. The potential for reinforcing stereotypes is high at public powwows in non-Plains regions, but at the same time, Native people can, and do, underscore the message of survival and growth in their communities. Powwow emcees often overtly speak about the contemporary cultural realities in Indian Country, and much effort is made to emphasize the role of children and young people both in the contest dances and in the gift giving and honoring that also happen at these events.

For many Native people, it would be unimaginable to attend a powwow and not enjoy a "Navajo taco" for lunch. In addition, I have attended many events at urban Indian resource centers, "Indian fairs," conferences, storytelling events, and rodeos whose attendees are from a variety of tribal nations, and frybread/bannock is nearly always served. Thus, the pan-Indian cultural elements—drumming, dance and regalia style, rhetorical imagery—provide a set of common touchstones that help to reinforce the traditional values sought at such events as they provide opportunities for Native people who lack the immersive community of a reservation or ranchería to have that experience.

When removal policies gave way to the modernizing effects of the "Indian New Deal," Indians of geographically distant tribal regions found themselves interacting in intimate cultural settings, many of whom came to urban centers from multitribal reservations, or reservations on which spiritual knowledge had experienced a lapse.[12] As these urban Indian communities continued to grow, it was through the lens of pan-Indianism that many members viewed their spiritual lives. In Indian Health Service offices, Veteran's Administration clinics, and independent agencies devoted to American Indian concerns, these urban Indian communities began to formulate tribal-style interactions outside of specific tribal circumstances.[13] The cultural implications of this process are significant, as this community-forming effort by urban and urbanized Indians revolves around culturally specific activities such as singing, dancing, storytelling, traditional arts, and so on, all of which have spiritual connotations in their specific tribal contexts. When placed in relation to other Indians of different tribes, however, these practices often adjust to accommodate these differences, rendering a set of common understandings of Indianness and Native spirituality via the participation in a set of common practices.[14] Thus, one can find Indians of various tribal backgrounds forming communities within which pan-Indian practices are a central feature, and frybread is inevitably connected to these practices and the associated ideals.[15]

While in many pan-Indian contexts Plains Indian traditions often play a large role in constructing experiential conditions suitable for a multitribal constituency, the pan-Indian co-optation of Plains-style dance, sweating, and the presence of the Sacred Pipe is not without controversy, and many Lakota, Cheyenne, Arapahoe, and Northern Cree (to name just a few implicated nations) object to what they view as co-option by other Native people that fails to honor the Plains origins of these cultural products. But the reality is that, given the concerted effort of the US and Canadian governments to force assimilation through a number of methods, Native people maintained a connection to their *indigeneity*, often by switching out signifiers as a way to forge a collective resistance. As American Indian and First Nation collectives grew in both population share and traditional knowledge in the latter years of the twentieth century, practices once common in tribal-specific contexts made, and continue to make, their way back into those communities. However, given the fact that most American Indians and First Nations people live off of reservation lands, and many have multiple tribal affiliations as well, pan-Indian symbolic elements remain important for many contemporary Native people who have struggled to maintain these cultural connections due to the effects of colonization on indigenous identity.

Social Power and Commodity Foods

The relationship between virtually all American Indian and First Nations tribes and the US and Canadian governments, respectively, thus has had a collectivizing effect as these official agents attempt to administer health care and other programs using a common system with a multitude of various nations. The response was for Native nations to form connections via common experiences, issues, and grievances shared among indigenous people that transcend specific tribal traditions. The bureaucratic apparatuses with which governments interact with Native people have produced many cultural products in Indian Country, including Indian Country itself, and many of these have become potent tropes for identity maintenance, cultural cohesion, and effective tools for critique of non-Natives. One of the most ubiquitous and widespread of these is the image of "commodity food."

As previously mentioned, the distribution of staple supplies to Native people has long been a practice in both the US and Canada. Now including such products as boxed meals and processed cheese, these programs are both a necessary service given the consistent presence of Native people at the bottom of the economic scale in both reservation and urban contexts relative to non-Natives, and a problematic imposition of often unhealthy food choices. Health issues are well documented among American Indians and First Nations people, and diet is implicated in many if not most of these health concerns.[16] Obesity levels are double that found among whites, the rate of type-2 diabetes are among the highest in the world, and frybread is often considered an aspect of this unhealthy diet foisted on Native people as a result of colonialism.[17] So why is there more of a sentimentalized view of frybread compared to, say, large blocks of processed cheese?

With the possible exception of canned meats such as Spam or Klik, commodity foods are generally seen as tasteless and disappointing, and fodder for derisive humor. The "commod bod" jokes regarding weight issues among reservation Indians, for example, are ever-present in Native humor from stand-up comics to powwow emcees. Frybread, however, occupics a much more nuanced place in the collective consciousness of American Indian and First Nations people.

For one thing . . . it's delicious.

While I can say from experience that while the commodity cheese blocks are often nearly inedible, and powdered milk is difficult to digest (especially since many Native people are lactose-intolerant), frybread is *deep-fried dough*. What's not to love? But beyond that, frybread embodies a particularly unique position in the signification system that forms the contemporary American and First Nations community taken as a whole. While I am arguing that frybread is a cultural touchstone, unique to Native people, that has obtained symbolic meaning and value inherent in traditional foods, I must attend to some subtle, but significant differences in frybread use between reservation or reservation-adjacent Native communities, and Natives who are not living in the concentrated atmosphere of a reservation or reserve.

For reservation and reserve communities, frybread often plays a much more frequent role in Native meals. Used as a classic flatbread, it is eaten with breakfast, lunch, or dinner, and though frequency of course varies, generally is a fairly common accompaniment. And it is therefore in these contexts that the health issues Harjo and others raise are most obvious, due to the cumulative effect of the high calorie and fat content of frybread. For urbanized communities, frybread is most commonly reserved for special occasions, when there is a desire for "traditional" food such as for a seasonal feast, or when eaten as a treat at powwows. Reservation communities are the primary recipients of the delivered commodity foods mentioned above, which accounts for it being more of a presence. But concentrated urbanized Native communities are often in the lower socioeconomic strata and therefore struggle financially. Frybread for these populations is often a way to make a filling meal with scarce resources. In both contexts, however, the dish is viewed as traditional and uniquely Native.

Though frybread can be seen as both exemplary of the commodity foods that represent the colonial control over Native people and the survival of those peoples, the undeniable truth is that commodity foods and the systems that make them both necessary and available are implicated in the social, political, financial, and educational marginalization suffered by American Indians and First Nations people. Colonial efforts to remove indigenous people from their land and the connected lifeways resulted in desperate poverty and ill health, and the US and Canadian governments responded with inadequate fixes that served to lock Native people in cycles of poverty and despair. Attempts by non-Natives to romanticize precontact Indian cultures tend to cement Native people in a perpetual state of stunted development, reinforced by the presence of bureaucratic systems such as the US government's Food Distribution Program on Indian Reservations (FDPIR) that seem to verify the apparent inadequacy of traditional Native cultures. The resulting malaise that arose in many Native communities, and indeed still lingers in the form of addiction and domestic violence, is an extremely difficult cycle from which to break free. Commodity foods in reservation/reserve communities can perpetuate ill health, both mental and physical, passing historical trauma from generation to generation.

However, the central feature of both Native outreach programs and Indian political activism is the valorization, rather than romanticizing, of traditional American Indian worldviews, providing community support and opportunities for regular community participation. Many programs dedicated specifically to issues in Indian Country value traditional Native identity as essential for Indian health and sovereignty, and regular communal religious practices as a method for maintaining that identity.[18] Cultural practices, both pan-Indian and tribal-specific, serve as reminders of ancestral ways that are seen as the antidote to modernity, a true medicine for what ails Indian Country. What I would argue is that, much like the way matzo is used in Passover commemoration, frybread is a cultural touchstone, ceremonial element, and potent reminder of the struggles Native people have undergone due to colonization.

In this way it is indeed uniquely representative of the Native experience—frybread connotes a particular expression of resistance that these other commodity-oriented foods don't. Frybread was an innovation born from necessity. It represents persistence and survival. It connotes cultural connections and uniquely Native roots. It connects us to home. But as it also makes us unhealthy when we overindulge, perhaps it is time to think of it as a special treat and celebratory. The social power inherent in the traditionalization of postcontact signs, such as American flag images in Lakota ledger art or cans of Spam at potlatch giveaways, serves as a cultivar for identity, an act of signification. Is frybread unhealthy? Clearly. But it can also be a ritual. A communion. As Thomas Builds-the-Fire says in *Smoke Signals*, "Way back when we were havin' a feast on our reservation. A good old feast. We didn't have a whole lot of food, just a little bit of deer meat, a huge vat of mashed potatoes, some coke, and frybread. But the frybread made all the difference in the world."[19]

For What It's Worth: My Frybread Recipe

Ingredients

- 4 cups white flour
- 2 tablespoons baking powder
- 1 teaspoon salt
- 2 cups warm water
- about 2 cups vegetable oil for frying

1. In a large bowl, mix together flour, salt, and baking powder. Gradually stir in the water until the dough becomes soft and workable (without sticking to the bowl).

2. Knead dough for 4 minutes, then cover the bowl with a clean towel and let the dough rest (it won't rise much, but it needs to rest) for about 30 minutes.

3. Heat the oil in a skillet deep enough that the frybread will be in about 2 inches of hot oil. Hot but not too hot, shimmery but not smoking.

4. Squeeze a small ball of dough up through your fist, through your curled pointer finger and thumb, about the size of a billiard ball and shape it into a thin disk, in your palms or on the counter with a rolling pin. The thinner the disk, the crispier the bread. I like them about ¼ of an inch thick. Make a hole in the center with the knuckle of your thumb (so the bread doesn't pop).
5. Fry in the oil one at a time until golden brown, flipping once halfway through. Frybread can be kept warm in the oven until enough is made to serve.
6. Think about the resilience of American Indians and First Nations people and what they have endured to keep their traditions alive.

Notes

1. Sherry B. Ortner, "On Key Symbols," *American Anthropologist*, New Series 75, no. 5 (October 1973): 1338.

2. Harjo, 2005.

3. Peter Iverson *Diné: A History of the Navajos* (New Mexico: University of New Mexico Press, 2002), 58–59.

4. Dana Vantrease, "Commod Bods and Frybread Power: Government Food Aid in American Indian Culture, *Journal of American Folklore* 126, no. 499 (2013): 57.

5. For an analytical treatment of this concept, see James B. Lagrand, "Introduction," *Indian Metropolis: Native American in Chicago, 1945–1975* (Urbana: University of Chicago Press, 2002), 1–16.

6. Stephen Cornell, *The Return of the Native: American Indian Political Resurgence* (New York: Oxford University Press, 1988), 14.

7. Ibid., 132.

8. For an historical treatment of this process and the relevant government actions, both legislative and militaristic, see Vine Deloria, *God Is Red: A Native View of Religion* (Golden, CO: North American Press, 1972); Vine Deloria Jr. and Clifford Lytle, *The Nations Within: The Past and Future of American Indian Sovereignty* (Austin, Texas: Pantheon, 1984); and Thomas W. Cowger, *The National Congress of American Indians: The Founding Years* (Lincoln: University of Nebraska Press, 1999).

9. See for an excellent example of this conceptual paradigm, Leo Panitch "Violence as a Tool of Order and Change: The War on Terrorism and the Anti-globalization Movement," *Monthly Review* 54, no. 2 (June 2002): 12–32.

10. Dennis Kelley, *Tradition, Performance, and Religion in Native America: Ancestral Ways, Modern Selves* (New York: Routledge Press, 2015), 23.

11. For an excellent overview of the dances and regalia associated with the intertribal powwow, see Tara Browner's excellent book, *The Heartbeat of the People: Music and Dance of the Northern Pow Wow* (Urbana: University of Illinois Press, 2004).

12. "Removal" generally refers to the US government actions in which tribal groups in the South were forcibly removed to "Indian Territory" as a result of the Indian Removal Act, passed by Congress in 1830. For an overview of this policy and its implications, see Ronald N. Satz, *American Indian Policy in the Jacksonian Era* (Norman, OK: University of Oklahoma Press, 2002 [[ED/AU: Should this bracketed information be deleted?]][Lincoln, Nebraska: University of Nebraska Press, 1975]); Anthony F. C. Wallace, *The Long, Bitter Trail: Andrew Jackson and the Indians* (New York: Hill and Wang, 1993); Graham D. Taylor, *The New Deal and American Indian Tribalism: The Administration of the Indian Reorganization Act, 1934–45* (Lincoln: University of Nebraska Press. 1980), 185.

13. Donald L. Fixico, *The Urban Indian Experience in America* (Albuquerque: University of New Mexico Press, 2000), 46–49.

14. Joan Albon, "Relocated American Indians in the San Francisco Bay Area: Social Interaction and Indian Identity," *Human Organization* 24 (1964): 296–304; and Arthur Margon, "Indians and Immigrants: A Comparison of Groups New to the City," *Journal of Ethnic Studies* 4, no. 4 (1977): 20.

15. James Treat, "Intertribal Traditionalism and the Spiritual Roots of Red Power," in Lee Irwin, ed., *Native American Spirituality: A Critical Reader* (Lincoln: University of Nebraska Press, 2000), 270–94.

16. Dana Vantrese, "Commod Bods," 55.

17. Michelle Chino, Darlene Haff, and Carolee Dodge-Francis, "Patterns of Commodity Food Use among American Indians," *Pimatisiwin: A Journal of Aboriginal and Indigenous Community Health* 7, no. 2 (2009): 280.

18. "SPNS Initiative: American Indian/Alaska Native, 2003–2007," Text, August 9, 2016, https://hab.hrsa.gov/about-ryan-white-hivaids-program/spns-initiative-american-indian-alaska-native.

19. Chris Eyre, *Smoke Signals* (Miramax, 1998).

Bibliography

Ablon, Joan. "Relocated American Indians in the San Francisco Bay Area: Social Interaction and Indian Identity." *Human Organization* 23, no. 4 (1964): 296–304.

Chino, Michelle, Darlene Haff, and Carolee Dodge-Francis. "Patterns of Commodity Food Use among American Indians." *Pimatisiwin: A Journal of Aboriginal and Indigenous Community Health* 7, no. 2 (2009): 279–89.

Cornell, Stephen. *The Return of the Native: American Indian Political Resurgence.* New York: Oxford University Press, 1988.

Eyre, Chris. *Smoke Signals.* Miramax, 1998.

Fixico, Donald L. *The Urban Indian Experience in America.* Albuquerque: University of New Mexico Press. 2000.

Harjo, Suzan Shown. "My New Year's Resolution: No More Fat 'Indian' Food." *Indian Country Today*, January 26, 2005. https://newsmaven.io/indiancountrytoday/archive/my-new-year-s-resolution-no-more-fat-indian-food-M6Fd3dv8tkWPjg383hjFyA/.

Iverson, Peter, and Monty Roessel. *Diné: A History of the Navajos.* 1st ed. Albuquerque: University of New Mexico Press, 2002.

Kelley, Dennis. *Tradition, Performance, and Religion in Native America: Ancestral Ways, Modern Selves.* New York: Routledge Press, 2015.

Margon, Arthur. Indians and Immigrants: A Comparison of Groups New to the City." *Journal of Ethnic Studies* 4(4)1977: 17–28.

Ortner, Sherry B. "On Key Symbols." *American Anthropologist*, New Series 75, no. 5 (October 1973): 1338–46.

"SPNS Initiative: American Indian/Alaska Native, 2003–2007." Accessed August 9, 2016. https://hab.hrsa.gov/about-ryan-white-hivaids-program/spns-initiative-american-indian-alaska-native.

Taylor, Graham D. *The New Deal and American Indian Tribalism: The Administration of the Indian Reorganization Act, 1934–45.* Lincoln: University of Nebraska Press, 1980.

Treat, James. "Intertribal Traditionalism and the Spiritual Roots of Red Power." In *Native American Spirituality: A Critical Reader*, edited by Lee Irwin, 270–94. Lincoln: University of Nebraska Press, 2000.

Vantrease, Dana. "Commod Bods and Frybread Power: Government Food Aid in American Indian Culture." *Journal of American Folklore* 126 (499) 2013: 55–69.

Epilogue

Michelene Pesantubbee

Numerous factors ranging from colonial ideologies and practices to global economies have impacted indigenous foodways in myriad complex and detrimental ways. Existing studies of indigenous foodways address these factors critiquing the practices and their impact on the economies, health, and cultures of Native peoples. Often left out of these discussions is their impact on the religious lives of Native peoples. From the smallest act of placing a seed in the ground to resource management, such as burning vast areas of grasslands, Native people understood the importance of assisting nature, of "keeping it living," as the Kwakwaka'wakw say, through "an entire system of resource maintenance, conservation, and enhancement" in order to live a good life.[1] They also understood their obligations to acknowledge the gifts of other-than-human persons, including those of the spirit world, whether creator, ancestor, or power. They understood that their good life depended on the well-being of the other-than-human persons who nourished their bodies. When they cared for the plants and animals they were as Apache woman Ellen Josay Tessay said of her corn plants, "looking after my children."[2] The consumption of food acknowledged this relationship in the form of ceremony welcoming and thanking the other-than-human people for making themselves available to humans. Among the Cherokee no one ate corn from the first harvest until the Green Corn Ceremony had taken place. The Yakama recognized the first salmon of the season before everyone had their first taste. Indigenous peoples thanked the grandparent plants for sharing their grandchildren with the human people.

Ceremonies around food did more than acknowledge the symbiotic relationship between humans and other-than-human persons. The sharing of food reinforced community values, supported shared cultural identities, and provided a means for acknowledging respect of honored people. Not just any food served that purpose. The food native to an area shaped and reflected cultures. Regional foods evidenced relationships established between the creator or spirit beings and specific peoples, which they expressed through stories, songs, and dances. For Lakota the stories of buffalo people or the Pte, their elder brothers, is significant to their understanding of annual pilgrimages through the Black Hills; their relationship to Skan, the creator and source of all power; and their emergence from Maka, the earth. To be selected as Buffalo Calf Woman for the Sun Dance is an honor of the highest order. The Tseshaht First Nation, a Nuu-chah-nulth group with a long tradition of whaling, received their name from their "former principal village, Ts'ishaa, meaning 'people from an island that reeks of whale remains.' "[3] Among the Nuu-chah-nulth, to kill a whale "was considered the highest glory."[4] The Cherokee stories of Selu, or Corn Woman, reminds them of the power and importance of women, of the need to sacrifice for the well-being of family and community. Those who gather and prepare the first corn for the Green Corn Ceremony are honored for their work. Every indigenous group has deep ties to the plant, animal, and bird peoples of their homelands and those relationships centered the people in a larger world in meaningful ways. Food is much more than sustenance for Native peoples.

To fully comprehend the impact of destroyed plant and animal habitats, eradicated or threatened populations of plants and animals, and the introduction of alien, genetically altered, and highly processed foods we must understand the effect of the loss of native foods on the spiritual well-being of Native peoples. Only by doing so can we fully apprehend the effect of generations of altered diets not only on the health of indigenous peoples but also on their cultural integrity and understanding of their place in a world, both physical and spiritual.

Most of the authors of this volume are scholars of religious studies, more specifically Native American religious traditions, or they have participated in sessions of the Native Traditions in the Americas Unit of the American Academy of Religion. They all have been trained, as Inés Talamantez taught, to direct their research toward the needs of the communities they study as those communities identify them. In more recent times tribal governments and grassroots people have focused significant attention to the food sovereignty of Native peoples, of improving the health of indigenous peoples by encouraging more traditional diets. Along with those concerns, many of the proponents of restored indigenous foodways point out the associated positive benefits of such efforts, including increased pride in indigenous identity, growing interest in learning traditional cultural ways and languages, and a strengthening of sense of community and mental well-being. Iris Gray Bull, an Assiniboine elder, tearfully noted the importance of the return of bison to Fort Peck Reservation in 2012, stating that "by bringing them back, we're bringing our identity back."[5] Similar sentiments are expressed on the Makah Nation's website, which states that whaling is "the subject and inspiration of Tribal songs, dances, designs, and basketry."[6] The return of gray whale hunting not only required relearning the art of whaling and associated rituals, but also led to a rise in interest in learning other aspects of Makah culture that had experienced a decline. Keith Johnson, president of the Makah Whaling Commission, in an open letter to the public on the importance of the planned whale hunt in 1999, described how, especially among young people, "we hope that the restoration of whaling will help to restore that discipline and pride."[7] The relationship between food, cultural identity, and community well-being is recognized by indigenous peoples across the continent who are vested in restoring indigenous foodways.

The authors in this volume have focused their attention on efforts to restore indigenous foodways and what this means for the health and well-being of indigenous peoples and their communities. As scholars of religion they also attend to the religious side of food management, harvesting, and preparation. Their work provides a much needed focus that complements the studies of colonial practices and ideologies that have impacted indigenous lifeways in so many negative ways. Native Americans have repeatedly demonstrated their resilience and adaptive abilities in the face of many hardships, including providing their communities with sustenance derived from monocultural approaches, modern ways of processing food, government food programs, and environmental threats. Their survival has come at a cost to their health, community well-being, and individual and family health. The inability to maintain symbiotic relationships with indigenous foods has interfered with the teaching of the stories, songs, and dances that shaped the moral and ethical world of Native peoples. These chapters introduce us to another expression of their resilience and encourage other indigenous peoples to explore ways of restoring traditional food ways that, in turn, support cultural vitality.

These authors also pave the way for more studies that further address the interrelated issues of global economies, climate change, population migrations, and political interests on efforts to restore Native foods for the health and well-being of Native peoples and the earth itself.

Notes

1. Nancy T. Turner, *The Earth's Blanket: Traditional Teachings for Sustainable Living* (Vancouver, BC: Douglas & McIntyre, 2005), 148.

2. Keith Basso, *Wisdom Sits in Places* (Albuquerque: University of New Mexico Press, 1996), 22.

3. Charlotte Coté, *Spirits of the Whaling Ancestors* (Seattle: University of Washington Press, 2010), 9.

4. Coté, *Spirits of the Whaling Ancestors*, 6.

5. Daniel Glick, "Bison Homecoming," *National Wildlife Federation* (September 19, 2012), https://www.nwf.org/Home/Magazines/National-Wildlife/2012/OctNov/Conservation/Bison-Homecoming.

6. "The Makah Whaling Tradition," http://Makah.com/makah-tribal-info/whaling/.

7. Robert Sullivan, *A Whale Hunt* (New York: Simon & Schuster, 2002), 13.

Bibliography

Basso, Keith H. *Wisdom Sits in Places: Landscape and Language Among the Western Apache*. 1st ed. Albuquerque: University of New Mexico Press, 1996.

Cote, Charlotte. *Spirits of Our Whaling Ancestors: Revitalizing Makah and Nuu-Chah-Nulth Traditions*. Seattle: University of Washington Press, 2010.

Glick, Daniel. "Bison Homecoming." *National Wildlife Federation*, September 19, 2012. https://www.nwf.org/Home/Magazines/National-Wildlife/2012/OctNov/Conservation/Bison-Homecoming.

"Makah Whaling & Whale Hunt—Makah Tribe (Neah Bay, Washington)." *Makah Tribe* (blog). Accessed September 3, 2019. https://makah.com/makah-tribal-info/whaling/.

Sullivan, Robert. *A Whale Hunt: How a Native-American Village Did What No One Thought It Could*. 1st paperback ed. New York: Scribner, 2002.

Turner, Nancy J. The Earth's Blanket: Traditional Teaching for Sustainable Living. Vancouver, BC: Douglas & McIntyre, 2005.

Contributors

Suzanne Crawford O'Brien is professor of religion and culture and chair of the Native American and Indigenous Studies Program at Pacific Lutheran University. Her work focuses on Coast Salish and other indigenous religious traditions in the Pacific Northwest, with particular attention to health and wellness, environmental activism, and religion and ecology. Other publications include *Religion and Culture in Native North America* (Rowman and Littlefield, 2020), *Coming Full Circle: Spirituality and Wellness Among Native Communities in the Pacific Northwest* (University of Nebraska, 2014), and *Religion and Healing in Native America: Pathways for Renewal* (Praeger, 2008). She lives in Seattle, Washington.

Lawrence Gross (Anishinaabe) is a member of the Minnesota Chippewa tribe, enrolled on the White Earth reservation. His primary research area is Anishinaabe culture and religion, with numerous publications in the field. His book, *Anishinaabe Ways of Knowing and Being*, was published by Ashgate Publishing in 2014. He has also published on using American Indian pedagogical methods in the university setting. He is an associate professor and serves as the San Manuel Band of Mission Indians Endowed Chair of Native American Studies at the University of Redlands in Redlands, CA.

Dennis Kelley is an associate professor in the Department of Religious Studies at the University of Missouri, Columbia. His work focuses on the role that religion plays in establishing identity, both individual and collective, ethnic in particular. Focusing on embodied practice, cultural performance, and the semiotics of practice as they apply to religion in modernity, his work uses the lens of indigeneity as a tool for the critique of the religious studies discourse.

Andrea McComb Sanchez is an assistant professor of religious studies at the University of Arizona. She specializes in Native American religious traditions, religion in the American southwest, religion and colonialism in North America, and religion and the environment. She is a member of the University of Arizona's American Indian Studies Graduate Interdisciplinary Program and an affiliate of the Institute of the Environment. She is the author of *Of Corn and Catholicism: Religion and Power in Pueblo Indian Patron Saint Feast Days*, forthcoming from the University of Nebraska Press.

Michael D. McNally is the John M. and Elizabeth W. Musser Professor of Religious Studies at Carleton College. He is the author of three books: *Ojibwe Singers: Hymns, Grief, and a Native Culture in Motion* (Minnesota Historical Society Press, [2000] 2009), *Honoring Elders: Aging, Authority and Ojibwe Religion* (Columbia University Press, 2009), and most recently, of *Defend the Sacred: Native American Religious Freedom beyond the First Amendment* (Princeton University Press, 2020).

Michelene E. Pesantubbee is professor emeritus at the University of Iowa. She joined the University of Iowa faculty in 2003, and retired in 2018. She regularly taught courses on Native American religious history and religious freedom issues, as well as courses on religion and violence in America. She is the author of *Choctaw Women in a Chaotic World: The Clash of Cultures in the Colonial Southeast* (Albuquerque: University of New Mexico Press, 2005), as well as several book chapters and journal articles. She also served as the executive secretary of the American Academy of Religion from December 2004 to December 2007.

R. Alfred Vick is the Georgia Power Professor in Environmental Ethics at the University of Georgia and director of the Environmental Ethics Certificate Program. He is a licensed landscape architect and a LEED Fellow. His work focuses on preserving and enhancing the functioning of natural systems while effectively and attractively integrating human use. At the University of Georgia's College of Environment & Design he teaches landscape ecology and sustainable design, collaborates with other researchers in the Sustainability and Landscape Performance Lab, and serves on the faculty of the Institute of Native American Studies. His academic research focuses on green infrastructure and sustainable site design, native plant communities, and American Indian ethnobotany. He earned a BS in Engineering Psychology from the University of Illinois and a Master of Landscape Architecture degree from the University of Georgia.

David S. Walsh is associate professor of religious studies at Gettysburg College, Pennsylvania, where he teaches courses on indigenous religious traditions, religion and the environment, colonialism, and method and theory. He holds a PhD in religious studies from Arizona State University and an MA from the University of Colorado, Boulder. He is currently completing a book manuscript pertaining to his ethnographic research with Tłı̨chǫ Dene on their traditional environmental relationships, spirituality, and foodways in the era of climate change.

Kimberly Wogahn is an organizer, activist, and nonprofit professional based in Seattle. She has worked on campaigns for fossil fuel divestment, indigenous sovereignty, equitable wealth redistribution, and prison abolition. She is particularly interested in envisioning a world without prisons and exploring what transformative justice on an interpersonal level can look like. Kimberly serves on the board of Books to Prisoners, where she worked as the program coordinator from 2017 to 2019, and is a member-organizer with the Seattle chapter of Resource Generation.

Michael J. Zogry is an associate professor in the Department of Religious Studies at the University of Kansas (KU), and currently serves as department chair. He was the director of the Indigenous Studies Program at KU from 2011 to 2016. He researches Native American religions and the historiography of religions in the United States, with particular attention to ritual practices and issues of representation. His book *Anetso, the Cherokee Ball Game: At the Center of Ceremony and Identity* (University of North Carolina Press, 2010), was an inaugural volume in the series First Peoples: New Directions in Indigenous Studies.

Index